MOHAWKS LOST

Flying in the
CIA's Secret War in Laos

1ST Edition (d) – June 2016

By Gerald Naekel
CW4 • US Army • Retired

NOTE: This is a *modified*, enhanced and grammatically improved rewrite and new edition of my previous great seller –

WAR STORIES
From an Army Pilot Flying in the
CIA's Secret War in Laos

© 2016 Gerald Naekel
All Worldwide Rights Reserved

All rights reserved. No part of this publication may be reproduced, stored in a retrieval system or transmitted, in any form or by any means, electronic, mechanical, photocopying, recording, or otherwise, without the prior permission of the author or publishers.

ISBN: 978-1533396174

Cataloging-in-Publication Data is available from the
Library of Congress

Online Links for This Book

There *may* be additional online links to many related pictures, some videos, background notes and more at the following link. As times change, and so also do domains and web servers, the shown web address may not be correct.

www.GeraldNaekel.com

"Someday the World Will Know What a Bunch of Army Pilots in Black Flight Suits Really Did"

— Spud Club Wall with Names

---

*"Spud IR - We Will Go Anywhere—**Once!**"*

— On the Wall at our CIA Operations Offices at the Udorn RTAFB

We know how all this ends . .

And here is the story of how it got to this . .

WHAT IS IN THIS BOOK

Dozens of short stories, some several pages long, of mostly combat flight events derived from over 500 combat missions that I flew in 22-1/2 months as a pilot in an ejection-seat, single-pilot, sometimes heavily armed, Grumman OV-1 Mohawk, and the events that happened to others in my Vietnam unit around my time frame.

My personal stories are only part of the story of one of the most unique Army aviation units in the world. For more than seven years, and tens of thousands of missions, with *huge losses* in men and aircraft, first the 20th ASTA, later as the 131st Aviation Company, flew armed and unarmed Grumman OV-1 Mohawks *exclusively* in North Vietnam and Laos until the ending months of the war.

At times, we wore black flight suits, *Baht chains of gold* around our necks, and always our personal *Blood Chits* tucked down inside our survival vests. Strapped to a Martin-Baker ejection seat and flying single-pilot, sometimes heavily armed aircraft in which we roamed all over Laos in some of the most intense fields of anti-aircraft fire in Southeast Asia—*and we paid a high price for it.*

We flew in the *CIA's Secret War in Northern Laos* for all these years, usually with three aircraft based at the Udorn RTAFB, Thailand and flying only at night up against (sometimes inadvertently across) the Chinese border to help attack truck and tank traffic moving across northern Laos and then going down into North Vietnam, towards Hanoi, or moving further directly onto the Ho Chi Minh Trail.

We also lost more aircraft and crewmembers than all the other Mohawk units—*combined*.

Of all our MIA's from shoot-downs and crashes in Laos and North Vietnam—even if we had contact with them after an ejection—*we never got a single man back after the war. Their fate, like so many, is unknown.*

MISTAKES AND ERRORS

There are surely some errors in facts and circumstances as this is a long book with limited official records to review. If you find mistakes or errors, I would like to correct them in the future versions. Do let me know. *The same with any grammar and spelling errors that seem to grow in the darkness after the computer screen is shut down.*

Gerald Naekel
Email: gnaekel@gmail.com

EVOLVING EDITION CHANGES AND UPDATES

This particular book has grown in distribution and sales as the years have gone by as more and as more men with additional information and details and corrections have emailed me with updates, and changes to things like Call Signs and missions and aircraft, particularly USAF pilots.

MY PERSONAL WRITING STYLE IN THIS BOOK

I write and publish a range of technical and non-fiction books. In *this book*, I am telling the stories as if we are sitting together, likely with something brewed in hand, and talking with you in the first-person—often in the present tense—even while recounting events from decades before. I often *step into the story*, the mission, the specific events and the writing tense will change or may vary from *was* to *is*—as you and I are right there, right now, and I am recounting what is going on or being felt.

My friends tell me I am writing just as I would be talking; absent the obligatory hand-waving needed by pilots to ensure the events are accurately being explained.

So, if one is expecting exacting literary prose as if writing a historical documentary work or a technical manual, then you will be surprised; hopefully in a positive way, as I draw you into the very essences for what the events were about—as if you are there yourself seeing, hearing and feeling the emotions of the moment.

While my literary style in this book is a bit unorthodox—at the minimum—I think you will find the sometimes colorful, even occasional humorous manner, sprinkled with more than a few politically incorrect expressions; *"Ah, shit..."* being the most commonly used, will help you get right into the mood of the book. This may sometimes bring a smile; but sadly, too, perhaps a tear as I pull at your emotions.

Enjoy.

Few people ever knew the real stories . .

OV-1A being armed with rockets and .50 cal machine gun.

    Mostly because at the time, during the Vietnam War, everything was a secret, including things about your own aviation unit, shoot downs or anything the enemy could use against us if *you* were shot down and captured. So it is not until decades later, with the internet mostly, that the history of this unique Army aviation unit could be better compiled, even with a lot of holes still in the story.

TABLE OF CONTENTS

What Is In This Book iv
Mistakes and Errors v
Evolving Edition Changes and Updates v
My Personal Writing Style in this Book v

Table of Contents vii

Chapter 1 1

It Was All Too Real 1
- 1-1 / It Was Not a Good Night At Pleiku 1
- 1-2 / SA-2 SAM Missile Over Southern North Vietnam 22
- 1-3 / Nurse Crashes Enroute To Her Phu Bai Hospital Assignment 42
- 1-4 / On the FUEL LOW Light - DaNang Approach Control Vectors Me Out Over The South China Sea to Eject 44
- 1-5 / Ubon Training Flight Nearly Ends Up a Burning Hole in the Ground 49
- 1-6 / Night Maintenance Test Flight Ends in Unplanned Ejection 54
- 1-7 / Two F-4s Collide in the DMZ 60
- 1-8 / Phu Bai Approach Control Vectors Army RU-21 Into Mountains ... 63
- 1-9 / VR Flight - He Took Three .30 cal Hits in the Chest—and Kept Flying the Mohawk Home 64
- 1-10 / UFO? Off the Coast of North Vietnam 65
- 1-11 / And Your Drop Tanks are Now Where? 71
- 1-12 / Triple Night Monsoon GCA Approach at Phu Bai — On the LOW FUEL Light 73
- 1-13 / One Engine, at Night, In the A Shau Valley, Damaged With a Hung Drop Tank 78
- 1-14 / Staff Officer Got More Than He Expected Flying With Me Over Laos to Vientiane 84
- 1-15 / Landing Gear Sucks Up Before Takeoff 89
- 1-16 / Overflying the NVA Artillery in North Vietnam For US Navy Precision Firing 90
- 1-17 / Four IR Flights One Night While US Marines are Trapped inside Quang Tri City 94

1-18 / There Were NVA Armored Vehicles on Highway 1 and a Resulting 131st Crewmember Mutiny 97
1-19 / My Last Flight and I Am in Trouble 99
1-20 / DaNang Graves Registration - Unreal 110

Chapter 2 115

Flying in the CIA's Secret War in Northern Laos 115

2-1 / Some Background Here 115
2-2 / How We Ran Our Mohawk Missions in Northern Laos 118
2-3 / WHO'S Damn Plan Was This Anyway? 121
2-4 / Special Forces Lost on POW Recovery Mission 130
2-5 / Wild Weasel Missed The Tanker and is Down in the PDJ 134
2-6 / George Follows the Crippled AC-119 Stinger Gunship to NKP 137
2-7 / Flight Operations at Long Tieng (Lima Site 20a) 139
2-8 / During the Siege on the CIA Base at Long Tieng (Lima Site-20a) . 142
2-9 / The Month of the White Elephants 146
2-10 / George and I Flying Out of Udorn 147
2-11 / Just Where the Hell Did I Snag a Cable on a Night IR Flight in the Mountains 149
2-12 / Thunderstorms Were Way Too Heavy 150
2-13 / The MiGCAP Missions 151
2-14 / IR Aircraft Getting Down in the Rainy Season 152
2-15 / Life at Udorn 154
2-16 / Alley Cat Capsule Crews 158

Chapter 3 161

These Ended Really Bad 161

3-1 / Ejection Seat Failure at Phu Bai - (1-Fatal) 161
3-2 / George is Lost on My IR Mission (2-Fatal/MIA) 167
3-3 / Identical Twin Brothers; One Lived, One Died - (2-Fatal) 171
3-4 / Deadly FSB Barbara Friendly Fire Hit Us (1-Fatal - Many Injured) 177
3-5 / Our Last Fatal Takeoff Crash - (1-Fatal) 181
3-6 / Mohawk Hits Ship in DaNang Harbor (2-Fatal) 182
3-7 / Jack and Al are Shot Down Near Tchepone - (2-Fatal/MIA) 185
3-8 / Don't Go To Tchepone 186
3-9 / Our Commander Dies on Training Crash at Phu Bai - (1-Fatal) 188
3-10 / Easter Bear is Lost on Medevac in Laos (Multiple Fatal and MIAs) 193
3-11 / Our IR or VR Mission Aircraft Lost in Laos - (2-Fatal/MIA) 197

3-12 / New and Old Unit Commanders Died in Fly-By Crash (2-Fatal) ...198
3-13 / IR Aircraft Ejection On Takeoff - (1-Fatal) 200
3-14 / IR/VR Aircraft Lost in Laos - (2-Fatal/MIAs)................................201
3-15 / VR Gunship Lost in Laos - (1-Fatal/MIA) 201
3-16 / VR Gunship Lost in Laos - (2-Fatal/MIA) 201
3-17 / Our Mohawk Shot Down By Soviet SA-2 SAM Missile - (2-Fatal/MIA) 201
3-18 / Still Another Mohawk IR/VR Aircraft Lost in Laos - (2-Fatal/MIA) 202
3-19 / Two Mohawk Gunships Lost in Laos on Same Mission - (2-Fatal/MIA, 2-Rescued) 203
3-20 / Mohawk Gunship Down in Laos (2-Fatal/MIA)........................204
3-21 / Mohawk Lost on IR Flight in Laos (2-Fatal/MIA) 204
3-22 / Chinook Crash Near Phu Bai - (Many Fatal) 204
3-23 / Head Into The Propeller After Emergency Landing - (1-Fatal)......205

Chapter 4 207

Tidbits and Other Screw-Ups.. 207

4-1 / The Bengal Tiger in the 131st Compound 207
4-2 / Rats in the Cockpit on Takeoff..208
4-3 / The Issue of Fear..209
4-4 / Seaboard World DC-8 Accidentally Lands at Marble Mountain Army Airfield - At Night!...211
4-5 / This Idiot (Me) Dives on Tiger Island off the Coast of North Vietnam..212
4-6 / My Assignment as the 131st Standardization Instructor Pilot......213
4-7 / This Just Had To Happen - Air Force Guys Lost 215
4-8 / Recon the Destroyed Cambodian Bridges 217
4-9 / Drug Control Officer..218
4-10 / Sending The New Pilots and TOs Back Home 220
4-11 / Dumping the 131st Compound Dogs Into The Ocean 221

Chapter 5 223

The 131st Missions and Areas of Operations 223

5-1 / The 131st Was Completely Unique 224
5-2 / About The Missions - We Flew Alone, Mostly 225
5-3 / The Fatals Were Too Many..227
5-4 / Number of Unit Missions Flown 228
5-5 / How Our IR, SLAR, and VR Missions Were Flown...................230

Chapter 6 239
Weapons We Faced 239
6-1 / Anti-aircraft Guns, Flak, and More 239

Chapter 7 251
About The Mohawk 251
7-1 / Mohawk - The Army's Widow Maker 251
7-2 / Martin-Baker Ejection Seats 263
7-3 / Aircraft Electronics 266

Chapter 8 269
Technical Stuff 269
8-1 / Getting Local Training 269
8-2 / Survival Vests & Gear 271
8-3 / Survival - Blood Chits, Safe Letters, and Rescues ... 273

Chapter 9 279
As It Was - Hue/Phu Bai 279
9-1 / The Vietnam Arrival Experience 279
9-2 / Checking Into The 131st 281
9-3 / The Spud Club 282
9-4 / Airborne TV Versus Our Porno Movies 288
9-5 / Rats - Everywhere in our Phu Bai Compound 289
9-6 / Bodies Left Hanging Along Side Our Compound Gate ... 291
9-7 / Our Hooches 292
9-8 / Bunkers, Culverts and Underground Holes 295
9-9 / Hooch Maids 298
9-10 / Mess Hall 299
9-11 / 85th Evac Hospital 300

Terms and Words 307
About The Author 315

Chapter 1

IT WAS ALL TOO REAL

This chapter goes through many of the non-fatal crash events we had in my two combat years of flying. While it is rare, I had made a note when it is not my particular event or was not a 131st unit event.

1-1 / IT WAS NOT A GOOD NIGHT AT PLEIKU

Event Comment: It is the second week of May 1972 and the NVA's massive *Easter Offensive*, the game changer as it was, is now about six weeks old. Part two of the three parts of their offensive is to come down the *Ho Chi Minh Trail*, (*the Trail*) and then cut to the east moving through the jungles and mountains into II Corps, near Pleiku, in the Central Highlands. From there they were to take the city of Kontum, about 30 miles to the north of Pleiku. After taking Kontum the NVA forces would move south and take over Pleiku, which the NVA eventually did, but just not this week.

By now the 131st Military Intelligence Company, (131st MI) my Mohawk unit of two one-year tours, had just weeks earlier *fled*, or moved, from Phu Bai, our airfield base of seven years, near the city of Hue, in I Corps just about 30 miles south of the DMZ.

We were now operating our Mohawks out of Marble Mountain Army Airfield (MMAAF), some 90 miles to the south and just a few miles *(but surely another world)* away from the huge DaNang AFB. Just a few miles to the north of our former base at Phu Bai, Quang Tri City and the Army base and Air Force airfield there, had already fallen to the NVA and shortly after that Phu Bai is mostly *abandoned* as quickly as possible. I was flying out of Udorn at the time so the guys at Phu Bai just swept through the hooches, grabbing what they could and throwing your things, some of them only, onto trucks and rapidly leaving Phu Bai: all the while hundreds of tanks were streaming south on Highway 1 past Hue and towards our airfield. Things were going to hell fast by then, and soon we would declare *"Victory with Honor"*—

> . . and flee Southeast Asia leaving behind millions of dead in another dead-end, sure-to-lose, ground war.

Not all was lost, though. The Vietnam War inevitably created thousands of new American multi-millionaires, a few more billionaires, and more jobs for makers of luxury cars, and homes and resorts and more—*the typical outcome of all of our war efforts, at least since World War II.*

131st OV-1D (IR ship) with Radar Jammers for North Vietnam

On this night, the stop in Pleiku is supposed to be a routine refueling stop for two of us, me in my IR ship and our SLAR aircraft, both of us coming out of a long, dangerous night of flying in *Steel Tiger South* in southern Laos. As was a nightly routine, our SLAR/IR combo had been helping in the attacks on the Soviet T-54/56 tanks that were now moving down *the Trail*. For this night, our SLAR aircraft and I just needed to refuel there, at the Air Force's Pleiku AFB in the Central Highlands, and then we would fly back to our base at Marble Mountain.

Usually, we would fly down into southern Laos (Steel Tiger South) from our new location at Marble Mountain Army Airfield (MMAAF / *Marble Mountain Rocket and Mortar Proving Grounds* some called it), run the SLAR/IR combo missions, and then fly home. But the attacks on *the Trail* were now so thick and target-rich that we were often staying in the hunter/killer attack mission longer than usual and as such needed to make the stop someplace, such as Pleiku AFB, to get fuel and then continue home.

I really needed a smoke.

On this night, there were dozens of these tanks continuing a deadly month-long siege on the South Vietnam (ARVN) forces at Kontum, just a short 30 km to the north of Pleiku.

By now Kontum is surrounded by NVA tanks positioned in the close in mountains and firing directly down onto the city and the Kontum airfield. The NVA military divisions led then by North Vietnamese Lt. Gen. Hoang Minh Thao, surely had the upper hand in the evolving battles. Their forces had been buoyed by their successes the year before during the disastrous *Operation Lam Son 719.* Operation Lam Son 719, being, for us, the ill-fated and deadly attempt to cut *the Trail* by streaming west from the reopened Marine base at Khe Sanh, at the north end of the *A Shau Valley* (the *Valley of Death*) as it were. Reportedly there were nearly ten thousand friendly casualties in those battles before the South Vietnamese RVN forces *fled* back into South Vietnam.

On this night, several aircraft, including at least one Air America, or perhaps it is a South Vietnamese Air Force, old four-engine DC-6 aircraft, is part of the forces of various aircraft that had been trying to airlift out of Kontum as many of the civilian and military wounded as they could.

Meanwhile, our Air Force, flying from Pleiku, is running nonstop bombing flights using mostly F-4 *Phantoms*, and many other strike aircraft, while waves of giant B-52s were running massive *Arc Light* strikes from their far away bases in Guam and Thailand. From Pleiku, the fighter planes, heavily bomb loaded, were going into full afterburner as they were rolling in earth-shaking and thundering pairs down the single 6,000-foot runway. An assortment of other aircraft from wars now long past are also working overhead at Kontum that night and—it is certainly *Showtime* at Pleiku.

To the far side of the runway is the US Army *Camp Holloway*. From there young guys flying AH-1 *Cobras*, and the UH-1 *Hog* gunships, now armed with the new anti-tank missiles, had been working around-the-clock, day-and-night, attacking the

NVA armored forces that had surrounded Kontum. It is a new game and one we were destined to lose within months with horrific losses on all sides.

However, for us—me with the IR aircraft and a unit captain in the SLAR aircraft—our long night we thought would soon to be over. We were in the Pleiku Air Force transit fueling revetment area, tankering enough JP-4 fuel to get us both back home to DaNang that night. The SLAR aircraft is already fully refueled, and the Air Force fuel truck had just started with the fueling hose attached to my plane.

We would routinely *tanker* home as much fuel as we could just in case of inclement weather at our base, or needing more fuel at home base, or even the risk that a crash at the airport, or perhaps that the airfield may be under attack (common) would delay us. The extra fuel could help us avoid diverting to someplace else. There is an old pilot saying—

> ***The only time you can have too much fuel is if you are on fire. True, true, true ..***

The Mohawk had the main fuel tank over the top of the fuselage, with armor plating offering some appreciated but surely just limited protection of the bottom side from any upward anti-aircraft firing. Additionally, under each wing we held an additional 150 gallons of fuel in each of two jettisonable drop tanks. The single-point fueling from the Air Force fueling truck would take maybe another 10-15 minutes.

In the darkness I am leaning back against the near side of the protective revetment, smoking, as I did then. I kept my survival vest and the ejection seat harness on as it is a hassle to take them off unless I had a crew chief to help me get dressed and then up and through the Mohawk's side canopy and into my Martin-Baker ejection seat.

Around my calves were the ejection seat leg garters with quick releases. The garter's straps went through the lower ejection seat and attached to breakaway pins in the cockpit floor, the method of pulling your legs solidly against the ejection seat as it blasted up and through the aircraft canopy.

So it was, as always, a bit of a struggle to get in and out of the Mohawk without our ground support guys, and hopefully with a maintenance-stand alongside the aircraft to climb up on and get through the swing open side canopy. Without the support stand, you had to get your boot toes into openings up the side of the fuselage and being very agile, or not, then get your knees onto your seat and work your legs into the cockpit, around the center flight control stick, and your boots maneuvered down to the armored protected flooring. It is *always a hassle* getting in and out of this aircraft.

Leaving the ejection seat's leg garters on during a short stop is easier and quicker than bending down in the ejection seat and working your boots through the straps.

1/ It Was All Too Real

You wore the ejection seat harness over your upper body survival vest. Straps went down through your crouch area with four harness attach points; two to the side on the ejection seat and two more attachments to the ejection seat parachute at the top of each shoulder point. Another attachment point is to the aircraft's oxygen hose and fed oxygen directly into your facemask in the case of a high-altitude ejection were the oxygen may be needed as you descended.

Your personal survival vest—the overland one for the Laos and overland North Vietnam missions—had a Smith & Wesson .38 caliber pistol, as much ammunition as could be sewn in strips all over the vest, two survival knives, two survival radios, four batteries, some flares and whatever else you customized your vest to carry. There were also pouches of medical stuff and injectable painkillers in the vest and then more carried in your flight suit pockets.

Also, under each ejection seat is a fiberglass survival container that had—for the overland seat packs—more food, water, a tent, fishing gear, ~~a guide to ordering wine with an Asian jungle meal~~, and medical supplies. The overwater seat packs had a small (!) raft, lots of shark repellant, water, food and medical supplies. After takeoff, you hooked up the seat pack so that it did not interfere with an ejection, and you disconnected the seat pack (a lanyard between your legs that then connected to your vest) usually when entering the traffic pattern, again so as to not interfere with a low altitude ejection. The seat pack then would hang down about 15-20 feet below you while you drifted down. If you ejected over water, the idea is to be able to pull up the container and auto-inflate the raft before you landed in the water.

When flying on the SLAR RP-1 (Route Pack-1) missions, just off the coast of North Vietnam, you wore a *different vest* that had more water survival stuff, starting with as much shark repellant as you could find places to put it with the assumption that you would try to limp to the coast and if you had to, to eject into the South China Sea. Shark bait is the issue, and I have several sections in this book about how that ended badly for some. There were already too many ways to die in this aircraft and its mission and more new ones were showing up every day.

Another .38 cal pistol—*my always-carry personal use one*—laid strapped to my right thigh from my holster belt with more ammunition packets. I strapped a large knife to my right calf and four plastic water—*or other liquid stuff*—flasks in my flight suit's thigh and calf pockets. With all this gear on you can see why even getting in or out of this aircraft is a chore and why you left your vest on if you could if you're exiting the plane for only a few minutes.

I was on a much-needed smoke break. For these past few hours, I had worked as the low-flying IR aircraft, as I nearly always did, taking coded target coordinate calls from a unit SLAR aircraft, flying some 10,000 feet above us and many miles away. The SLAR aircraft flew a box pattern with the Side-Looking-Airborne-Radar looking down and finding targets or *Movers* as they were called, on *the Trail*.

After receiving coded coordinates of the location of the *Movers* from the overhead SLAR ship, the IR crews job is to go down in the (invisible) mountains and valleys, running along *the Trail*, usually flying at only about 600-800 feet above the jungle floor. We would use the IR system to find the *hot spots*; the vehicle exhaust and hopefully see enough on the IR screen to know if this is a truck or a tank. Even if the vehicles had stopped and shut off their engines, we could still find their heat signatures for several hours. If the targets were considered worthy, then in the *Box* with us were an assortment of other Service's aircraft to attack the tanks or trucks.

Sometimes the *Movers* were just sensitive radar returns even from people just pushing bicycles loaded with supplies along *the Trail* or a series of radar reflections from small waterfalls and river rapids. A good TO (and they were all good) would know the difference in regards the water returns, but *Movers* that were showing up on *the Trail* itself had to be checked out for targeting.

Generally, in each hunter/killer box, at night, in Steel Tiger North and South in southern Laos, we had an Air Force AC-130 *Spectre* gunship that is flying out of Ubon RTAFB and offering high-level attacks using laser-tracked 40 mm cannons and a variety of mini-guns—and later even with a 105 mm cannon firing from above.

Air Force AC-130 *Spectre* Gunships used in Steel Tiger
(southern Laos)

Less accurate, but very deadly also, would be an assortment of *fast-movers;* mostly Navy A-6 *Intruders* and Air Force F-4 *Phantoms*, but others also, with a variety of ordinance.

Ever unseen, unknowingly where, would be the Air Force EC-130 *Command and Control* capsule aircraft from Udorn RTAFB. If there were active downed airman rescues in the works— or anticipated to be— we would also have Air Force OV-10 *Broncos*, or Cessna O-2 *Skymasters* (usually call sign *Nail*), as the FAC aircraft. And as always, some older Air Force A-1 *Skyraiders* (usually call sign *Sandy*) used for both *CS gas* dropping and close air support. Plus, an assortment of helicopters and other Air Force KC-130 aircraft there that could be fuel tankering the rescue helicopters. It is a wonder there were not more midair collisions considering how many aircraft we had in the air at any given time and with each doing their own thing, at night, with the lights out and not saying in the clear where they were working.

From those calls, I would go down into a blacked valley, along *the Trail*, find what the target is and in doing so also try to make a judgment call on the anti-aircraft weapons that the attack aircraft would be taking. All of Laos was full of Soviet 23 & 37 mm flak weapons, along with more than a few radar-directed 57 mm *heavy* flak guns. On top of that were many .30 cal machine guns, dangerous mostly if very close, and of course, the most dangerous weapon—*the .51 cal (12.7 mm) heavy machine guns.*

The other part of individual IR missions is flying onto predetermined targets using the IR system to find enemy camps, ammunition sites and more. If we had many of these types of targets, then a separate IR mission is flown in the *Box* at the same time we were there with the SLAR/IR combo flights. Otherwise, the IR ship would fly a mixture of checking the *Movers* and running the predetermined targets.

Making things worse is just a couple, just a couple we knew of, of the most feared quad-.51 cal anti-aircraft guns—and no defense there for if they find you— *they have you*. The muzzle velocity of the .51 cal and its projectile's large physical size made it possible for a gunner, if he even sees you, to start firing and then literally *walk the tracer rounds right into you*. The other weapons, mostly the flak, took more luck for the shooters as they had to *lead* the aircraft. The slower flak-type tracer rounds made it easier to avoid being hit, *sometimes*. Finding a .51 cal on or near my targeted site and we would move away. It was like fighting with a Cobra snake— *don't do it.*

As the low-flying IR aircraft, we would pinpoint the target, tell the Air Force C&C aircraft, *Moonbeam* in Steel Tiger South, (night time, otherwise is *Hillsboro* in the daytime) what we thought the target is, any anti-aircraft fire I am taking, and my recommendation for entry and exit paths if need be, though that is usually an Air Force FAC function. For us, working on *the Trail* at night, we were usually feeding this targeting information only to a high AC-130 *Spectre* gunship for them to make the decision to press the attack.

If there is no anti-aircraft firing on me (rare as that was) I would sometimes turn on my position lights and rotating beacon, going *Christmas Tree* as it was called, to try and draw out any anti-aircraft fire, so the bombing run guys, when they were around, and whom I always suspected were sitting down so low in the armored cockpit of the jet that could barely see the ground, much less a tank or truck under a jungle canopy, at night, thousands of feet below, would at least have an idea of what the anti-aircraft gun and flak situation might be on their bomb run.

It was our tasking, if we wanted, *if we dared*, to make a few runs and see who would start firing on you and how many guns there were and what types—machine guns, flak, or the usual combination of both. Sometimes the NVA would coordinate their firing so I that could make a couple passes with either no ground fire or maybe a single .30 cal, or two, and maybe a 23 or 37 mm flak gun are tagging me. Then on the *real target run,* there are the other six flak guns and a .51 cal in waiting. This is like trolling for alligators in a Georgia swamp— *right*? There is a certain bit of *insanity* related to doing this, but as the rest of the book spells out—*that was only a small part of our mindset.*

> *You may assure yourself that a couple of hours of intentionally trolling for anti-aircraft fire is like a direct injection of adrenalin—a hefty dose I might mention that would last for hours and hours after you got home.*

Sometimes the trolling for gunfire scenario played out differently such as when faced with a target run where we *knew* there were a lot of guns; you might go *Christmas Tree* and start into the blackened valley along *the Trail*. The NVA, having already been lured more than a few times into a bait-and-switch with this trolling scheme, would hold off on the flak thinking there is a gunship overhead waiting to smite them, and thus we would have made an unhampered IR pass (or two), pulled up, not been shot at, and then headed on to safer targets, or to a much deserved and needed smoke break.

On this night, it had been long, dangerous and with many hot and valuable targets. There was, on this night, as usual, much gunfire and no moon, which is why the NVA were attacking Kontum, under the near total blackness of a moonless night. A moonless night also made dodging mountain ridges more than a bit risky. It is always a tradeoff, for if there were no moonlight, then the flak and machine gun fire would be less as they could not easily see you, but then you could not see the mountain ridges. As an IR pilot, mostly, I would rather take the flak and see the mountains, as not, while to the SLAR ships, up high, a black night is better and safer for them.

I needed that smoke break during the refueling. While working on *the Trail,* I would move a few miles off to the side, usually to the west towards Thailand where there is no real anti-aircraft threat, have a smoke, get my nerve back up, signal my TO for the next target, and roll the Mohawk down into another dark and dangerous valley. It seems to me my cigarette lighter of that time had an inscription something about—

"As I Fly Through the Valley of the Shadow of Death"

At the time, the *A Shau Valley* **was** the *Valley of Death,* and I had just months before left parts of my crippled Mohawk there, including a single drop tank, there one night. See the *Bomber* event in this chapter.

These actions then described much of our nightly working terrain—mountains that we could not see, and valleys we were never sure of.

While the Air Force fuel tanker truck is attached to my ship, my SLAR pilot partner is working up an outbound artillery clearance for us to get from Pleiku to the east, or north to DaNang, to Marble Mountain. An *artillery clearance* would direct us to fly outbound on a particular TACAN course for X-miles, then fly an arch over to another radial and fly that outbound for another X-miles. The artillery clearances were supposed to keep us out of known friendly artillery firing paths. These artillery clearances, though usually simple, could, at times be quite complicated. I never heard of an aircraft getting hit by artillery fire, but am sure it did happen. With all the other uncontrolled risks this is one we could partially control ourselves.

I needed to get home. I was so looking forward to a couple of beers in the upcoming wee hours of what is left of the night and then get some sleep before starting this all over the next afternoon. It just is not to be that night.

Quite suddenly, but not entirely unexpected, the constant roar of the Air Force's F-4 Phantoms racing down the runway in full thundering afterburner is now broken by a series of rapid exploding impacts of heavy NVA 122 mm rocket fire raining down on the airfield. The objective, of course, is to stop the bombing aircraft going off to hit the NVA at Kontum. Dozens of those big and poorly guided NVA rockets were now impacting around the airfield. The air base is large enough that the usual few hundred 82 mm mortar rounds could not get close enough to the perimeter to do much damage, but the 122 mm rockets more than made up for it.

A significant problem with the 122 mm rockets, besides their size of explosives versus the 82 mm mortars, is that they are just pointed toward an area, set to launch, and where they hit is very scattered and uncertain. The enemy's 82 mm mortars would be precision aimed and usually, if mortars were hitting a particular area on the base, then that is where they were meant to impact. But where the 122 mm rockets impacted is much more random, and thus much more dangerous.

X-The Rocket Attack Starts

Damn. As the first rounds of 122 mm rocket explosions started I snapped my look over to the fueler, who is at least *not running* and leaving me there, but is quickly pulling the just-attached fueling hose from my Mohawk. *I needed that fuel*, the cushion to get home and not be worried about other emergencies. He is pulling out fast as being in a fuel pit area with two aircraft and a truck loaded with explosive JP-4 jet fuel, is surely not where anyone wanted to be right then.

The *smart thing for us to do* would have been to leave the aircraft, find a protective bunker (bunkers were everywhere), and wait this out as it would surely now be going on for some time, probably on and off for hours. That would be the smart thing to do—but the logic of it escaped me that night, as it often did, and I made the snap decision to fly out—*right away.*

At the 131st, the IR pilot was *usually* a warrant officer and would thus call the shots on a SLAR/IR combo flight mission. There were only a few warrant officer pilots, and later only four of us, and we were all IR pilots, the unit instructor pilots, and usually the most experienced of all the pilots, so rank made no difference. The SLAR aircraft, mostly being safe high and away, were usually flown by one of the captains or majors, often because those guys had other unit duties and as such their duties were not totally committed to the nightly missions while the warrant officer pilots were. As it was then, the IR aircraft had the most mission-experienced pilots. The dangerous stuff to be sure.

I dropped the cigarette, with one last quick puff, and am bounding like a waddling duck to the side of my Mohawk. We were leaving—***now***.

With my boots poked into the forward fuselage step plates, I climbed the side of the cockpit, awkwardly, very much so, and swung a leg inside and over the Mohawk's short control stick. With just one leg inside I reached up to the pilot's eyebrow panel, switched on the battery and pressed the right engine START button—even as I am struggling to drag my left leg into the cockpit. The engines start better with large ground power APU carts, but a battery start, while workable, is much slower to initiate the engine compressors spinning.

The right-side Lycoming T53 turbine engine started turning ever so slowly; black jet fuel exhaust now filling the air—with the screaming of the turbines coming alive like an old and slow man awakening from a deep sleep. Ever so slowly the right propeller is picking up the jet compression exhaust and starting to spin up—too slowly it seemed right now.

It is an awkward scramble to get the ejection seat connections in place; the seat's harness points pinned in, the two leg garter connections fastened, the communications plugged in, and the oxygen mask and all the radios brought to life.

I had to wait several long minutes for the battery to recover its charge before I could use it to start the second engine. One could do this while being able to taxi with just the one engine, a task to be sure, but we did it when we were in a hurry—this being one of those times. The one-engine taxi would get us moving toward the

1/ It Was All Too Real

runway while waiting for the second engine, the left side, to be started. Otherwise, an APU start would have gotten both engines running before we moved out of the revetments.

Increasingly, the 122 mm rocket fire is exploding randomly around the base. It would be dicey, getting out of there now. Maybe staying at Pleiku, an Air Force base with real food and *beds with mattresses* would have been better.

The Air Force Pleiku tower guys were down into their bunker now and controlling what traffic there might be just by radio contact and limited visual observations. I advised them that we would make a rolling takeoff from a midfield intersection, and we would be ready in about two minutes—*two very, very long minutes.*

From Kontum there is now an inbound Air America DC-6 with many wounded aboard, coming in, blacked out, and they would, like us, have to take his chances with the rocket explosions. Timing as it was, the inbound DC-6 is too close for us to get all our engines running, make a running start, and still clear the runway area in time for them to land. We were going to have to delay a few more incredibly slow seconds.

With all engines turning I called for the SLAR pilot to plan to move to the left side of the runway and initiate a rolling takeoff with me on the right side. We would take the runway just as the DC-6 passes the intersection we were coming up on as our starting point. This *ill-conceived plan* is that we would make a running takeoff and then liftoff over the top of the DC-6 as it is still rolling out, and still on the runway. Then we would do a high-performance climb out, steep as it may be, to avoid what would surely be much small arms *sparkler* gunfire from just outside the perimeter.

I did not see this as a problem as even from the intersection takeoff the climb would have us at least 500 feet at the end of the runway. I would be staying tucked down and to the right of the SLAR aircraft and then piggyback with him to the coast and north to DaNang. It is not to be, so, as fate would play its hand in but a moment.

What kind of idiot had come up with this plan?

I am, of course, on drugs at the time – the adrenalin being nearly straight injected into us not only from the rocket attack but lingering from on from the several hours we had just spent in Laos dodging a LOT of flak and gunfire and the mountains that stalked us all the time.

We moved rapidly down the taxiway toward the nearest runway access. I peered into the darkness to the south, time having stood still as it was, sitting ducks we were on the receiving end of this rocket attack, as the unlighted DC-6, already in a landing configuration, slowly materialized out of the darkness.

I knew we could not get onto the runway ahead of the DC-6. Looking over to the side of the airfield towards Camp Holloway, and now under the glow of many large flares, were Army Cobra and Huey gunships lifting up from their revetments and rolling, literally from the liftoff, directly into firing rockets and machinegun fire into the perimeter.

Army pilots—mostly young warrant officers like me; few probably were even old enough to drink or vote. Combat command pilots only in their teenage years. Most were young enough to have the quick responses needed in combat, but with the still misplaced feelings of being bulletproof and not worrying about the wife and kids and mortgage back home.

The DC-6 is dropping in short of our runway intersection point. The SLAR aircraft and I both spooled up the engines as we started rolling, with me moving to the right side, our wing flaps set at takeoff, and the engines now screaming against the oversized propellers.

Inside our cockpits, both of the individual ejection seat arming switches, one, a flip-down lever just above our helmet, and the other a throw-over lever between my legs, now went *hot*. A pull of the overhead looped rope hanging above our eyes, or a pull-up on the rope between our legs—and we would be leaving the aircraft—and as it was, maybe a less than 50% chance of surviving any ejection.

For the takeoffs, the TOs put their left hand just below the power console and grasped onto a yellow and black stripped T-handle; the external stores manual jettison handle. In the case of an engine failure on takeoff, the external stores had to be dropped *immediately,* or we could not make the sustained flight on just one engine. Lose an engine on takeoff, *as happened too often*, and it is an immediate jettison of all the wing stores; the 150-gallon fuel drop tanks, the rocket pods, or machine guns or whatever we had hung on the aircraft for that flight. The underwing radar jammers, mounted when working in North Vietnam, could not be jettisoned due to security issues. The IR and SLAR aircraft did not carry any external armaments or weapons, only fuel drop tanks, radar jammers, and flare or light pods.

X-The DC-6 Is Hit On the Runway

As the approaching DC-6 is touching down just before our intersection, we started a roll to get in behind him. We were leaving—*now*! But that was not to be. Unfortunately, *Luck* is not anywhere in sight that night. Not any *Good Luck* as it were.

I had the throttles to *full*, the prop levers to the *max*, and the engine torque is surely approaching the red bars as our Mohawks were rapidly accelerating down the runway.

The SLAR aircraft is running as the lead aircraft, offset to the left of the 200-foot wide runway centerline. I am staggered back by about two-aircraft lengths and rolling to the right of the centerline. We were now only about 400 yards from the DC-6. We were accelerating to liftoff speed and planning to leap over the top of the old DC-6 and *get the hell out of Dodge.*

We were almost at lift off speed, maybe now only 10-12 seconds down the blacked-out runway, and suddenly there is—*a massive explosion*—a 122 mm rocket had hit the runway in front of the right inboard engine of the DC-6.

JFC!

I think the copilot died instantly as parts of the rocket, runway, and engine parts blasted into the DC-6's cockpit. The flight engineer, sitting at a panel seat just behind the copilot, maybe taken out too. The right side inboard engine, the number three, is on fire and pieces of that engine had come through the cockpit—*where the carnage must have been surreal.*

In front of us, the explosion of the rocket blew concrete runway pieces into the air, along with parts of the DC-6, all in a flash and a blast maybe only a few hundred yards immediately in front of us—and we were barreling into that. Forget about overflying the DC-6 and leaving. The rapidly unfolding events were unreal! We were just seconds behind and were now coming into the falling debris.

Maybe the DC-6 should have stopped, but I am not one to second guess, especially considering what the horrific scene in the cockpit is then with just the captain at the controls. The pilot pushed the throttles forward, and the DC-6 accelerated back to a takeoff speed and staggered into the air. Not a good plan, in my view, but then I did not have the remains of my copilot, a close friend probably, all over my lap either.

Some even more dramatic video of similar, or worse runway hits, is on YouTube when you search for a video about the siege at the Marine base at Khe Sanh, in 1968.

See Air Power at Khe Sanh 1968.

http://www.youtube.com/watch?v=8vDgBNFpQEs

Damn! There were frantic radio calls to the Pleiku tower bunker that the DC-6 is hit, *dangerously as it is,* with fire, and they were taking off again. The tower controllers had seen it happen from their bunker position. *Incredible*.

I squeezed my control stick trigger microphone and told the SLAR aircraft that we would stay with the DC-6. **That was a mistake**, to be sure, but things were happening now in mere fractions of seconds, interweaved with a hundred other things—we were already rolling, power immediately full to the panel, with more explosions clouding everything. We had already started to lift off, the plan being to climb over the top of the DC-6 and to climb then out of the perimeter small arms sparkler fire, is now trashed. Instead we both throttled back and were barely staggering into the air, to stay with the damaged DC-6.

We had barely lifted off the runway and were staying just feet above the concrete. I pulled my hand from holding the throttles full forward—like I am pushing them through the instrument panel—and shifted just inches to the left of the power quadrant and slammed the landing gear handle forward, throwing three thousand pounds of hydraulic pressure to the actuators and sucked the landing gear up, closing gear doors banging as they did in mere seconds.

We would typically follow the gear retraction with a climb and pull up the flaps from the takeoff position, but now we left the flaps at the takeoff position and giving us not only the extra lift needed for this now unexpected slow flight, but at that setting we had additional flight control ability through two large, hydraulically actuating inboard ailerons that were only available when the flaps were in any down position, either on takeoff of landing. Without the added flight control derived from these inboard ailerons, many a Mohawk had only rolled over, crashed in an exploding ball of flames and killed whoever is unlucky enough to be flying them. If they did eject, they had only maybe a 50-50 chance of surviving that too as most of these low-level ejections were well outside of the safe ejection seat performance envelope.

The SLAR aircraft drifted left, downward, and to the lower left side of the DC-6 while I pulled back and down to the right. We were now no more than just 80-feet off the ground, with no lights, and no obstacles marked. Meanwhile, the sky in our little corner of the airfield is now filling with tracers and flares while a half dozen Cobras and Huey gunships were working their guns near to my right. Surreal, absolutely surreal how quickly, in just seconds, what had happened—*just seconds.*

JFC!

The DC-6 is staggering back into the air. In a quick exchange of calls, we decided the SLAR aircraft would stay with and support the DC-6 for their safety and support *as he had fuel to do so* while I did not have any spare fuel at all. I would break off and head toward home to DaNang, to Marble Mountain. As to the artillery clearances we needed, or usually liked to have—*forget it.*

The new reality is that we passed the outer airfield perimeter and into the NVA and Viet Cong small arms fire, mostly AK-47s in target range as it was. We were maybe a mere 100-150 feet above the ground, flying *low and slow*, with the wing flaps still in the takeoff position, and barely staggering into the air while trying to stay in position with the DC-6.

Viet Cong and NVA small arms fire (*sparklers* we called them) from dozens of weapons pointed up at us as we now drifted overhead. *Time stood still*—like one is suspended in a nightmare, but, it is still better than the cockpit of the DC-6 that is not more than a few hundred yards in front of me.

To my right side, from the corner of my eye, were the Army gunships making point-blank firing nearly right below us; to the obvious favorite Viet Cong hang out for aircraft target practice. They got what they wanted that night. Damn, we were low and slow. The tracer fire from the mini-guns on the gunships is bouncing back up around us as we slowly moved like a lumbering whale over the outer perimeter.

This is not good . . .

The SLAR aircraft and the Pleiku tower guys had some chatter with the DC-6 captain, and I think he said his co-pilot is dead and the flight engineer, sitting at the control panel behind the copilot in those aircraft, is severely hurt but working. Within a few miles the DC-6 had staggered into the air on three engines and is slowly climbing—very slowly. Our SLAR aircraft would follow the DC-6 to the coast, but I lacked the fuel to linger around; I had to take the most direct route to DaNang or risk going to the coast and finding some other place to land and refuel, which was not likely that night. I turned to the north, toward Kontum, and continued my climb.

Wow! Okay, so this is a very intense what, maybe only three to five minutes at the most? Caught in a time capsule we were. It is time for a cigarette. Two of the plastic water flasks in my flight suit thigh and calf leg pockets had Scotch in them, not water, but this is not the time, not right now, for that relief.

Most of us carried in half of our four small water bottles something alcoholic with the logic (a word I use very loosely throughout my books I might add) that, if we had to eject over bad guy land—which is everywhere—that a good stiff drink after drifting down under the ejection seat's parachute might do more to settle our nerves for survival than more water would! Alternately, we could use the alcohol for wound cleaning. That was the logic, but occasionally I understand some of my comrades in arms had to refill the liquor bottles, if they had them, after a particularly trying day at the airborne office. I never touched the non-water bottles, as right now I needed all the clear *mindset* I could muster.

The shortcut with my now limited fuel would take us nearly right over the besieged city of Kontum. That was all right. Overhead Kontum is probably the safest place considering the artillery arching patterns going in and out. The cigarette hit the spot, and the Scotch in my flight suit water bottles stayed put, for a while. However, this night is young and about to get a lot worse.

In the right seat, my TO had spoken hardly a word since the first rocket hit while we were still in the fueling area. Only the best, *really the very best*, of the technical sergeants and specialists (they were all excellent) would fly with us on IR missions, whether they wanted to or not. The TO is so vital to every minute of every flight that even under intense gunfire, with flak everywhere, there is a quiet, *if not absolutely professional job*, on working together in near silence; each of us knowing what is happening, listening to the war around us, knowing what the other would say or do, so that little cockpit communication is need, other than more than a few *"Ah shit . . ."* comments, well deserved as they would be.

Within maybe only twelve minutes after the surreal departure from Pleiku we were near and almost over Kontum. Clearly the war is alive and running full steam down there. The NVA had three divisions surrounding Kontum and intended to take it, but ultimately did not in that sequence. Besides the F-4 Phantom bombers and Army gunship support from Pleiku, there is also these waves of B-52 heavy bombers running *Arc Light* strikes working through the mountains. Thousands would die there, those weeks, and as usual, *all for nothing*.

There is an interesting account in Wikipedia about **John Paul Vann,** the civilian *General of the American II Corps*, the man that was running things on our side. Sadly, though, he too would be dead within just a few days and within only a few miles of where I am right then. Vann died when his Army aircraft was shot down while doing a low-level observation of the battle at Kontum.

We had been lucky coming out of Pleiku. Things could have gone badly on several more fronts. While my fuel status would be critical getting back, the weather is workable at Marble Mountain, and I could get a fuel emergency priority handling for landing.

Such a night it is already. So lucky we had been. That is the way war is—*mostly luck*, but ours is about to change again. As we started to fly silently just to the east of Kontum, I made some comments about not wanting to be down there, like the DC-6 had been, trying to get the wounded out.

Then disaster struck us.

We Had to Go Back to Pleiku— or Eject Near Kontum

The small arms gunfire at the Pleiku airfield perimeter had, in fact, found us that night. Small arms fire from likely dozens of the *sparklers* had found us as we dragged our butts low and slow over the perimeter while all these guys are were shooting at us.

* * AFT CAMERA BAY HOT * *

What? The MASTER CAUTION light jumped alive as this annunciator light came on. Hot camera bay? This particular warning is usually not a cause for great concern, but I did not have any cameras there and—

Then there is sudden **BLACKNESS** in the cockpit.

Instantly, the autopilot kicked off as my Mohawk lurched to one side and everything went black for just an instant—and then the white, cockpit emergency lights above and to the side of the ejection seats, came on full bright.

Ah, shit . . .

From warning light to blackness was what—*two seconds?*

AM I ON FIRE?

Was I hit by ground fire coming out of Pleiku? Was something now burning in the rear section of my Mohawk, which is below the aft end of my main fuel tank? Whatever had happened now somehow gave me the camera bay hot indicator and is bad enough that my electrical power boards in that area were now out.

I am running on *Emergency Battery Power* only, and that would only last at most maybe 25-minutes, and then I would have nothing at all for electrical power.

AM I BURNING?

Oh, to have my SLAR aircraft with me now so he could slide up near and under me and see if I am burning and if so—

My TO and I both simultaneously, and without any talking on the intercom, pulled our individual ejection seat harness attach points down tighter.

If we are burning, we are going to punch out rather than wait for an explosion. I glanced down to the left as the Kontum airfield is drifting back under my left engine cowling. Below me, I could see near constant explosions on the ground. Only moments, or is it many minutes ago; I was looking down and thinking how lucky we were *that we were not there*. Be that as it may, right now the thought of rolling back to the left and diving toward a landing on the imploding Kontum runway had sort of interest to me—sort of at the time and the now new circumstances.

It is now maybe five seconds, *no more* since the warning light came on and things had gone black in the cockpit.

Damn it .. were we burning? Do we eject? If we eject, this is seriously bad guy land right now as we were directly over where many thousands of NVA and VC soldiers are amassed for the upcoming sweeping attacks to seize Kontum. Like any ejection, we faced a potentially fatal outcome from the ejection itself; the limited flight envelope not being the immediate issue, but rather the coming down into the mountains. Many bad things can happen on any ejection, planned or otherwise.

Are there many Bengal tigers here too?
Strange what goes through your mind at times . . .

Maybe ten seconds now, maybe less have passed—or has time just stopped again?

I rolled my Mohawk to the left and had a brief chat with my TO that if he wanted to step out, *to eject before potentially blowing up in flight*, that I fully understood, but if we have not exploded by now or are not flaming, maybe we can limp back to Pleiku. The aircraft is flying okay though the noticeable and uneven shaking is most likely from the direct nervous pilot input as I am now hand flying the plane. We were running on the Mohawk's limited Emergency Power Bus so many electrical things were not working that were not on this electrical bus.

I switched my UHF radio back to Pleiku tower, who were still in their tower bunker someplace, and told them I had a possible fire and am going to be landing in about ten minutes.

What they did not want, right then, is to have a crippled aircraft on the runway when they had dozens of aircraft involved in this fight and only this one runway to use, so their hope would be that—

If I thought I might crash on the runway, to then instead point my Mohawk away from the airport—and eject.

Frankly, I did not quite see the obvious merit in that. There is a similar account in this chapter about DaNang approach control once sending me, and likely others, out over the South China Sea to eject just to keep crashes off the runways while they were trying to recover damaged strike aircraft themselves coming back out of raids in North Vietnam. Some of these crippled planes likely could have wounded pilots that could themselves not survive an ejection and needed to be on the runway.

By way of some history, one of my very good unit warrant officer friends had a similar situation many years later in Korea on a SLAR mission when he got into adverse weather, and he could not get a good GCA radar talk-down to a landing. He and his TO elected to eject rather than risk a crash. With half the ejections fatal, for a variety of reasons, any reason to eject, whether decided within the few *milliseconds* of your likely remaining life during a failed takeoff, or a shoot down, or whatever, or even if you have some time to decide, was often not successful—*and often fatal.*

Some years later, during the first Gulf War, two more Mohawks were lost together when they recovered together to a Saudi desert airfield that had such high crosswinds that a successful landing looked more than just difficult. The lead aircraft decided to go ahead and try a landing—*and then crashed onto the runway.* The second plane's crew, now fuel critical, and with no runway below them, elected to point the aircraft away from the airport and punch out. So this scenario is not so unusual and my account of DaNang approach control one day leading me 45 miles out to the South China Sea to eject rather than crashing on one of the recovery runways at DaNang was another example.

While running on the Emergency Bus battery power only I had limited items that functioned off that bus. When the reserve emergency electrical power is done with, and that would not be long, we would be down to flying with a mini-flashlight in our mouths! The landing lights I could have, if I had any battery power left, only when the wheels are down. The ejection seats' vertical adjustments (*the Army had bought the optional LSe version of the Mohawk that included, amongst other features such as armor plating, the instantly removable, two-way power seats, unheated as they were*) are now fixed at whatever position they were last in, which is not an issue. Cockpit illumination is now just twin bright white overhead lights—and that *is an issue*, but it is all I had available to see the flight instruments as the panel lights were out. We were in good weather, so this is still not a big issue.

In less than 15-minutes, I am back at Pleiku. I turned onto my final approach and told the tower I am a minute out. My TO and I both made sure our ejection seat packs were unhooked anticipating a possible low-altitude ejection even at this point.

As we came out of the darkness, blacked out, there were still multiple 122 mm rocket explosions about the base, but none onto the runway in front of me, at least I think the runway is in front of me as there were no runway lights either, everything is still blacked out.

To think that just twenty-five minutes ago, or so in my now long, long past, that I had taken a sigh of relief as I pushed the throttles forward to get flying *out* and *over* the DC-6.

How quickly things and perspectives can change.

On short final approach back at Pleiku; my landing gear is down and locked, and I have enough overhead flare illumination that I can leave my landing lights off and touch down on this wide, blacked-out runway.

Immediately on touchdown I have both engine controls pulled back to the fuel off position while still doing maybe 80-90 knots on the runway. At the same time, my TO and I are snapping off the ejection seat quick disconnects. We are getting out of this Mohawk *fast*, just as it is still not sure that we were *not burning?*

I had enough rolling speed to take a turn onto a high-speed exit and rolled clear of the active runway. We set our ejection seat's two safety latches to safe/cold, the harnesses unstrapped, the side canopies are swung out, and we are getting out of this aircraft even as both unpowered propellers were still winding down.

As it is, this flight is my first, my very first flight, with my helmet that I had custom painted to match the gold color scheme that is now, on this ship, painted on the tips of the fuel drop tanks and also onto the nose pan camera cover. This plane is *my* IR aircraft. We did not paint pilot names on the aircraft like other units might have, but on this plane, I had everything working and in perfect condition. Now I had broken it.

I came swinging out of the cockpit, jumping to the ground and ignoring trying to look for my foot into the step that would trigger the boarding ladder to drop out—I am getting out.

In my frustration, I took my helmet off and tossed it toward the cockpit where it is caught by the still moving left engine propeller blades and flung several feet away. I had now chipped my custom painted helmet to top things off.

An Air Force vehicle showed up a few minutes later to see if we needed medical attention while the crash rescue guys had stayed in their bunkers through all of this. They said it might be some time until this rocket attack ends before they send out someone to tow us to the ramp.

My TO and I were now sitting in this very wet ditch between the runway and taxiway and looking to stay low and quiet until this is all over.

X-*Now the Rest of the Story*

It was then, in that ditch that the issue of the **For Emergency Use Only** *Scotch* came out of my flight suit. And about 45-minutes later, during a brief lull in the rocket attack, an Air Force tug showed up to pull us to the ramp.

It is now past midnight on a blackened Air Force base and, well, what to do now? Where would we stay that night? Spud Operations (131st call-signs are "*Spud*") at Marble Mountain had been notified that we were crippled, and grounded at the Pleiku AFB. Sometime overnight they would be sending another aircraft with maintenance support and to retrieve the IR film. And who knows where the SLAR aircraft had gone with the DC-6?

As this very strange night moved along I got a ride to an Air Force officer's club; by then a bit tipsy of course, and wandered inside looking for, well, for whatever there is at this late hour. I had no place to sleep and no one around to help with where to sleep, so, frankly, finding the officer's club had several good points, for even at this late hour I could get food and maybe just sleep there, in the club.

Being sociable as I am, and already a great night of war stories to tell, I did start drinking with these guy. Along the way, I got dragged into some stupid drinking game called *Bears Around the Ice Hole*, which I assumed was *made up on the go* that night as I lost continually.

One thing did stand out, and that is that some Air Force pilot and I had taken possession of, or commandeered, an Air Force field ambulance—*of all things*. Surely there would be someone that needed that ambulance, but the last I saw of it, it is stuck in a muddy ditch near where this guy had a room and a place for me to sleep off what little remains of the night. I am not sure who was driving either.

1/ It Was All Too Real

Often, there is this undefined sense of the surreal, as here we are on an Air Force base, in Vietnam, under a pounding rocket attack, while hundreds of young men and boys are dying just miles away, jets are coming and going, more explosions, and we are playing drinking games and driving around drunk in a commandeered ambulance.

It would be some years later when the epic war movie *Apocalypse Now* starring Marlon Brando and Martin Sheen had the effect of pulling this sense of the surreal into something that is visual. You find that you can blindly drift into, almost seamlessly, into an entirely different reality.

The section in this chapter about my very last Vietnam Mohawk flight is really about the effect of the very intensity of the mindset in combat; be it chronic or acute, it exists. Once you get started on an adrenaline high you are as doped up as any drug addict is, or maybe even more and this is running in your veins for hours and hours after you come down from your flight.

By early morning, the 131st had another Mohawk down to Pleiku with our maintenance guys to see what happened to my aircraft and to give me an aircraft to take back home.

What I do remember, and I am pretty confident this is recounted from a *slightly different perspective* in more than a few Air Force clubs, is that about mid-morning—too early actually considering the night before—that I am on the flight line by my replacement Mohawk and thinking about going home when a half dozen Air Force guys walked up to look at my Mohawk, my replacement one.

I am wearing a flight suit that is more than somewhat tainted in mud from our time waiting first in the runway ditch and then later trying to get away from our ambulance. I had not shaved in a couple of days, of course, and I probably smelled like a skid row bum—*and admittedly looked every bit the part*—when walking towards me are these Air Force guys: pilots, and crew members, from a neat, clean, big Air Force C-141 cargo plane that is sitting down the ramp from my replacement Mohawk.

These guys were all wearing clean and neat *Zoomie Flight Suits,* and each man wore matching colored scarfs neatly tucked in exactly the correct position around their neck and down into the front of their flight suits. Polished boots, clean shaven and probably smelling good topped off the picture that morning. Surely this is the very image of our fighting men at war.

What a different picture this is. I am leaning against my replacement Mohawk like Lee Marvin was leaning with his horse against the side of the saloon in the movie *Cat Ballou*. And I am sucking on the pure oxygen from the O2 outlet beside the ejection seat. Here is this Army bum, me, *surely not an Army **officer***, in a dirty, muddy flight suit, unshaved, smelling bad just as these guys from the C-141 walked up.

I am certain their description of this encounter has been heard over and over and over at Air Force clubs. There was no sense trying to enlighten them. ***To my defense,*** within the past 16-hours I had spent hours on end flying dangerously low altitude IR runs in the mountains, slow, under intense anti-aircraft gun and flak fire in Laos; had got into a rocket and mortar attack just hours ago; had taken off under the falling pieces of the runway and pieces of DC-6 just a few hundred yards in front of me; had flown low and slow through the perimeter gunfire, taken hits, and came back somewhat crippled under fear of being on fire.

That is hardly the whole story.

There was a gunfire triggered electrical short up through an electronics panel in the aft camera bay that had taken out enough of the electrical to trigger the high-temperature light and loss of my primary electrical bus. What could not be found is an entry hole? Ultimately the maintenance guys figured that a *single small arms round*—probably from an AK-47—likely had come up through a four-inch vent opening under the aft camera bay. **How ironic is that?** For all the flak, the SA-2 SAM from a year before, anti-aircraft fire night-after-night, and here I am almost buying my way out from just a single AK-47 round!

1-2 / SA-2 SAM Missile Over Southern North Vietnam

Event Note: In late 1966 we had lost one of our SLAR aircraft off the coast of North Vietnam from a 42-foot Soviet SA-2 SAM missile. In writing this book, I found online other pieces of the 20th ASTA/131st accounts of other SAMs possibly downing our Mohawks in years before I got there. For me, it was during the start of the ill-fated, and very deadly, *Operation Lam Son 719* into Laos, in the spring of 1971, just weeks before the end of my first tour.

> *"There is nothing, absolutely nothing, to describe what goes on inside a pilot's gut when he sees a SAM get airborne."*
>
> — *Author and Source Unknown*

More than 241 aircraft were shot down with Soviet SA-2 missiles.

On the previous three nights, Dan and I were working multiple spot and strip IR targets into Steel Tiger North, near Tchepone (*dirty, deadly Tchepone*), into southern

North Vietnam, and then down into the DMZ just north of the old Marine base at Khe Sanh—when a Soviet-built SA-2 SAM targeted and attacked us. *At the time, we were flying on our **third** back-to-back IR flight of that night.*

Just after our attack many other small aircraft were lost in the following days, including helicopters, and even what I think was an Australian C-7 Caribou cargo plane blown down on March 14, 1971, in daylight, at the Quang Tri airfield and right out of the traffic pattern. That got our attention—in daylight—in the traffic pattern!

An Army U-21 from our base at Phu Bai, flight school classmates and friends of ours, is blown down on March 4, 1971, shortly after Dan and I took the missile. If you read my brief mention of Lam Son 719 elsewhere here, about the loss of Easter Bear, a *Dustoff* pilot friend of mine from Phu Bai, in just a few ill-fated and disastrous weeks, we lost over **800+** Army aircraft down, or severely damaged, and a staggering **106** of them destroyed. Lam Son 719 was real ugly.

We also lost an incredible **173** Army crewmembers dead, another **818** wounded, and **42** more crewmembers MIA, including my friend Easter Bear. Another online summary had the overall flight crewmembers lost from all the Services, airplanes, and helicopters, just in Lam Son 719 alone, *and just in a few weeks*, at a staggering 1,942, mostly helicopter crew members, wounded. The intensity of the war in that location, then, was the heaviest of the entire war. There were over 10,000 South Vietnamese RVN troops dead or injured. This escalation now *is* all out war.

The Lam Son 719 disaster involved reopening the old Marine base at Khe Sanh and to then move some 20,000 RVN troops to the west, into Laos, and attempt to cut off the supply traffic on *the Trail* at a point to the south to Tchepone in central Laos. This mostly South Vietnamese Army ground operation was supported by US Army aircraft for gunships, transports, medevac, and other support, and by US field artillery.

At the time, I am just a couple weeks from going home at the end of my first combat tour. Over the past week or so I was training another warrant officer to be an IR pilot in this target area. We could not possibly have started this at a worse time of the war. So, for several of the past nights, and usually a couple of times each night, Dan and I had launched out of Phu Bai into the same target areas. These were mostly to the north, and west of the old Marine base at Khe Sanh, which had just been reopened by the RVNs as a ground pathway to the west, into Laos and on toward Tchepone. For several of the past days and nights, there is a steady stream of many hundreds of ground vehicles coming up from the South, mostly through Phu Bai, to Hue, to Quang Tri and then to the west to Khe Sanh and beyond.

Dan is a *highly qualified pilot* and already flying IR missions, but this is a new—and very hostile area—and as I am going home in just a few weeks, I needed to get another warrant officer IR pilot up to speed on the targets and bad guy weapons in this area.

The SAM Missile Threat and Our ECM Gear

As far as the SAM threat was concerned, we had lost a SLAR aircraft on RP-2 to an SA-2 SAM a couple of years before. Additionally, other 20th ASTA Mohawks were thought to be lost to the SAMs. Mostly this large, trailer-mounted, 42-foot missile, pushing a nearly 288-pound explosive warhead at speeds of Mach 3.5 had been kept farther, much farther, into North Vietnam. Hundreds of SAMs were operating in the Hanoi and Haiphong areas.

The Air Force and Navy stories of missiles fired up north, taking down everything from the attack aircraft to the large B-52 bombers were certainly far worse than what we might have to deal with, but they also had other ECM help, such as the Wild Weasel aircraft. **In just one night**, *on one mission*, the Air Force lost **8** B-52 bombers to SAMs over the Hanoi area, even with all their electronic gear and other Wild Weasel aircraft for radar jamming, plus another **six** were severely damaged and limped home. That was during the Christmas bombing of 1972.

In just 11 days the Air Force lost 15 B-52 bombers to the SA-2 missiles, inside of the nearly 250 aircraft shot down by this deadly missile.

The Soviet SA-2 missile had an effective engagement range of roughly 8-28 miles. Often an effective attack, that once fired, the missile is guided into position behind the target. This maneuver might be by just shooting at a passing aircraft, even a very high one like the B-52 bombers they successfully took down, or by aiming at an angle that is not directly towards a plane and then turning the missile so as to come from behind. The SA-2 could reach up to 60,000 feet, thus the shooting down of our U-2 spy plane over Russia (Frances Gary Powers) in 1960 and again over Cuba in 1962.

Just a few seconds after the SAM launches there is a first-stage booster separation and the main part of the missile is on its way and is guided by the SAM's ground site radar systems. The missile's warhead can be manually exploded. This technique was used later on the B-52s over Hanoi when the Wild Weasel jamming was otherwise active in jamming some of the signals on board the warhead. The missile has a proximity warhead capability, so while the intent is to use the blast to take down an aircraft, the missile did not have actually to hit the target. That is what 288-pounds of high explosive in a warhead can do.

The time from a launch until reaching the aircraft is only a matter of seconds so an evasive maneuver—if it even could be used—had to be done *immediately*,

One of the limitations of the missile is that supposedly the flexing guidance fins could only affect a maximum of a 4G turn, or pull-up, giving just a very brief window that an aircraft might escape with a High-G evasive maneuver of its own. If the target aircraft suddenly pulled up too soon, the missile would make an easy adjustment and blow it down. If one waited too long, just a few seconds more at most, and then, of course, the missile wins also. Somewhere in there is a window of only a few seconds that an aircraft may be able to blindly and reactively maneuver to be outside of the 4G turn or redirect ability of the SAM.

For us, after our SLAR aircraft disappeared on RP-2, (and others from the days of the 20th ASTA), the conventional wisdom was, in both the case of an SA-2 SAM missile and an air-to-air engagement with a heat-seeking missile from a MiG, was to turn towards the oncoming missile and—

"When the sweat blinds you . . .

Pull up!"

We all harbored some severe doubts that would have ever worked.

Until this night, the overall saving grace for us was that the NVA would not waste a huge, expensive, and limited number of these big missiles on any small aircraft target that could otherwise simply be shot down by ground fire or flak. Because we had Air Force or Navy Wild Weasel fighters to attack a SAM sites, why waste the missiles and immediate retaliation on a meaningless smaller target?

This assumption turned out to be a serious misjudgment in our thinking.

The defense against the SA-2 SAM missile sites were attacks by what are known as *Wild Weasel* aircraft: Air Force and Navy aircraft with wing-mounted electronic packages that can go in and themselves lock onto a missile site's radar signals and send weapons down at the sites. These attacks are often flown just ahead of and during an active airstrike deeper inside of North Vietnam.

To this end, the Air Force flew several versions of the F-4G *Phantom* out of DaNang AFB with a Wild Weasel package of electronics and missiles. Later they added more dedicated groups of various versions of the F-105 *Thunderchief* and themselves usually paired with other Air Force attack fighters as escorts. The Navy often used the A-6 *Intruder*, or other aircraft with a Wild Weasel package and were flown from aircraft carriers somewhere out in the South China Sea.

The Air Force F-105 Wild Weasel aircraft out of Takhli RTAFB.

I have a firsthand account in Chapter 2 of an F-105 WW crew who could not mate up with a KC-135 tanker while they were coming back from strikes in North Vietnam and ended up ejecting in northern Laos, near the Plain of Jars where I was working IR targets that night. This Air Force flight group had an interesting patch with the words Wild Weasel on the top, a startled looking weasel in the middle and across the bottom just the letters Y-G-B-S-M, which is allegedly short for—

<u>Y</u>ou <u>G</u>otta <u>B</u>e <u>S</u>hitting <u>M</u>e

These guys lost a lot of aircraft and crews on these attacks and if you Google *Wild Weasel* you come up with some great stories.

The SA-2 SAM sites had six to eight missiles arranged in a circular pattern so they could fire in any direction. These sites could be fully setup or taken down and moved in about four hours, which was common because if a Wild Weasel strike did not take them down, surely a B-52 *Arc Light* strike would wipe out all traces of them and anything else in the neighborhood to boot.

At the 131st, we had some of our VR mission photos of our Mohawks running nose pan camera missions right over these SAM sites while coming at treetop level. Great pictures!

For an attack, the SAM site has to make a radar lock on an aircraft and thus our APR 24/25 ECM (passive Electronic Counter Measures) electronic equipment was used to let us know trouble is brewing nearby.

The Mohawk's ECM had a glare shield mounted round screen above two rows of illuminating buttons. The ECM light panel showed either an I SAM LO or E SAM LO light (not sure what the difference is other than perhaps the radar frequency). At the same time, there would be a particular type of strobe on the scope with a unique audio into our headsets. The length of the SAM strobe (different patterns of the strobes depending upon the radar system) flickering on the scope is an indication of the direction towards and perhaps of the distance (signal strength) to the launch site. Any SAM *lock on* was a cause for *immediate* evasive maneuvers and a need to move away from the site—*now!*

The I/E SAM LO lights step up to I/E SAM HI when the ECM detects that more power is being fed to the missile. At this point, the missile is also being turned towards the target. The ECM system is sensitive enough to detect the small changes in electronic power that changed the ECM lights and strobes—and had an *immediate impact* on one's breathing and heart rate.

The next step up is a bright yellow ACTIVITY light along with louder strobes on the ECM scope and more frightening screeching alerts in our helmet earphones. The ACTIVITY light meant they were at the last phase of preparing to fire and were exercising the missile fins. From the first radar lock on to the aircraft target with an LO light to the HI light, to ACTIVITY could be only 4-7 seconds. FAST!

The ECM shows a RED, *screaming, flashing* LAUNCH light when the missile is launched.

Our ECM scope and warning lights are
mounted on the upper left of the glare shield.

Each of these steps required our ECM gear to detect a slight power change at the radar site as it is sending more preparatory electronic signals to the missile guidance. Later, on the OV-1D model Mohawk, the 131st aircraft we did have a radar jamming pod mounted under the wing at the most outboard hardpoint and is hardwired (could not jettison them in an emergency) to the wing. A radar-jamming control panel, located just above the throttles, showed us indications of the *type of radar* sensed, and tracked, and some electronic jamming; but this is surely not for a SAM, or why have all these dedicated Wild Weasel aircraft for the Air Force and Navy?

Only the 131st Mohawks had any ECM sensors or radar jammers because we were the only ones flying in North Vietnam and Laos. The radar jamming gear, shown in this book with black pods under the wings at the most outboard wing station, did not come about until the deployment of the OV-1D aircraft on my second tour.

Did it work like that? We would never know. At the earliest sign of the E SAM LO, and hopefully before the E SAM HI light, we would be diving lower. ***Plus,*** they would never waste a large missile on us—*never*.

On This Fateful Night during the Start of Operation Lam Son 719

Dan and I had flown most of these IR targets for four of the past five nights. Each launch would be run on 6-8 strip targets, mostly being roads to the north of Khe Sanh coming down from North Vietnam, and more roads a bit further to the west, toward the Laotian border, the tri-border region as it were, and then further west towards Tchepone. We were now looking mostly for tanks, *hundreds* of the Soviet-built T-54/56 light tanks that could move through the jungles and along *the Trail* or infiltrate down through the DMZ to attack Khe Sanh from the north, in force.

Dan and I would fly these IR missions, run the strip targets, and take the aircraft back, refuel, get new IR film loaded and launch again. Each of these missions is for *read-out* intelligence. In most IR missions, other than the heat-of-the-battle during Lam Son 719, we would usually only be using the solo IR aircraft to find NVA camps and vehicles, but mostly for the IR film to be read-out upon our return. Those missions were usually flown between about 2100-2400 hours when the NVA camped out, stopped, and we could find where the ground camps were.

Tens of thousands of NVA soldiers were on the move along with hundreds and hundreds of trucks and tanks, and now on the move 24-hours a day. With this fast evolving situation, we would run the mostly targeted IR missions, return to Phu Bai, refuel and reload new film, then do another one, and then a last one into the very early morning hours as there was a constantly changing battlefield deep into the jungle.

For the past few nights, I flew as the pilot and Dan ran the IR system to see how I planned and ran targets. Then a couple of nights earlier I put Dan into the pilot seat, and I am the IR system operator.

On this night, I am finishing Dan's IR training, and I am working just in the right seat on both of the earlier launches. On our last launch, Captain Al Musil, my hooch mate, and our SPUD Intel officer, gave us a troubling update on the IR mission brief concerning the movement and location of two new SAM sites that were now just above the DMZ. These new sites were the closest we had seen these missiles to our working airspace. More troubling, these SAM sites were not on the two earlier briefings of this night, so the sites had just been set up and detected within the past few hours.

A few weeks later, Captain Musil, and my classmate, Warrant Officer Jack Brunson, were both brought down in Laos, in Steel Tiger North, near Tchepone during an armed VR flight with another ship. Almost immediately, the aircraft wreckage is found by their wingman, but no radio contact is made with either of the guys. Sadly, their downed Mohawk is not in an area where a ground insertion could safely be performed, as we had been able to do while looking for George Rogalla just a few weeks before. Al and Jack then went into an MIA status for many decades.

One of the two new sites is to the west end of the DMZ, near the tri-border region and south of Mu Gia Pass, while the other site is also just above the DMZ, but located northeast of Khe Sanh. There were maybe 40 miles or so between the SAM sites. Clearly, in retrospect, the intent was to attack the hundreds of slow-moving aircraft, like our Mohawks, which were supporting the hundreds of vehicles we had been moving westward through Khe Sanh toward *the Trail*.

Our typical detailed IR mission briefing is about any heavy machine guns, any of the .51 cals, and the *known* 23/37/57 mm gun locations. There is also a troubling rapid change in our *Safe Letters*, meaning there were multiple pilots down in the past days and this *Safe Letter*, unique to a downed pilot, is being changed with some frequency—*now several times in only a few days.*

It is about 0300 hours as Dan, and I walked out to the IR aircraft for the third launch of that night. The ground guys were great, knowing what we were going through, and all of them put out the very best individual efforts to be sure the aircraft is perfect, the windshields were spotless inside and out and every detail of the cockpit and IR systems already setup and ready for a launch. On these pilot qualification flights, the regular TOs took care of the IR system setups and checking, including the IR film, something the TO would normally do. But none of the TOs wanted to go on *these flights.*

The SAM missiles now worried me for the first time. This area, on this flight, is where we had been flying too many recent nights already, so they knew our pattern and how we moved from target-to-target. But, no one is going to waste a SAM on a little Mohawk, right—*or would they?*

As we walked down the blackened aircraft ramp to the revetment to our plane, I told Dan to take a break and that I would fly this last launch as the pilot. I am more than a bit uneasy as this is now the biggest and fiercest time of the war to date, *Lam Son 719.*

Navy Fighters Took the First Two SAMs That Night

We were about half an hour onto the targets north of Khe Sanh, going down into the blackened valleys, running the IR strips on the roads, taking some machine gun fire only, and then pulling up, reorienting ourselves and then going down to the next target. Early on we picked up some 23 & 37 mm flak, but it is light, in my view. By staying down as low as we could keep out of most of the flak, but it did give the machine gunners a chance to work on us over and over.

While we flew the IR runs themselves over the targets at only about 600-700 above the ground, our optimum IR sensor altitude, on this night I am staying below 3,000 feet on my climb-ups (to pull up and over the mountain ridgelines) from an IR run out of the hills. I considered this lower altitude to be safer from the missile threats and I then only had to deal with some light flak. The real *Light Show* of heavy machine guns and flak-filled skies is already up and running farther to my west, to the tri-border area and towards Tchepone.

Then the first SAM came up at a flight of Navy aircraft. The nighttime explosion of the warhead is **MASSIVE**! There were 288-pounds of high explosives going off nearby in the night sky. I had never, ever, been anywhere close to a SAM missile fire or explosions. This SAM had come up from the site just to the northeast of Khe Sanh. The radios were going rapidly now, and Red Crown is on UHF Guard 243 MHz with—

"SAM . . . SAM . . .

Vicinity of Khe Sanh . . .

SAM . . . SAM . . .

Red Crown on Guard out."

JFC!

I had heard a hundred of these *in-the-blind call outs* on the UHF Guard frequency from Red Crown or Deep Sea, but they were usually near Vinh, or much further to the north, with many of them BULLS EYE (Hanoi and Haiphong area). Near Khe Sanh? Again, sometimes it is Red Crown or Deep Sea calling out—

"Bandits . . Bandits . .

Vicinity [wherever] . .

Bandits . . Bandits!"

But not down here! Near us! Never.

Within just a few minutes or so—**ANOTHER SAM CAME UP!** Again, fired at this flight of Navy jets that were somewhere near me. There were now two massive explosions within a few minutes! This back to back set of missiles might have been a game changer. This one also came from the same site to the northeast of Khe Sanh and north of the DMZ.

But, indeed, the North Vietnamese would not waste a big missile on a slow-moving target like a Mohawk? *Right?*

Because the North Vietnamese had moved these two SAM sites into place in such quick order just in the past hours that I don't think we yet had any Wild Weasel support to press the attack against them.

What the NVA had decided to do is reflected a few pages down in this account about the Army helicopters and others brought down over the next few days, was to use these big missiles to *force* the helicopters and other *slow-movers* down into the heavy machine gun range.

Until now, a helicopter, a twin-rotor CH-47 Chinook, or Air Force C-130, or C-119 or C-123s flying cargo, could stay above 1,500 feet and feel relatively safe from the ground fire, assuming you were not operating in the area of the flak guns. So now, over the next weeks, the SAMs would be used to force downward the small aircraft and thus increase the plane losses. The NVA were now using these missiles for the nearly assured shoot downs of our *slow-movers* and to run fear into the pilots of the smaller, slow-moving, aircraft—*and it worked very well at that.*

I still had a few IR spot targets and strip runs in the area generally north and east of Khe Sanh and starting or ending north of the DMZ. It is tanks we were looking for, just as had been done during the 77-day long and deadly siege of the Marine base at Khe Sanh in 1968 when the Marines lost over 248 men KIA just defending this base at the head of the *A Shau Valley*.

As revealed years later, this is the only situation during Vietnam were the US command had *considered the use of battlefield nuclear weapons*. Khe Sanh was just that important to us, and to the North Vietnamese, and we would protect it at any cost. Now, in the current battle, hundreds of tanks were making their way south through the DMZ and toward Khe Sanh, our forces new staging area for Lam Son 719.

This fast developing situation is why I could not abandon the mission that night and go back to Phu Bai after the two SAMs had come up. No one would believe that they would use the SAMs on the smaller aircraft, and the missions were just that important—too many lives were at stake.

Dan and I would be the first small aircraft to take the SAMs. Unfortunately, that was only the beginning for the SAM sites that upped and moved the mobile missile launchers several times a day.

Repeatedly, over the next thirty minutes as I came up through a series of IR runs my ECM started to come alive, (!!) going through an E SAM LO several times, and once to an E SAM HI, but nothing more. Each time I quickly dropped down masking myself below a blackened ridgeline that I really could not see.

I am getting radar tracked, painted, and repeatedly locked on now by *both* the SAM sites, but I could not tell which one is the site that is running up my ECM missile signals. My ECM is alive with strobes and locks, the lights running, the screeching in our headsets, but still not sure which site is on me with the *hard locks*.

Each time I came up above the mountain ridges, the ECM running now much faster than my heartbeat, and I would make a climbing turn *towards the SAM site to the northeast*. I am maybe less than 15 miles from that site and about 25 miles from the one near the tri-border. My intent is to try to stay closer and closer to the most eastern SAM site, to remain so close that I would be inside, or at least near to, the closest firing range of about 8 miles.

Maybe three times we came up—*got the hard radar locks on us*—the lights, my heart stopped, and probably Dan's too, and then each time I rolled toward the missile site that I *thought* is the immediate danger.

About the fourth time up—*and surely three times past when I should have gone home and had a not uncommon early breakfast of Jack Daniels and Coke*—I had climbed above the blackened ridges, the ECM is screeching in our headsets, and **the scope has strobes of two SAM sites locked on us**.

Ah, shit...

Everything is now alive and flashing on the ECM's screen while the mixed audios were screeching in our headsets. There is now clearly too much information screaming at us visually on the ECM scope on my glareshield and the flashing lights and the mixture of so many loud audio alerts in our helmets.

It is now difficult to make reasoned and instant decisions when I have no blood flow to my brain.

My ECM scope becomes flooded with a variety of ground and airborne radars from aircraft near us and some land and long-range airborne tracking sites. Maybe a dozen or more radar paints were running at any given time, each of them taking more of our attention even as we were working on the increasingly heavy enemy ground fire and the deadlier mountain ridges where we would sweep down past while going into the valleys on an IR run.

Both SAM sites had us, but I am only concerned with the *close one*, and I felt I had to be very close for them to risk firing on me.

E SAM HI - Trouble now—three times in maybe 5-8 minutes and never this deep into an ECM signal in all my flying.

LAUNCH – Is screaming in our headsets; the red **LAUNCH** light is flashing, and the radar strobes are now running wild on the ECM scope.

Ah shit..

There is no yellow **ACTIVITY** light, no last warning to call **TIME OUT**; we are picking up our toys and going home. It is too late.

I am climbing to the north, just maybe 10 miles or so north of the DMZ when the screeching and flashing red **LAUNCH** light exploded into our world.

I rolled hard to the right—toward the site I thought had fired on me.

My right hand had already gone down to the external wing stores jettison, and I glanced out my left window as I saw my left fuel drop tank disappear into the jungle. At least it worked *this time* because the account here of the BOMBER story is about losing an engine in the *A Shau Valley* (*The Valley of Death*) and jettisoning my external fuel tanks—only to have a full underwing tank hung up under the right side wing!

As I turned to the right intending to continue the roll further and down toward the mountains, I caught a large flash out my *left side*.

The SAM is screaming toward us at Mach 3.5 from the remote site to the west—*not the near site!* Damn! The flash I first saw from the corner of my left eye, the Air Force debriefers told us later, was the first-stage booster separation. ***It's coming for us.***

Apparently, the two sites had been trading radar information so that while the strongest radar locks were coming from the near site, the one I felt I could hug close to and not get fired at, they were feeding launch information to the one to the west. That explained why I got an **E SAM LO** light, then an **E SAM HI** light, but no **ACTIVITY** light—*and a 42-foot Soviet-built missile coming from the wrong direction.*

I am solidly in this far missile's prime engagement range. Why a *slow-mover,* like me? When I rolled right and caught the flash of the booster separation back to my left, not my right as I expected it, I had wrongly turned my backside toward the real missile—*the one coming with our name on it—*

"SAM . . . SAM . . .

North of Khe Sanh . . .

Spud 11 . . . Spud 22

> *[In the blinding rush of those seconds I had changed from my mission call sign, the Spud 11, to my personal flight call sign, Spud 22]*

SAM . . . SAM!"

Bear in mind, all this is going on in seconds, seconds that seem like time standing still or moving a thousand miles an hour, all at the same time.

In my turn around I am now full throttled and in a diving roll down and to the right. This missile is now like a flaming basketball coming at us—*just that fast!*

The dive could not now have been much more than five or so seconds. We could not survive doing that as I am descending directly into pitch-blackness and I am already close to the mountain ridges, the ones I could not see. If the missile did not get us, a crash into an unseeable mountainside is only seconds away. Screw the anti-aircraft ground fire that is coming up at us; it did not matter right then.

At this time, in retrospect, and in several follow-on briefings I gave over the next couple of weeks, is that *we should have ejected*. The attack on a slow-mover like me, without an active (jamming) ECM, and certainly no Wild Weasel on the scene—*was technically not survivable*.

A large number of ejections are fatal, even when things are going right, but there is no time to think about that. We were in North Vietnam. We were running targets right over thousands and thousands of enemy soldiers, so we might survive the ejection and surely be killed on the ground. The NVA was not in the habit of taking any prisoners in this type of active field fighting situation. Also, there probably could be no rescue attempt in this area—*none*. Like Dan and I had figured all that out in two or three milliseconds of our spare time—with no blood flow to the brain?

For the *slow-movers*, like us, using this ECM gear without a Wild Weasel, or real active radar jamming, they needed to add another flashing panel light to the system—something like—

Kiss Your Ass Goodbye, Buddy!

Thinking back, after having been a Mohawk pilot, civil now and military, for most of my 27-years of Army flying, and being an instructor pilot in both the US Army and the Argentina Army, that we have had so many fatal crashes from pilots trying to outfly some event, such as an engine failure on takeoff.

It is human nature I suspect, to attempt to fly something out. Not a conscious thing, because I had no time to think through anything any more than the guys that lost engines on takeoff and crashed did. Just the way it is. Emergency checklists work great in training, and on checkrides when you expect an emergency event, and you are not likely to die, but not so much in real life.

Obviously, we did not eject.

Only seconds now into this steep, full power, right-diving death turn that apparently this missile, *our missile*, has come around to us. I can see it as I look up to the right and backward through the overhead canopy—and it is fast, growing from a burning light to a flaming basketball in only these few seconds.

At about the same time, we figured later, out of the corner of my eye, Dan snaps back hard into his Martin-Baker ejection seat and goes for the upper ejection seat firing rope. Later, Dan said he was not going to eject until we were hit, which would have been too late.

At the same time, my right hand had come off the throttles I am pushing through the instrument panel, and with both hands, I snapped the Mohawk's small control stick hard into my gut.

The Mohawk lurched upward into a high-speed, high G-force accelerated rolling climb and stalled, and tumbled, we figured, onto our back. We were so screwed!

There is this HUGE explosion, and we had not a clue of what kind of rolling, tumbling, accelerated stall situation we were in when this 288-pounds of explosives blew up above or behind us. I think, but am not sure because already we were tumbling, rolling at the same time, and the explosion is so shocking, so close, that we had no idea, in the blackened night, just what flight attitude the Mohawk is in.

Opening our eyes might have added some details right then, but . . .

For several very long seconds, with time standing still again, our Mohawk tumbled out-of-control. There were no outside references, no horizon—*no anything.* Dan is still holding onto the upper firing rope, and I am jockeying the control stick still trying to get some control of the aircraft. My moving the control stick is not doing any good because of the tumbling stall and the complete lack of air flow over the wing and tail control surfaces. That is a deep stall situation, mostly likely an inverted accelerated stall, and we were in it, and until we were pointed downward, stalled or not, we would not get any flight controls until we had smooth airflow over the wings and tail.

Some decades later, I am in Argentina, training an Argentina Army instructor pilot in a mixed language cockpit (not a great plan), and we lost control, rolled into a high-speed, overspeed situation—*during which I instantly forgot all of my Spanish*—and the pilot did a similar thing: jamming the stick hard full back and truly doing a near vertical accelerated stall. I was in the right seat then. My visor snapped down; my microphone dropped to my throat, and I went into a full gray out condition and could not stop this guy or get control of the aircraft.

Back at the Argentina air base, we found that due to the excessive G-forces we had shed the entire left engine outboard cowlings, and the landing light was expelled (!) out of its retracted position. The three G-meters in the Mohawk's belly could record up to 8-Gs, and each of them had maxed out—so we had no idea how many G's we had put on the aircraft. When we got back to the airfield at Campo de Mayo, that particular Mohawk became a spare parts bird—and it never flew again.

Something like that happened to us that night, north of Khe Sanh. My full force, overspeed, full power jerk up and away had saved us, but it bent this Mohawk too. It was all blind luck—*all of it.* Had I waited maybe a couple more seconds the blast would have destroyed us with no chance for an ejection; had I pulled up a few seconds earlier the missile's 4-G maneuver limit could have easily adjusted to destroy us.

Luck, all of it—nothing more. Like so many of the fatal events in this book, luck is so often the decider—or, is it that *Fate is the Hunter?*

As we came out of the tumbling near vertical stall, I got enough airflow to take back control of the aircraft, but it is still shaking badly. The shaking is most likely from pilot induced hand shaking, but again, I don't think this plane ever flew again either.

We are out! *Alive*. Not out of danger yet by a long shot, but right now just facing some heavy machine guns from below seemed almost welcoming.

Dan came off the ejection rope, and I remember we were—*We're out! We're out!*

By then Red Crown is up on UHF Guard with the warning call I had heard so many times in the past, only now it is about us—

"SAM . . . SAM . . .

North of Khe Sanh . . .

SAM . . . SAM . . .

Red Crown on Guard out!"

The Air Force ATC radar guy at Quang Tri is calling me in the blind while there is another call, or series of calls, from an Air Force OV-10 *Covey* FAC, which is somewhere near us. The Covey FAC is telling Quang Tri that a missile had just come past him and exploded, but that he could not see if we were gone. I am now calling the Quang Tri Air Force radar controller in a rather rushed and breathless first call—

"Quang Tri . . .

Spud 22 . . . Spud 22 . . .

We are out . . . possible SAM missile damage!"

The night, though, is far from over. I had a crippled Mohawk to the extent we did not know with no external fuel tanks and we needed to get on the ground soon.

Probably some 60-90 miles to our east an Air Force HH-53 Jolly Green rescue helicopter is likely sliding down and unplugging from a KC-130 refueling tanker. He and another HH-53 would be holding on to the fueling hoses waiting for a new rescue, as ours is perhaps about to start. Silently, *professionally*, the Jolly Green would be starting in our direction, but from below the DMZ.

1/ It Was All Too Real

Rescue helicopters stayed with the tankers until needed.

Within minutes, Red Crown is grabbing Navy *fast-movers,* and I hear him starting to stack them off some Quang Tri TACAN radials. He is asking, *fast and professionally*, as I had heard too so many times, the Call Sign, the ordnance they had for attacking and their *Bingo Fuel* time.

Bingo Fuel is a slang term about when they have to leave to get home comfortably. There are times someone can stay past his Bingo Fuel, but usually only in a combat emergency. Red Crown is grabbing the guys that were on their way to support bombing to our west, in Lam Son 719, and putting them into stacked orbits to use for suppression of ground fire during a rescue—our possible rescue just north of the DMZ.

Within minutes, and probably before we had crossed the DMZ, Air Force A-1 Skyraiders, call sign *Sandy*, were probably already starting to crank their powerful Wright-series radial engines, billowing black smoke as the propellers start to come to life. The Skyraiders, heavily loaded with CS gas and bombs, become the principal close air cover aircraft for many rescues.

The real problem is that if we were down, or yet may go down; we were right over some really, really, really bad guy land full of everything they could throw at an aircraft, now from multiple SAM sites on down to thousands of enemy soldiers on the ground. The missile hit on us would have been just as sure a death–*and a whole lot quicker.*

The Air Force lost a staggering number of some **74** Jolly Green and Pedro rescue helicopters in the war. And an even more incredible, **191** A-1 *Skyraiders*, the prime support aircraft for rescues, plus many more assorted FAC and other attack aircraft used just during rescue operations. The numbers of lost aircraft are staggering: Wikipedia has a good list of lost aircraft at "Aircraft Losses of the Vietnam War."

Meanwhile, on our RP-1 mission, just off the coast of North Vietnam, our 131st SLAR aircraft heard the calls from Red Crown and the follow-on that this is a Mohawk, a *Spud* call-sign. He immediately broke off the mission, let down out toward the open sea, and then turned to come back to Phu Bai. Meanwhile, it is still in the early morning darkness as dozens of events were running at the same time.

Spud Operations got an urgent land-line call from the Air Force controllers at Quang Tri that Spud 22 had taken a SAM over North Vietnam; is still in the air, and that I am coming back across the DMZ, possibly with missile damage to the aircraft.

More people were pulled into the process at Phu Bai even as it is probably not yet 0500 hours. Quickly, an already fueled Mohawk readied for another mission is prepped and fired up to be aloft and vectored towards our Mohawk. The developing plan is to have some daylight on us and get the other Mohawk up close enough in flight to examine the aircraft, something that needed to be done to determine whether I could land safely or Dan and I may have yet to eject if there were damages that could cause a runway crash.

Across the runway at Phu Bai, the helicopter units got a call that one of the Mohawks is coming back out of North Vietnam and may be damaged, and if so, may have to eject. To be sure, no one wanted to be on the ground in this area, even near Phu Bai, so a dual post-ejection pickup rescue would need to be *immediate* and require several helicopters with multiple Cobra gunship support.

Likely an Army helicopter Pink Fire Team, usually made up of an OH-6 Loach and two AH-1 Cobra gunships, each piloted by kids like me, were called out and standing by so that if there is an ejection, hopefully, there would be a rescue within minutes of parachuting to the ground; if not even having a helicopter already sitting there as we came down.

Another Army Dustoff Huey from Easter Bear's unit over on our side of the runway would be cranking up to go out with the fire team helicopters. The helicopters would be running, blades turning, and ground guys by the aft end of the Cobra's rocket tubes, there waiting to pull the 2.75" folding fin rocket's arming pins, waiting until they knew the helicopter is going up.

As we got nearer to Phu Bai, whatever Air Force rescue aircraft that might have been managed, were released, or never launched while Red Crown let his stack of holding ordinance aircraft go back onto their assigned missions.

It is breaking dawn by the time we reached Phu Bai and one of our unit Mohawks is in the air with us. As far as could be seen, in the breaking daylight, my aircraft is okay to go ahead and make a landing. But the plane is not flying well, which is probably a combination of my still shaking hands on the control stick and the clean configuration of the wings—no external stores or drop tanks, and a bent tail section to boot. It is jointly decided, amongst the pilots, ops guys and maintenance chief to go ahead with a landing.

The landing at Phu Bain, in the now breaking dawn, is itself uneventful. The crash crew is out in force, and many of the 131st unit guys were out on the ramp or up on the revetments, most likely waiting to see another crash. *Just the way it was.*

It is only about two hours later that several Air Force Intel guys from DaNang AFB arrived to debrief Dan and me. I am not sure about the debrief contents, because by then what they found were two rather already semi-drunk Army warrant officers. I recall that the issue of how the two sites had coordinated the radar linking so that we were locked hard on by one SAM site and expecting a launch from there while another missile is already on its way to us from the other site. The missile's on again, off again launch sequence had confused our reading of the ECM gear to the point that it was not reliable whether any launch *is* imminent.

Over the next couple of weeks, I traveled a bit and gave several brief descriptions to other pilots about what had happened. My words of wisdom and guidance were simple—*eject*, or get down and out because our survival was *completely luck*. **No skill was involved.** I should have ejected and at least given Dan and me maybe *a slight chance* of survival versus what should have been a 100-percent assured blowup of the Mohawk.

The Next Weeks Were an Even More Deadly Disaster

In just the next weeks of Operations Lam Son 719, until the SAM sites were either destroyed or used up their missiles, they were useful in taking down many aircraft that would not otherwise have been subject to a SAM attack.

The NVA would fire several missiles and then quickly, on portable launchers, move some distance away and rapidly setup to be able to fire again. The hasty shoot-and-move tactics made Wild Weasel attacks on the sites difficult, just as trying to attack the ever-moving flak guns were. They would fire, move, and fire and in the day and age of a lack of precision-guided weapons, just moving a hundred yards is enough to thwart retaliatory attacks from our aircraft or ground-based artillery.

Not all the events are accurate, I know, because even during these times no one is given any more information than they had to know, and finding out how many other aircraft were taken down is not high on the list. One critical example not given us is that an Australian C-7 Caribou cargo plane was blasted right out of the traffic pattern at Quang Tri—*in daylight*: taking a missile from the more eastern of the two sites we knew were working in that area. That struck the most fear; the right-into-the-traffic-pattern kill with this missile at an airfield just a few miles to our north.

With us in Phu Bai, an Army U-21 radio intelligence aircraft, call sign *Vanguard 216* from the 138th Aviation Company (Radio Research) took a SAM head-on and is destroyed along with the loss of all five men on board. So shocking is that, that within just a few hours of taking down the U-21 we were listening to the controller tapes while the pilot described how he had turned to face the missile, and the last words on the ATC audio tape were something like—

"We're dead!"

At least one of the CH-47 aircraft with troops is taken down.

Several UH-1 Huey's and AH-1 Cobras were taken down.

An F-4 Phantom out of DaNang, amongst many of them.

Perhaps five or more that were downed by these big missiles.

Then . . .

About ten days after our encounter, an Air Force OV-10 Bronco FAC aircraft (I think), successfully engaged a SAM; his aircraft also without an active ECM capability, and survived. At the end of the war supposedly he and I were the only two small aircraft that had successfully engaged an SA-2—*without an active ECM capability*—and had survived. *However*, in my Internet searches, I found references to other 20th ASTA Mohawks that had engaged SAMs, but I found no further details. I also received several emails from pilots with the 20th ASTA and the 131st before I got there, that SAMs were an issue. On the Amazon book site, one of the comments stated—with some sound of authority—that no Mohawks were known to have been downed by SAMs: I think that is incorrect, but again, all this is secret for security reasons even if you are right there. To say nothing of moral issues with the pilots!

1-3 / NURSE CRASHES ENROUTE TO HER PHU BAI HOSPITAL ASSIGNMENT

Everyone knows this wonderful young woman, one of the many great nurses (they all were) at the Phu Bai 85th Evac Hospital. Her story of how she was medevac'd into the hospital, her Vietnam assignment, arriving as a patient *after being shot down* on the helicopter flight up from DaNang is fascinating.

She had arrived in Saigon and processed through whatever was the situation of the day, and is assigned to the 85th Evac Hospital at Phu Bai (our airfield), in I Corps—*the last stop going north*. To get to Phu Bai she gets booked onto an Air Force C-130 transport for her ride far north to DaNang AFB, and then either a jeep or helicopter ride over to the Marble Mountain Army Air Field (MMAAF, or *Marble Mountain Rocket & Mortar Proving Grounds* depending on one's experiences). From MMAAF, it would be an Army helicopter flight north to Phu Bai. Most of the administrative organizations, even our unit's higher headquarters, and support, had their last base no further north than MMAAF. She would take a helicopter from Marble Mountain to Phu Bai and directly into her assignment. Seemed easy, but it certainly is not—*not for her this fateful day.*

Her helicopter trip in an Army UH-1 Huey departed Marble Mountain for the 90-mile flight north to Phu Bai. In doing so the helicopter, unescorted at the time, had to go over the dangerous Hai Van Pass. You could fly around the pass to the east, but the mountains went down into the ocean, and this did not give a downed helicopter any beach to land on. They got through the pass without incident, but just to the north the helicopter developed an emergency mechanical problem (typical helicopter!) and had to be put down on the beach area. *Immediately* the people set up a perimeter for protective cover and soon Army Cobra gunships from Phu Bai would be overhead for protective cover. Another Huey is there on the beach for a pickup within about 25-minutes. That seemed okay.

While the folks had not taken any ground fire, or even any indication of enemy presence during the wait, the VC had been there, waiting, waiting to get the pickup crew.

The recovery Huey came in and with Cobra gunships overhead, picked up the people from the beach and left a helicopter mechanical recovery team with the first helicopter. Then, when they lifted off—all hell broke loose. The local enemy troops, VC or NVA, had been lying in wait and opened up with multiple guns just as the recovery helicopter lifted off with the passengers.

Groundfire hits her helicopter! And then hit again—*and it went down*, crashed and then rolled on the beach. The initial downing of the first aircraft had been mechanically okay and routine, but now she is one of the passengers in this downed Huey that rolled itself up on the beach.

Ah shit . .

The Cobra gunships immediately started to work attacking whomever they could find while more gunships and additional air cover were called in. The helicopter crews on the ground set up a protected area with the two aircraft while the gunships kept the VC/NVA at bay. This time, the wait is about an hour to ensure that the next helicopter would itself not also be shot down.

The third aircraft picked her and the others up from the beach and landed at the 85th Evac Hospital's hot pad with her as a medical patient—arriving as it were, to her duty assignment as a combat injured patient! Wow!

What stories she must have for her kids and grandkids!

1-4 / ON THE FUEL LOW LIGHT - DaNANG APPROACH CONTROL VECTORS ME OUT OVER THE SOUTH CHINA SEA TO EJECT

Event Note: One day with intense bombing in North Vietnam and with multiple Air Force aircraft that were battle damaged trying to recover to DaNang AFB, I wiped out my reserve fuel coming out of North Vietnam, could not get a tanker (?) and am vectored 45 miles out over the South China Sea for ejection and a helicopter pickup—or most likely picked up by a hungry shark!

Numerous air strikes in the North were running at the time. It is mid-1972 and I had come off a SLAR mission, in the monsoons, with less fuel than I should have. When we moved the 131st a few months earlier from Phu Bai to Marble Mountain— did I say *moved*, when I meant *fled* ahead of the hundreds of tanks that had come across the DMZ, we now added a bit too much extra time to each RP-1 SLAR mission. The logic is that while a bad-weather recovery followed by a low approach to Marble Mountain might be risky—at best, two large runways are sitting just four miles away at DaNang AFB, and there with a great Air Force GCA group ready to talk you right down to the runway surface—*in theory anyway.*

What we should have done, in my view, was take the eight-a-day standard RP-1 SLAR flights and added two more so that instead of making the regular three loops on RP-1 and heading home, to make only two loops and come back with enough fuel, especially in the monsoons, to give you some options. This plan would have included a diversion across Laos, to the southern end of Steel Tiger South, well south of Tchepone, go into Ubon, ~~get laid~~ . . . err . . . get refueled, a *Kobe Steak* for sure, some cases of Thai beer put in the belly avionics bay and *only then* come back with the SLAR film.

I had come back that day, in the daylight, thankfully, and a bit lower on fuel that I had anticipated. The monsoons were running hard. There is no chance for a GCI radar approach to Marble Mountain. Even if there were, a radar approach to Marble Mountain is only down to maybe 400-500 feet as a vectored surveillance approach, not a GCA to touchdown on a runway. We needed that vectored approach to be sure we did not crash into Monkey Mountain, which is near the runway final approach area.

When I got word that the weather ceiling is too low for any vectored approach to Marble Mountain, I told approach control that I would need to recover to DaNang AFB. Good luck getting that! That was the plan, but the fly-in-the-ointment is that the Air Force had multiple aircraft with battle damage that had priority for recovery ahead of anyone else.

Over and over the calls for assistance came in and I think they would put a damaged aircraft down on one runway and use the other runway for a few minutes while dragging or towing the damaged plane clear.

It was shaping up as a hell of a day there.

Too Many Damaged Aircraft Recoveries in Progress

Today there were way too many battle-damaged planes and recoveries in progress. To allow for extra time working during these many emergency recoveries, there was an assortment of refueling tankers in the air off the coast from DaNang. You never saw them, but you did hear clearances and requests regarding a particular *anchor*, such as vectors to the *Hickory Anchor*. These tankers were KC-135s (Boeing 707s as tankers) for the *fast-movers* or KC-130s that were used to refuel rescue helicopters or other *slow-movers* with a refueling probe. As needed, aircraft were vectored out to sit on (fuel tethered) or fly a pattern near the tanker, drawing fuel as needed until a slot is available to pick up a recovery GCA to DaNang AFB.

The Mohawk, the production models, used in Vietnam, did not have the refueling probes that the early test ones did. I could not take extra fuel to stay aloft. I had to get down—*and soon.*

I am holding in the weather off the coast for about ten minutes when the LOW FUEL warning light illuminated, and the RED upper panel annunciator came on. I now had about 15-20 minutes of fuel, at most, and am solidly in an emergency fuel state. I pressed the sweep second timer on the panel clock for my timing reference. With the ATC radios running nonstop with approach control and multiple emergencies in progress, I did break in and told DaNang approach control that I had an emergency. He asked what type of emergency I had? I advised him: I am in a Low Fuel state. He had me wait a few seconds and then gave me a new frequency to go over to the *Emergency Controller*. It is so busy at DaNang that day that they had separate *Emergency Only Controllers*.

DaNang Approach Vectors Me Out to Sea to Eject

I switched over to the emergency controller, made contact, and told him I am at about 15-minutes of fuel. He asked if I could take an aerial refueling tanker and I said—*No*. All the while this controller is talking to several aircraft, seemingly at once.

I could have used a refueling tanker that day, but we did not have air-to-air refueling in our Vietnam Mohawks

With that, he fired back a clearance to go to the DaNang TACAN 360-degree radial at 45 miles and hold with an expected approach clearance time about thirty minutes in the future—about 15 minutes past my zero fuel time.

I broke in and told him I would be out of fuel. He is fast and thoroughly professional as multiple aircraft were on the frequency and told me to give him a five minutes' heads-up call just before my ejection and he would *try* to have a Jolly Green nearby when we go out.

WHAT!?

Then he ignored my follow-on calls. I am to fly out to the north, wait until I ran out of fuel, and eject into the shark-infested South China Sea. Frankly, this was the fate of several aircraft and helicopters over the years, including a helicopter from our base at Phu Bai.

I am not going down so easy; I called Spud Operations at Marble Mountain and told them DaNang wanted me to eject to the north, over the water.

DaNang had an ILS to both runways and used the GCA to speed things up. I tuned in the DaNang runway ILS and turned inbound on the localizer and started to let down. My intent is to get down below the extended ILS glideslope and follow it as close to DaNang as possible and then either land illegally or break it off and eject right there, not 40 miles out over the ocean! Of course, that would have left my 20,000 pounds of Mohawk to hit a friendly ship near the harbor and maybe kill some more people.

There is a certain deadly irony that played into this. The year before, at Phu Bai, we had a local helicopter that was in the weather, an Army Huey that could not get down, so they too turned out to the east of Phu Bai to get down over open water and follow that back to the coast. A helicopter should be able to pull that off easier because they can go real slow, but while they did get past the coast and had then turned back to let down, the weather went down literally right to the waves—and they flew into the water. My account in this book of a triple-GCA at Phu Bai on the **LOW FUEL** light is typical of the severe weather issues we faced, mostly during the six-month monsoon season.

The helicopter broke up upon impacting the water and while I heard that everyone got out okay, as they all had personal floatation (water-wings), *only one crew member survived,* and he is found holding onto a floating rotor blade when a rescue is made just about a half-hour later.

The sharks had gotten the other guys. The absolute horror of the hundreds of US sailors that were eaten by the sharks when the USS *Indianapolis* sank was always something that played in our minds. Of the over **900** sailors on that ship that went into the shark infested waters, only **317** survived to be rescued—*History's Greatest Shark Attack.*

I had no intention of punching out that day—or any day!

DaNang approach control is irritated and called me repeatedly to get off the inbound ILS course, as there are multiple damaged aircraft on recovery on that same glidepath. I ignored his calls. I had no choice. I set the radar altimeter to 200 feet and started my let down over open water, still on the ILS localizer but well below the glideslope, so I did not get run over by *fast-movers* from above and behind me. I am still solid in the monsoon rains and clouds: I am glad it is not at night too!

The radar altimeter showed I am just two hundred feet above the water, and I still saw *nothing.* Solid in the monsoon rains and the clock running out on the timer I had started. Marble Mountain tower said they thought they had 300-500 feet of ceiling there, and that I may land if I could find the coast in time. It would be close, too close. It is not safe, surely, that I am dragging in 20,000 pounds of Mohawk that may end up crashing into—well, maybe at the last minute—into our base and killing many others when I am supposed to be out nose-bumping with the sharks and only two of us dying: *I am coming in anyway . . .*

The risk of now flying low, and with almost no visibility, and then diverting to Marble Mountain is perilous, even if I had the fuel time to do it. Near Phu Bai, there were several miles of flat coastal beach and farmland between the water and the airfield, while Marble Mountain had mountains, including Monkey Mountain, right down to the coast and going into the water. So coming in fast, and low, and with only limited forward visibility, posed the danger that by the time we saw the coast we would be a smoking hole in one of the low-lying mountains. China Beach is at DaNang, but that is near the port area, not over to where Marble Mountain is.

We strapped tighter down into the ejection seats and silently figured that from the time of seeing something in front of us, that until an ejection would, if we were quick, maybe only 3-5 seconds. The adrenaline running through one's veins would keep you sharp, alert and keyed up.

I reset the radar altimeter to just 100 feet and am now maybe 12-15 miles out from DaNang. I am about six minutes I figured from a landing, but not sure I would make it. The DaNang emergency controller, now instead of demanding I get off the ILS localizer, is now giving me advisory calls. I had descended to just above the water so as to stay out of the way of the jets coming past me and only a few hundred feet above me. It would be close.

At about 100 feet above the water, I saw the first wave action—but it is not good. Maybe another half minute and the cloud ceilings were indeed higher. I climbed a bit and asked Marble Mountain tower now what the weather is. Maybe, just maybe, I could do it. DaNang approach is calling my turn to Marble Mountain, so now I had a chance, except that Monkey Mountain is still between me and the runway at Marble Mountain.

Low-Level in the Rain to Find Marble Mountain

Now I had perhaps 300, to no more than 400 feet of a ragged cloud ceiling— and this is like a clear day to me! I turned off the DaNang runway inbound localizer to the left, desperately searching to find the coast and to avoid smacking into Monkey Mountain. The GCA Final Controller at DaNang could not see me after I had left the inbound course and there is no time to get over to the GCI controller to warn me of the coastal mountains.

I am at or right near the 15 minutes of the **LOW FUEL** light. I am close, really close. I had the NDB radio beacon from Marble Mountain for guidance in the rain and sort of offset aligned for the short 4,300-foot runway.

I put down the landing gear and set the flaps to approach, still not sure how far away now—two miles? A mile? The risk now is that my approach flight profile is too flat, and this would hurt being able to flare and to land and not overrun off the other end of the runway. If I am descending to the runway, with full flaps, I could throw out the speed boards, flare, land, throw on the reversers and stop. I am at approach flaps only: a flat run in approach. Could I land like this?

Out of the rain swept windshield the coastline near Monkey Mountain came rapidly toward me. I needed only a minute, just one minute now.

We unhooked the ejection seat under-seat survival packs (overwater rafts and things), left the flaps at the approach setting, and told Marble Mountain tower that I am on short final, but still no runway is in sight. The runway materialized as fast as the coast had in my windshield. Full flaps now, speed boards popped out, as the

Mohawk swerved a bit from the configuration change. The end of the runway is there. I am approaching very flat—not good for a flared landing—and the short runway is wet; then with the rain pounding—*I am down.*

Both props to reverse idle now, not risking that going to full reverse would, as had sometimes happened, cause the Mohawk to swerve from uneven application of the reverse prop speeds— find me off the runway or collapsing the gear from side-load stresses.

I am down, and the sharks had lost—*this time, as it was.* The lesson learned from that is to go back to our old process of coming out of North Vietnam with minimal fuel and with the uncertain weather for landing now at Marble Mountain that we would again divert across Laos, take the anti-aircraft flak as it was, and get fuel, food, and maybe laid at Ubon. Maybe even an overnighter on real beds with real food.

1-5 / UBON TRAINING FLIGHT NEARLY ENDS UP A BURNING HOLE IN THE GROUND

Event Note: This is entirely my screw-up, as were most of them, and I nearly had us ejecting from a perfectly good, but uncontrollable, Mohawk on a bright sunny day over the rice fields of Thailand, just a few miles from the Ubon RTAFB.

It is my second tour, and I am our lead flight instructor at the time, the SIP if you will, with two other warrant officer IPs (unit Instructor Pilots) under me for both mission and aircraft training, checkrides, and new pilot orientation work. Because of the Northeast Monsoons covering Phu Bai, I would take the pilots that needed training or a periodic flight checkride and head for the USAF base at Ubon RTAFB, Thailand, along the southeast border with Laos.

OV-1D Dual-Stick with only a few right-side instruments

It was checkride time, not training so much, and we had flown over to Thailand and gotten *real food*, some fuel, and then headed out about 30 miles southeast of Ubon to do upper air work: emergency flight training events, and then try to do the entire checkride all in one flight. I am coordinating closely with the Ubon ATC approach controllers to be sure that I stayed in a *box,* so to speak, about 15 x 15 miles in size and from the surface up to 12,000 feet. Our heads and attention would be mostly in the cockpit as the other pilot is often wearing a plastic hood obscuring his vision only to see the flight instruments to simulate flying in the weather. With so much climbing and descending and turning and some aerobatics to boot, having the controllers watching us is a great help—plus, it is during the daylight hours and the real *War Show* in Laos did not start until the lights were turned down at night.

On this particular day, in southeastern Thailand, and to the east and just across the border into southern Laos, the sky is officially *clear,* but with very limited flight visibility due to haze and smoke. I had maybe, at most, three miles of horizontal flight visibility, which is not much at flight speeds. I could look up and see the outline of the sun through the haze and look down, like being in a tunnel, and see the ground right below us just fine. Officially this is good weather and with Ubon ATC handling any air traffic issues, I am fine—just do not expect me to try to navigate anywhere in the haze nor to see the horizon so as to be able to adjust our flight attitude.

As expected, most of the checkride went just fine. We did standard flight procedures, routine emergencies, shut down and then later restarted an engine. The plan at Ubon is that we could do an hour or so of the runway patterns and single-engine emergencies, but here we were just doing the upper air work as high as 12,000 feet above the ground and maybe in the aerobatic parts, doing aileron rolls, some barrel rolls, inside loops and Immelmanns. These are all great aerobatic maneuvers that made flying the Mohawk so much fun.

Another required training maneuver is the *Emergency Recovery* (under the hood as if flying in the clouds) from unusual and vertical attitudes. The way to do this is to have the pilot put his head down, and I would turn the aircraft back and forth to get the inner ear fluids all confused and then I would suddenly pull the Mohawk into a near vertical flight, preferably somewhere close to coming over on its back and say—

"You have it!"

—And let the pilot, either visually, or completely relying on instruments, to make a recovery by allowing the aircraft nose to always *fall through the horizon*, never pushing it there, but letting the plane, *even if over on its back*, slide the nose down through the horizon, maybe just a bit below the horizon to avoid an aerodynamic stall and then roll it upright to a wings level attitude. Remembering all this time that the inner ear, confused by the turning with pilot's head down, would betray you. It is fun—*if you did not mind maybe puking sometimes*—so we always had plastic bags on hand just in case. No matter how experienced you were, one had to be careful what is eaten during the 24-hours or so before one of these checkrides, or you may get the opportunity to reexamine your stomach contents.

Most of the aerobatics are not needed in a mission flight except on a VR camera flight—and especially carrying our rockets and .50 cal machine guns under the wings. That was only in the OV-1A model aircraft, and those had already left the unit the year before. Our daytime VR flights now were usually flown in the OV-1 Super-Cs, (dedicated IR aircraft otherwise with cameras though) without any armaments. There is always some maneuvering, maybe aileron rolls involved with dodging flak over Laos, but that was the extent of the violent maneuvering. On our gun runs or a camera shot, you might make a half loop out: otherwise known as half of a Cuban-8 maneuver. If too slow or too heavy (early into the day's mission) the Mohawk would stall, inverted, at the top of an Immelmann maneuver.

That would represent another *"Ah, shit . . . to be sure!"*

On a day like this, doing a checkride, I might move about in the airspace box from a low of 5,000 feet AGL on up. Nothing too dangerous could go wrong . . . *could go wrong . . . could go wrong . . .*

If something could be screwed up—*I could do it.* My main talent at the time was finding new ways to bring one right up against the face of a horrible death and then back away. These things always get the pilot's *fight-or-flight* instincts going and the adrenaline rushing. You do stuff like that when you are only 20, or 21, or by the time I had over 500 combat missions, maybe an old man at 22.

I am using one of the dual controlled Super-C Mohawks, but unlike the OV-1A model gunships, we had, the Super-C, at least this one, did have dual controls *but did not have any flight instruments on the right side*. Later, most of the dual control aircraft, we would have the avionics guys install at least an airspeed indicator, altimeter, turn needle and a small gyro attitude indicator on to the open panel in front of the right seat. The basic instrumentation of a Piper PA-18 Super Cub I might add.

In the single-pilot Mohawk, in front of the pilot is the 1950's era Collins FD-105 Flight Director, itself moved about an inch outward from the instrument panel. Below the flight director is the HIS (Horizontal Situation Indicator). In standard aircraft cockpit configurations, Mohawks through anything else that flies, the airspeed indicator would sit to the left of the flight director and a turn needle usually just below that. The altimeter would be to the immediate right of flight director or attitude indicator if you were not flying with a flight director system. The aviation term of—*flying on the needle, ball, and airspeed*—referred to controlled flight in instrument conditions relying only on a turn needle and the airspeed to keep you right side up. This can be very trying and sometimes, nearly impossible. Remembering that this aircraft and avionics were designed and built at the end of the 1950's.

The upper air work is okay, and while we were up in the 10,000-foot range I had the pilot put on the plastic hood over his eyes and put his face down with eyes closed while I would do turns and some relatively minor unusual attitudes working my way up to an inverted climb and saying—

"You've got it."

But, nothing could go wrong, on a VFR day at 10,000 feet—*well, maybe not*.

The easy recoveries were going fine. The pilot would look up, his hood still obstructing outside vision, and would check the flight director and decide which way is up and get control of the aircraft. After two of these, I put the pilot's head back down, started some turns to the left and right, so his inner ear fluids were totally confused, and then I started into a very mild maneuver—while he is usually expecting another pitch up or rapid aileron roll. I reached up to the upper circuit breaker panel between our heads and pulled the *flight director* circuit breaker, with the Mohawk still in a medium-banked turn. That locked the flight director, showing an attitude to be something other than what is the aircraft's flight attitude. Doing this left the indication of the flight director showing one configuration and the *needle, ball, and airspeed* showing something else.

Generally, after jerking the aircraft around, I would go into a slow turn, let the inner ear fluids then think we were right side up, and then pull over into maybe a 30-degree bank, something relatively mild, and give it back to the pilot to perform a very smooth recovery. I needed the pilot to be sure that he is *reconciling the flight director*, an electrical instrument known to fail, with the indications of the turn needle and airspeed. These were very basic airmanship skills—all very necessary.

Well, that day, the pilot did just fine on the first couple of events. In the last one—nearly the last one for us forever I might add—he raised his head and started to pull the aircraft back from where it was, just straight and level, and towards a turn because the flight director had been turned off by me while in the turn. No sweat; a quick partial turn and we were looking good . . . *for all of about two seconds.*

He had it right, and I am just about to push in the flight director circuit breaker when the pilot rapidly jerks the control stick to the left side, misreading the flight director that is in a failure mode, and rolled us inverted.

No sweat, this is ~~routine~~ *. . . err . . . well, maybe not so routine that sunny, hazy day over the edge of Laos.*

Within Seconds, I Knew We Were in Trouble

Big trouble now. With the flight director set out about an inch from the panel, as they all were in our aircraft, the airspeed indicator and turn indicator were blocked from my view and the flight director is nonfunctional. *Oops . . .*

We rolled and started to twist. In just a second the adrenaline is flowing, maybe even rushing. The Mohawk stalled as we rolled over on our back, or what I thought was our back side because now all I could see, after I had taken the controls, is that as we twisted and rolled the glowing blob that is likely the sun exchanging itself with the criss-cross view of the rice paddies far below. As I flip-flopped the controls, the sun is coming through *this way*, then seconds later it is rice paddies, more sun but coming from someplace else across the canopy—or from the nose to tail

I had no idea of the flight configuration of the aircraft.
***That** was a clue not to be ignored . . .*

I had no outside horizon references and none inside and without being able to see the turn needle and airspeed—not a clue as to what is happening.

In a surreal episode of complete disorientation, I could not find left from right nor up from down. First, the sun, then the ground, then the sun, *must be a **different sun** as this one is coming through the cockpit from a place the **other sun** was just seconds ago.*

Ah, shit . . .

The altimeter is unwinding. Within seconds, it and the rest of this beautiful aircraft were just going to be a hole in some rice paddy—preferably without any human organic material still embedded in the mess.

Our flight rule was if you were out of control and not *right-side-up* by 5,000 feet—*eject*. From 5,000 feet, if upside down and out of control, you probably do not have enough time to get the greasy side down and keep flying.

I should have just shouted—

"Eject. Eject!"

—and stepped out for some fresh air while hanging under the ejection seat canopy. It is not to be. Sometime after passing 5,000 feet on the *apparently faulty altimeter* that is rolling itself backward, I only shouted—

"Off the controls!"

—And within seconds, we had stopped fighting the tumbling with no visibility, and I had gotten back control of the aircraft—at less than 1,000 feet above the then rushing towards us rice paddies. It still took a heavy G-load to pull up from a near vertical dive with the high airspeed, still invisible to me, surely into the danger zone. If falling and tumbling like that, an ejection would have most likely simply sent us following this aircraft into the same smoking hole in the ground.

I am quick, with a bit of quivering voice to be sure, to point out what the purpose of this particular training maneuver was (whatever ***that*** might be). Then we flew back to Ubon, had a few drinks, got a room for the night, and went back to rainy Phu Bai the next day.

1-6 / NIGHT MAINTENANCE TEST FLIGHT ENDS IN UNPLANNED EJECTION

Event Note: Murphy's Law was alive and well this night. A night maintenance flight in the weather (all against rules) after an urgent engine swap to get an IR aircraft ready ended up with a low-level, into the minefields, ejection at Phu Bai when everything that could go wrong did go wrong.

We were *always* chronically short of spare engines and engine parts, mostly I suspect because we were at the end of the supply line. Anything, including food and liquor that managed to get from a supply ship far to the south end of Vietnam and not get picked off in the journey to Phu Bai, was a miracle. Thus, the sometimes eating hot dogs for breakfast, lunch and supper is part of many of the typical problems we faced in our shortages of *everything*.

1/ It Was All Too Real

At one point on my second tour, we were grounding aircraft because of a lack of workable engine vertical tape instruments, a new design on the OV-1D model Mohawk that had replaced the round engine gauges. The problem is that they failed, *a lot*, and thus, we had no instruments and no flying.

At one point, our CO sent one of the officers back to the states to get a suitcase full of the new tape instruments, and then rush and hand-carry them back to Phu Bai—all within a week's time.

One of our most critical issues was a sometimes lack of workable engines. From time-to-time, the maintenance guys—working day-and-night endlessly as they had too—would swap engines from a day flight, say a SLAR plane, and put one, or even both engines, on a night flying IR or SLAR aircraft and then send that one out on a mission. Then, after midnight, they would start to swap the engines back off *that* aircraft for a daytime SLAR flight. *These hastily performed engine swaps were surely courting disaster.*

There are many of the engine, fuel, oil, and hydraulic connections that needed to be done correctly and tested on an engine change. If working stateside that might be something they did over a few days' time, not over a few hours at night, sometimes in the rain and sometimes with mortars coming in from time-to-time just to keep you on your toes.

Things can be missed, or not connected properly. With a complete engine change, there is also a mandatory maintenance test flight with one of the maintenance check pilots and a senior mechanic to run about an hour's flight, start and stop the engine, change the power, and other issues and be sure everything is set right.

Besides the check flight, the other criteria are that the engine change test flight must be done in *daylight* and *VMC* (visual) flight conditions in case something went badly, as it did that night.

The maintenance guys had made an engine swap, a single swap I think, and headed out for the test flight very late in the afternoon. It is monsoon season, pouring rain and the darkness had started to settle in. Well, things could be worse—*and it would be very soon.*

They departed on this ill-conceived, necessary flight test: up into the night monsoon rains and clouds. Sometime during the flight, while performing changes of the engine power and the propeller controls, the engine apparently had the propeller controls not correctly set and after pulling back the prop and the power and then going forward—in the weather, at night—the propeller on one side went into reverse with the other in the forward mode—and the Mohawk rolled. I am sure the—

Ah, shit . . .

—Was loud and clear as the aircraft now rolled and tumbled while in the weather. The problem, *one of many*, with doing this at night and in the weather is that you are stuck on using only the instruments to gain control of the flight attitude instead of one's whole visual field with your eyes. So you are very limited with just relying on the FD-105 flight director.

The Mohawk tumbled while the pilot is scrambling to get control of the plane, and the run-away engine at the same time.

Of course an emergency call, one engine shut down, at night, and in the weather while being radar vectored back for an emergency GCA approach to Phu Bai is about as bad as it gets.

The airfield sirens sounded, and the crash crews headed out. The rest of us poured out of the Spud Club, or our hooches, and climbed on the revetments to see what is going to happen. We certainly had our share of crashes at Phu Bai, many of them fatal including our own CO just months before, and from our unit, but also others had shared the same fate. Phu Bai, had as most airfields in Vietnam, an aircraft bone yard of wrecked planes, up to transport size aircraft, that had crashed there or were destroyed on the ground in rocket and mortar attacks—and even more helicopter wreckage piled off to the side of the approach end of the runway.

We were looking for another crash. None of us would admit that, but it is like going to a hockey game and saying you are only there for the game issues. Not so.

X-They Had Multiple Aircraft Failures in Progress

We were lined up on the backside of the Mohawk revetments facing the runway. There were a half dozen crash vehicles seen moving about the airfield. Near to the end of the runway, a 571st Dustoff Huey is already cranking their rotors. Across the runway a light Pink Fire Team consisting of an OH-6 Loach (Hughes 369) and at least one, probably two, AH-1 Cobra gunships, were probably cranking up with the anticipation that the Mohawk would not make it to the runway: That this would quickly become a nearly impossible, at night, in the rain, search, and rescue, looking hopefully for a crew that had ejected. It is not to be.

1/ It Was All Too Real

Waiting for a fly-by or another crash at Phu Bai.

The cloud ceiling is low and wet: typical monsoon weather. This situation is dangerous even with two engines and with a crew not scared from the already severe in-flight loss of control. Now it is one engine and a shook-up crew. More can go wrong—*and would within minutes.*

With the limited power of a single-engine approach, the pilot would set the flaps only for the first notch, the approach flap setting around 15-degrees, and this would give him not only more stability but also brings on the large, inboard hydraulic ailerons, critical now for limited power and control.

Instead of lowering the landing gear a few miles out at the start of the final approach, it would be delayed until right before the touchdown; because while on a single-engine approach, once the landing gear is lowered—the Mohawk is *committed*—and there had better be a strip of something hard right in front of the aircraft because the landing is the only option at that point. Full landing flaps, if used, would only come at the last few seconds before touchdown. On a long runway it is best to stay at approach flaps, but at the short Phu Bai runway full flaps would be the norm, so there not going to be any single-engine go-arounds—and no single-engine reverse thrust, of course.

Trying to make a *go-around,* single-engine, with approach flaps and the gear down is nearly impossible. You would have had to add power, while still descending toward the runway, pull the gear up and try to transition back to a climb before you hit the runway, or worse, the minefields that are just short of the runway. This technique is clearly not possible in a night, IFR GCA approach, on one engine—so the gear had to be held until you had the runway and the landing is *assured*.

It is not to be. The flaps had been put down to the approach setting: the GCA final controller had taken over, and the crew is making an incredible effort on this approach.

If the landing gear does not come down with the use of the gear handle and the 3,000 pounds of hydraulic pressure, then the backup is a *one-time pneumatic high-pressure air charge* that routes the air around the hydraulic system, unlatches the gear doors and blows down the three landing gears. It is a one-time use only and is undoable. The blowdown activation is a small T-handle on the upper right side of the engine control power quadrant. Pull the handle and the landing gear, *hopefully*, blows down and you get the three green lights showing the gear is down and locked. Supposedly, hopefully—*but not always*.

Times were very tense as this played out that night. Seconds surely seemed liked minutes for this crew. The windshield wipers would have been pounding at the rain-smeared windshield hoping for the early view of a lighted landing runway. While still several miles out, the GCA final controller would have called for approach configuration and the flaps would be set. They were holding on lowering the landing gear because of the one-engine emergency.

Down they came, while the GCA final controller is giving constant, uninterrupted calls of quick, short turns and the aircraft's position above or below the glideslope. A GCA is *tense*, even in good times, and is worse on that night—*on just one engine*.

Fortunately, the cloud ceiling gave the crew a few extra hundreds of feet and some seconds to see the runway in front of them. It is short final. Dozens of us were sitting on the revetments. It is raining. There were crash crew vehicles spread along the outside of the runway area. The Dustoff and the Pink Fire Team had their rotor blades already turning in anticipation. The 85th Evac Hospital, located at the far end of the runway, is ready for whatever the crew's fate is to be.

The Mohawk is now on a short final approach with the flaps just at the approach setting. It is still raining hard. To those of us by then sitting out on top of the revetments waiting for another ~~crash~~, *err*, another miraculous landing—as aircraft landing lights started to show as a glow that is growing out of the rain darkened skies outward from the end of the runway. Within seconds, the Mohawk came into view like something walking out of the shadows in a movie.

They were coming into the short final and approaching the three rings of minefields which were protecting our outer perimeter. There is no gear: Okay, that was planned, now put the gear handle down and complete the landing.

Silently we gasped, sensing that a crash, with the landing gear up, is surely imminent. Then there is a sudden ejection, right on short final. Were they going to crash into the minefields?

Only one of the crew ejected. The seat is sent into the air surely too close to the ground to get a full chute deployment, but it did, miraculously. The Mohawk hung in the air, right on short final, with the nose rose up only slightly, and as the aircraft is passing abeam of where we perched on top of the revetments, the gear unfolded and locked almost at the very instant of touchdown.

The ejected crewmember, the maintenance guy in the right seat, got a partial chute deployment and seat separation and came down into the no man's land of the three rings of minefields. The Mohawk is then still rolling out with the remaining engine already shut down on the runway. Our great maintenance ground crew was standing by to safety pin the landing gear and hook up the tow bar to get the Mohawk off the runway just as quickly as possible. The *careful* rescue of the maintenance guy is already underway.

Apparently, what happened is that these guys, having already done a fantastic job with this crippled aircraft, at night, in the weather, and suffering from the shock of the loss of in-flight control, had come out of the low clouds, on the GCA, on a stable approach (more than I might had done), had the flaps in approach, as they should be, and while approaching the outer perimeter had reached to lower the gear, with hydraulic power from the one remaining engine. **But it failed.** Murphy's Law was alive and well. The gear is still up, and the touchdown is only seconds away.

With the landing gear failure, the pilot had called—

"Blow it!"

—Meaning, at that point, to have the maintenance guy reach aside the power levers and manually pull the emergency gear blow down T-handle.

Times are tense. They had been through a lot the past twenty minutes; it is very intense to make this approach, at night, in the weather, with a GCA and then—*no gear!*

The maintenance guy, maybe expecting, subconsciously even, to anticipate a possible ejection on short final, is tense, probably breathing hard . . . and then the call out—

"Blow it!"

—And reacted automatically and ejected instead of reaching over to the power quadrant and pulling out the emergency gear T-handle. The maintenance guys were not regular flight crewmembers, so the process on things like the blowing of the gear is likely not something he had anticipated. You see, hear, and react like your mind is set to do, and when something is out of the ordinary, well, then these things happen.

They were both lucky to be alive. Am thinking we maybe started to go back and demand that the safety rule of daylight and VFR only engine change test flights came back into being. Maybe even the whole idea that we could make such quick entire engine changes was rethought.

1-7 / Two F-4s Collide in the DMZ

A short story about just one of the 445 Air Force F-4 Phantom jets lost only to combat in Vietnam.

I had come out of an armed VR mission in Laos, coming back to the east and just below the DMZ when the emergency calls started in about a collision in the DMZ, which we later determined or heard were two F-4 Phantoms from DaNang. One aircraft limped back to DaNang AFB, but the two crewmembers of the other Phantom had ejected into the DMZ—and a rescue begins.

I am low on fuel, and I had to get into Phu Bai. I went ahead and refueled, rearmed and went back up to see if I could be of help. This downing only about 30 miles from Phu Bai, and we worked in the DMZ area on a regular basis.

By the time I got back up and into the area Red Crown is on 243 MHz Guard channel and is stacking whatever ordnance aircraft he had to prep for an armed recovery. Red Crown being one of the coordinating aircraft with a crew of people working radars and other things similar to what the Air Force EC-130 command and control capsule crew did around the clock.

Red Crown is grabbing whoever is in the air, mostly *fast-movers*, and asking about what ordnance they had, and their fuel state and then is parking them at designated orbiting radials at various altitudes off of the Quang Tri TACAN station. Cool, fast and professional Red Crown was grabbing a variety of Air Force and Navy *fastmovers* that were otherwise on their way to some other targets—but a rescue is a priority, always.

An Air Force rescue operation in that part of the AO, and down into Laos with us, often included up to four A-1 Skyraiders—Call Sign *Sandy*—whom would carry both ordnance and a version of *CS gas* to be used to incapacitate people on the ground that were near a rescue site: including incapacitating the pilot on the ground whom then had to be collected up by a rescue guy that is let down to get them.

The HH-53 Jolly Green helicopter was by then the standard for rescues. They would be refueling from a nearby rescue-dedicated KC-130 tanker. An Air Force FAC, usually by then an OV-10 Bronco call sign *Covey* or *Nail*, would direct the rescue, depending on where it is. Thus, any rescue is a well-oiled organization and heavily armed and supported by any aircraft in the area.

Usually, there would be two rescue helicopters on scene and an Air Force KC-130 tanker nearby for continued refueling.

The intensity of these rescue missions and the great and immediate danger is shown, in that **74** Air Force rescue helicopters were lost in the war with **40** of them destroyed in combat while. Of the often used support aircraft, the Air Force lost a staggering number of **191** Douglas A-1 Skyraider aircraft, with **150** them being direct combat losses.

The FAC support aircraft, usually right in there, were the Air Force's OV-10 Broncos, the O-1 Bird Dog and O-2 Skymasters. War losses of just these were **339** aircraft!

For some good reasons, any aircraft not part of the rescue is not wanted in the area: the first being to avoid a midair collision and another is that uncoordinated aircraft risked drawing undue attention from enemy ground forces. As is typical, a rescue or insertion helicopter would routinely fly about and make several sweeping down maneuvers that would look to observers as if they, the helicopter, were doing an insertion or pickup at a certain point, but not the right point. By making a half dozen sweeping let downs or stops the enemy, unless they were very close, could not know where the rescue is actually about to take place.

So it was that day that by the time I am back in the air in a position to the eastern end of the DMZ that the rescue of these two pilots had begun in earnest. There is much gunfire: mostly .30 cals, but in that particular area, not much heavy antiaircraft weapons. Still, ground fire to a Jolly Green with 6-9 crewmembers and gunners is a high-risk event, thus, the reason to have the CS gas in the Skyraiders always available and Red Crown stacking and holding as many ordnance carrying aircraft as had been happening by right then.

They were having trouble finding the guys; I suspect because of the ground fire, the pilots were either hiding and could not get into the open, or they were on the move.

As more ordinance is needed, Red Crown is making calls on Guard for more attack aircraft. I had not heard the *Sandy* guys with the CS gas get involved yet.

While the chatter on the newly assigned emergency recovery channel, now off of the regularly open 243 MHz emergency frequency, is very fast and without a break. There were now increasingly more aircraft—and more ground fire. It was getting interesting in a standoffish way.

Then I heard something amusing. A young Army helicopter pilot is trying to break into the constant radio calls. He tried several times, and Red Crown is clearly getting impatient and demanding that he stay off the emergency Guard frequency as there is a rescue *in progress*.

When the young helicopter pilot would key the microphone, you would hear his speaking like he is beating his chest from the whop-whop of the chopper.

Maybe two more calls were rebuffed by Red Crown. Then—

The helicopter pilot came back on the radio, on Guard, loud and clear, left a brief message and then went silent—

> "Army Scout 44 (I made that up) . . .
>
> With two gunships (a pair of AH-1 Cobra snakes) . . .
>
> On short final at Quang Tri . . .
>
> Two Air Force in the back. **Out**."

Dead silence. This event was way, way too funny.

In the midst of all the massive air armada, and the confusion surrounding all this, the kid in the Huey, with a pair of Cobras, likely also teenage pilots, had flown in, picked up the first guy, got him on board: found the other man and picked him up too, and came out of the DMZ and is now landing at Quang Tri.

There had been so much confusion going on that no one had even apparently been close enough to the Air Force guys even to see that a Huey had swept in, made a pickup, moved over, made another pickup and is already out and about to land.

1-8 / PHU BAI APPROACH CONTROL VECTORS ARMY RU-21 INTO MOUNTAINS

The Phu Bai approach controllers were Army men and were usually excellent and very careful. Normally, the worst of our issues were some RVN aircraft coming in, not speaking any English, and just making their calls in the blind like—

"I turn now."

"Oh, and from where are you?" Or,

"I land now."

Again, who and where there are, and what type of aircraft to be looking out for, was usually a mystery.

An Army U-21. The J&R/U-21 was a version with electronic sensors and monitors and had large distinguishing antennae on the aircraft and also out on the wings.

There was an incident on a day during the monsoons that ended with great luck and no one dead when Phu Bai Approach Control misidentified one of the RU-8's or JU-21's, (Call Sign Vanguard) from the 138th Radio Research Aviation Company in Phu Bai.

Approach Control had the aircraft's radar blip mixed up with someone else that is east of the airfield, towards the coast. They then vectored the guys to the west, the wrong guys, around towards the mountains. In the process of vectoring the wrong aircraft, in a flash, they saw a mountain and rocks and trees in the windshield, pulled up, hit the trees and then went immediately back into the clouds—without a clue as to where they were and if there is now another rock pile maybe just seconds in their future!

What luck they had—*all of it bad to that point.* They quickly got correctly identified on the approach control radar. I would assume there were some nervous and loud communications with approach control: And then they limped back over to Phu Bai with some of the antenna and external pieces missing, but still flying. *Lucky... lucky... lucky!*

1-9 / VR Flight - He Took Three .30 cal Hits in the Chest—and Kept Flying the Mohawk Home

This event was not at the 131st, but at one of our four sister units, the 73rd SAC at Vung Tao, I think. I had been sent down to where they were to run another mission into Cambodia and stayed a couple of days with them—in real beds with real food as it was.

It was one of the warrant officers that I knew from Army flight school that had been flying a VR mission with another non-pilot officer in the right seat doing this mission. He had been dancing around for some time with the ground fire and in this case as he pulled up from a run against a hillside and started to turn out there were rows of streaming tracers, but nothing more—at least for a few seconds. He did not know right then that the aircraft had been hit straight on.

There is extensive damage to the pilot instruments from gunfire coming in. The guy in the right seat apparently had the initial shock, maybe only seconds into this, and the pilot, seeing the shot up flight panel, but not sensing anything, looked down to see the wetness on his survival vest. He pulled off a glove and stuck it under his vest and came up—RED—bloody red as it was. I saw his scars when I stayed there.

He had taken three hits in the chest and neck from a .30 cal machine gun, and more to the aircraft, but being so tightly strapped to the ejection seat there was no sudden notice of being shot.

He flew back to Vung Tao and is taken to the evac hospital where he recovered and was back flying in about two weeks or so, but with a large area of scars across his back from the bullet exits. Lucky, lucky, lucky!

1-10 / UFO? Off the Coast of North Vietnam

By the time this was over, I was a believer—but of what I am not certain?

Well, maybe not **MY** UFO.

It is not a stretch to say that I, and most other pilots I am fairly sure, flying on a lone, night, solo combat mission, have from time-to-time easily misidentified common phenomena, such as the stars, the moon, cloud shapes illuminated, as threats to them.

I know I have had that sort of run in with stars or the moon coming after me, or other events that take the quick visual from the eye and recasts it into something entirely different in your mind.

I am flying a routine, at night, partially in and out of the weather, SLAR run on RP-1 just a few miles off the coast of North Vietnam. I had checked in with Red Crown by the time I crossed the extended line eastward from the DMZ and started on the mission.

Besides my cockpit transponder squawking a four-digit Mode 3 ATC code, and the Mode 4 is ON (for IFF—Identification Friend or Foe), I am, as we always were, squawking a secret mission-unique Mode 2 code. The Mode 2 code is manually loaded into a black box, located back to the aft electronics bay, with a unique coding device, but only after the engines are started. The Mode 2 code would disappear if the aircraft electrical power is lost; so if you shut down someplace, it was not possible to reset your Mode 2 codes. Fortunately, the Mode 2 was only for our combat missions in North Vietnam and sometimes, but not always, in Laos.

North Vietnamese MiGs were sometimes an issue, but no Mohawk had recently been attacked by any MiG, though we had lost a SLAR aircraft up here to an SA-2 SAM. As the MiGs would come out of the Hanoi or Haiphong area, we would start getting the calls in-the-blind on UHF Guard, 243 MHz from Red Crown—

"Bandits . . Bandits . .

Vicinity BULLSEYE (Hanoi area) . .

Bandits . . Bandits . .

Red Crown on Guard out!"

Like their constant SAM calls, the voices of Red Crown and Deep Sea were always calm, bold, clear, and ultimately professional. During times of intense Air Force and Navy fighter attacks on these areas, the MiG, and SAM calls were a near constant on the always-monitored UHF and VHF Guard frequencies.

Usually, the MiGs were on flights out of *Bullseye* (Hanoi) and then down the coast some miles. Then they would apparently turn to the east and go to the large Chinese island of Hainan.

Our guidance in regards a MiG threat was that we would abort a mission if a Bandit is within 80 miles of our location *and* heading our way. We were to turn to the east, further out to sea and be in a dive down from our usual mission altitude of about 10,000 feet and get as close as possible to the water, which could be done in just a couple minutes if the need arose.

If the MiG is close in on us, we were to come around face-to-face to the threat so as to not get a heat-seeking missile up our tailpipe and from there, if there is a head-on, air-to-air firing to do the—

"When the sweat blinds you . .

Pull up!"

This technique is the same maneuver one was supposed to use in the case of a SAM missile attack. Of course, **none of us had any belief at all that this would work in the real world.** To the best of my knowledge, none of our aircraft ever had to make any evasive maneuver or divert down to the water because of a MiG threat.

What we did have to do is keep our SLAR aircraft on the RP-1 mission 24/7 to keep track of the vehicle movements in the southern part of North Vietnam. If we had to abort a mission for a maintenance issue with either the aircraft or some problem with the SLAR (not unusual), then another Mohawk is on its way up to the RP-1 track within 30-minutes to take over that mission. The replacement aircraft would pick up where the usual three round trips up and down the coast were left off, and then things would continue on schedule for the next launches out of Phu Bai.

X-The First Indication of Trouble

It is in the very early morning hours, and I am in and out of the scattered clouds, not really on top, but not fully in IFR conditions either. What was perhaps an omen that I had missed, but whatever is about to be sitting off my wing in just a few minutes, was never part of any BANDIT calls on the UHF and VHF radio *Guard* frequencies.

My first indication that something was up is a call from Red Crown, and my only individual call *ever* from Red Crown, that they had a *target* moving south, *fast*, in my area at a high rate of speed.

I got the same type of call from Deep Sea. In over 500 combat missions, of all sorts, *this is the first time either Deep Sea or Red Crown had ever called to me directly:* otherwise, we would check-in on each flight, but that was it.

But no BANDIT call was made?

Then came a series of back and forth calls between Red Crown and the radar ships that were someplace else off the North Vietnam coast. *These were excited calls in very rapid order;* now missing the usually calm, clear, measured SAM and BANDIT calls I had heard so many times before. Something is up, and I am apparently the only aircraft in the area.

*Rod Serling's theme music from **The Twilight Zone** was about to start . . .*

Red Crown interrupted his excited batter with the radar ship controllers and told me they had this *fast-mover* coming south and that I should be prepared to abort my mission.

Well, I think *this* is still maybe a couple of hundred miles to the north yet, and I have some time to spare, so I alerted Red Crown to call me if it looked like the *target* is going to cross my 80-mile safety zone. For me to abort just at this time would have gotten me in trouble back at Phu Bai as there is, *at that point*, no actual threat. And there had never been one that developed in the past, so an abort, right then, was not in the cards.

It should have been . . .

In what was maybe just a couple of minutes or so, Red Crown interrupts this radio banter that he has ongoing with Deep Sea and tells me that—

"We have aircraft on the deck . . .

And will have escorts airborne momentarily."

WHAT!?

It was time to abort this SLAR mission, but not with me diving into the darkened ocean about two miles below me.

Within seconds, Deep Sea calls *me* to say they have aircraft in the air, and that the *target* had crossed my 80-mile ring.

That was fast!

Two Navy fighters are now airborne off some carrier in the South China Sea and were heading toward me with great haste.

I started to get calls directly from the airborne radar aircraft, which I thought was Deep Sea. The Call Sign Deep Sea was the one of the same possibly EC-121 aircraft that the North Korean's had shot down some months before while they were fifty miles off the coast of North Korea. All 31 US military crewmembers died in that attack, for which the US did not retaliate.

How quickly we forget!

Whether it was Red Crown or a similar call, this is the first of my direct contact with this ship.

We had Red Crown, Deep Sea, and the Navy flight leader all on the radios at about the same time on the same frequency, on Guard, on open mics.

They were excited! *I am worried.*

I am now down probably to 5,000 feet and headed to the south when Red Crown told me the target, *It*, is now less than 20 miles behind me. That was way too fast. I turned now to get into a face-to-face position from what surely had to be a hostile aircraft.

I could hear the Navy jets being vectored on the Guard frequency, knowing this is probably unusual, but it did allow all of us, me, Deep Sea, Red Crown and the fighters to all be talking and listening together.

I turned back around and headed toward the target that Red Crown is calling the position of.

I did not see *It*, whatever *It* was, and Red Crown was still calling—

"Spud 12, target now your 12 o'clock fifteen miles. **Do you see It?**"

I did not see anything and could not turn my back on this again.

I could hear the Navy fighters on Guard saying they had a radar paint on *It*.

"Spud 12, your target is . . . now stopped . . .

Your 12 o'clock less than four miles . . .

*Do you see **It**?"*

WHAT? Stopped?

The Navy fighters confirmed they have the target, on their radar, but did not have any target altitude information. The fighters were to the west of the target, between the coast and my position and had swung around to the east now, gotten a radar lock and were coming fast from my left rear.

I could see no aircraft and certainly not this other *Bandit*, for surely ***It*** must be a Bandit.

I turned hard to the right, to the east, now level at about 5,000 feet.

The target started moving off my left wing, less two miles away (just a long runway length off my wing). I saw nothing, nothing at all.

"Spud 12, your target is now at your 9 o'clock, less than two miles.

*Do you see **It**?"*

No!

Both Navy fighters have a radar lock on ***It***. They are to my back left side and descending, having perhaps expected to find us at a higher altitude. Red Crown is calling me their position.

There is a lot of *excited radio chatter* as Red Crown, and Deep Sea are both talking *fast* that this—***It***, had been moving at over 2,000 miles per hour (or knots perhaps) and had then, with me right nose-to-nose with whatever the target is, ***It*** had STOPPED, or near so. I turned hard to the right, towards the open ocean. ***It*** stayed on my left side, close where I should have been easily able to see it, and ***It*** is tracking to the east with me only about a mile off the side—but I still could not see ***It*** even as I am not in the clouds.

For maybe a *long, long, long* 30-seconds this target hung on my left side. ***It*** had come out of nowhere, moved south at what is an *impossible speed*, and then had, impossibly, stopped when I turned to face it. Stopped? Impossible! ***It*** is moving slowly with me less than a mile off my left wing.

The Navy fighters are excited! They are close now and have a solid radar paint of me *and* the target (***It***) and then, suddenly, the target speeded up and—

. . and disappeared!

Ah, shit . . .

Gone. There is more radio chatter as the fighters passed on my left wing in full afterburner looking to catch up with—with something that is no longer there.

Impossible. Gone as quickly as it had appeared.

Whether this target, this UFO as it was, ***It***, as in something that is admittedly unidentified and flying was an object painted onto multiple radars, not as radar ghosting, had now started, just briefly, to move with me and then is—*gone*.

Did it drop down into the ocean? Climbed so fast it could not be tracked—or moved forward or laterally so quickly it was lost in an instant, or, what? Where? How?

For the next Twilight Zone Episode . . .

Everyone is talking on Guard: Fast and lacking the usually calm, cool, calls I had become used to the past year. Where had ***It*** gone? Deep Sea, the fighters, Red Crown . . ? How this had gone from the 2,000 plus speed to zero, then slowly off my wing, and then moved so fast it is gone—*without a trace?*

I headed back to Phu Bai, now down at about 1,500 feet and more miles off the coast than I had ever been. I called Spud Operations about the abort and told them **NOT** to launch another replacement SLAR aircraft. They wanted to know more; they needed to launch the replacement aircraft, as it was our mission requirement. I convinced them that I had to get down and debrief *before* they did anything at all.

There were a couple of clues of events that happened that early morning. The first is that we did not launch another RP-1 SLAR aircraft for about **eight hours.** We skipped three or four mandatory launches, so whoever our Spud Intel guys had communicated with, someone far above our pay grades, or theirs, had made the call to keep our aircraft off the RP-1 missions.

This event was on my first tour, in early 1971. But it is during my second tour, in 1972, that I am at the Udorn RTAFB officer's club, a bit drunk, and talking about this with one of the EC-130 C&C capsule crew guys and he recounted to me that they had, or had heard of, similar events with UFOs—whatever that might be—*being mixed up in the combat flights.*

So, I have become a believer. But not a clue of what ***It*** is that I might be believing. Surely, this could not have been Soviet, not with this capability, the high, *hypersonic speed* too and then down to basically, zero, almost instantly, and then moving again and *disappeared.*

We never had any discussions about this matter, either with our unit guys or anyone else asking for details. They did not have to as I think, especially after the conversation with the capsule guys, that this was something one just did not discuss. The most probable reason is likely—

It is sometimes better to remain silent and thought a fool.
Than to speak up and remove all doubt...
This was probably one of those times...

1-11 / AND YOUR DROP TANKS ARE NOW WHERE?

Half of our 597 gallons of JP-4 fuel is carried in two 150-gallon *drop tanks* that hung under the wings. That fuel fed from there to the main fuel tank, located on the top of the fuselage, and then out to the engines. For a ferry flight, and used routinely as mission fuel in the first Gulf War, the Mohawk could carry the larger 300-gallon drop tanks.

To jettison the tanks, and anything under the wings from rockets, to machine guns, to flare pods and other things, there is a black and yellow T-handle located just below the engine throttles on the power quadrant. Pull the handle and the wings should clean themselves. *Should* is the word, as my story of a hung drop tank on my IR ship down in the *A Shau Valley* is one of my personal stories here. The wing stores could also be jettisoned using a lower center counsel panel selector and a button on the pilot's control stick that would fire an electrical squid to release anything on the wing's hardpoints.

You set the selector and pressed the control stick button to run an electrical charge to fire the rockets or machine guns, or drop any individual item from one of the six under wing hard points. No one ever used that method because a decision to clean off the wings is usually a near instant one, like during an engine failure on takeoff.

On takeoff, the right-seater—the TO or another pilot—puts his hand physically on the stripped handle, so that in the event of an engine failure the wings could be instantly cleaned, or the Mohawk is not going to keep flying. So, that stripped handle is always a big deal—*and marked accordingly.*

In the design of the Mohawk, unpressurized as it is, there is a built-in message drop chute, a small tube: a cylinder between the pilot's legs meant for a message container to be dropped to someone on the ground. A good idea as it was.

The message tube jettison is a *smaller* gray, T-handle down and to the left of the power quadrant. Pull the *lower* handle and a spring-loaded flap opened on the bottom of the aircraft and out would go the message tube.

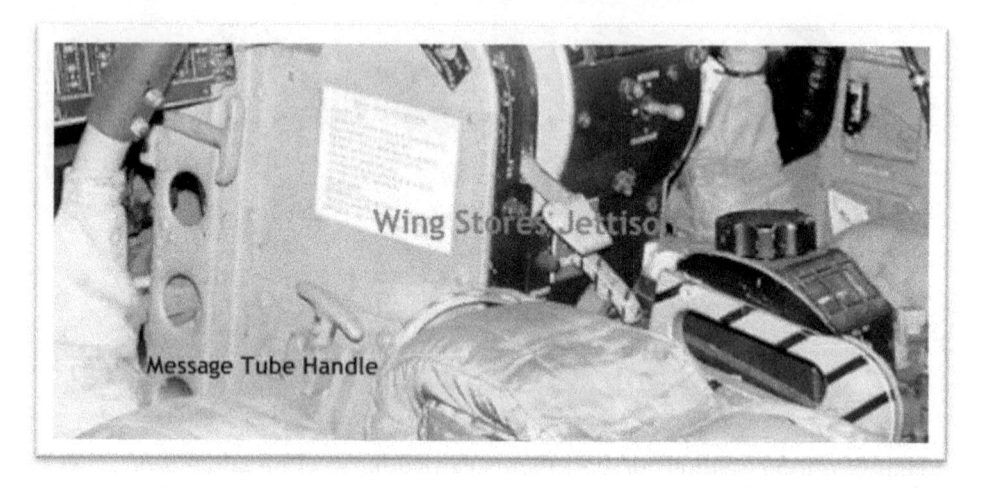

One Message Tube Handle drops the pop cans, the other T-Handle . . .

What we *used it for* was to drop our empty soda cans during a flight.

It Just Had to Happen—and it did one day to a new guy that departed on an RP-1 SLAR mission up the coast of North Vietnam. Not so long into the flight, while he is cleaning up the cockpit clutter, he put one of the pop cans into the drop chute—*and pulled the handle.*

Perhaps it was the unexpected slight *up-tick* of the aircraft, the effect of losing two nearly full 150-gallon drop tanks that were the first clue that—*he had pulled the wrong handle!*

Ah, shit . . .

1-12 / Triple Night Monsoon GCA Approach at Phu Bai — On the Low Fuel Light

Event Note: This was a few seconds from becoming flaming wreckage and it resulted because I had stayed on target too long and tried to recover to Phu Bai, in the monsoon night rains with minimum fuel.

It is the Northeast Monsoon season, and I am running a SLAR mission on RP-1 just off the coast of North Vietnam. Routine but for the fact that we had a shortage of critical aircraft avionics, not the least of which was our TACAN receivers, something we needed for navigation, position locating, and IFR approaches. As things were, we sometimes launched combat SLAR flights, in IFR weather, onto RP-1 with only a transponder working and no other navigation gear. **Nuts it was to do this.** The transponder is not a navigation device, only a radar interrogation responder to identify us. But, with that we would get the Air Force, or Navy, as we moved farther north, to give us vectors to get into our starting position on RP-1 and from there we could use our SLAR ground mapping screen to figure out where we were. *Sometimes*.

If the weather conditions at Phu Bai are too bad when coming off an RP-1 mission, the planning is that we are to divert to the west across the flak-covered skies Laos and go to the base at Ubon RTAFB in Thailand. From there we could refuel and decide whether to come back, as the aircraft would be needed for more missions, or wait for better weather. On this night, I made a *serious mistake* in not diverting to Ubon.

Anyway, I had come back from a night RP-1 SLAR mission with no working navigation equipment other than the transponder (!), a*nd a transponder is not navigation,* but it is all I had that night as I had taken the aircraft with no working TACAN, no working VOR, and a marginal, at best, ADF. Disregard that I had a working Doppler system, but that only put you in the AO, not a navigation tool in our world. I had worked my way with only radar vectors back towards Phu Bai. Making matters so much worse that night is that Phu Bai had been taking on-and-off mortar attacks, which is not unusual at all, so the airfield is in a blackout status, and no runway lights could be turned on. Okay, so this is going to be a full GCA right down to an invisible runway, at night, in the rain.

And we did this why . . . ?

I made the first approach with the GCA guys and am surely sweating just how I was to come out on the bottom side. The GCA can put you right on the runway, pretty much, *usually . . .* most of the time—

"Spud 22 this is your GCA final controller . . .

Do not acknowledge any further transmissions . . .

Approaching glidepath . . your wheels should be down . .

Begin descent . . .

On glidepath . . .

Slightly right of course . . .

Turn left . . . Stop turn . . .

Correcting . . . Drifting slightly below glidepath . . .

Correct rate of descent . . .

Now 900 feet above touchdown . . .

Slightly right of course . . .

On glidepath . . .

800 feet above touchdown . . .

Slightly below glidepath . . .

Correcting."

The tense moments of this GCA approach are going second-by-second. Your attention and vision are glued—***glued***—to the turn needle, rate-of-climb gauge, and the airspeed indicator. Constant small corrections in start- and stop-turns, usually in the same breath and trying to adjust the rate of descent with the calls of being slightly above or below the glidepath.

It is raining hard, and my wipers were banging a steady drumbeat across my windshield while, from the wet darkness and clouds, sometimes very heavy, sometimes lighter, comes the occasional flashes of mortar rounds impacting on the base to the right of the runway and usually on the helicopter side of the airfield. In the dark, wet, raining and low, very low, clouds right down to the ground the VC could be sure that there would not be any Cobra gunships coming out to return fire.

Occasionally, in the darkness, there would be tracer rounds bouncing up through the clouds that come from our perimeter defense gunners shooting at a suspected area of nearby mortar fire and having the large size .50 cal tracer bullets ricochet up into the air. Great, not only am I descending on to my blacked out airfield while it is taking mortars, but our guns may be shooting me down.

What would (should) I be doing in Ubon right now? Like getting refueled, eating real food, maybe getting laid if I had the time . . .

> *"On glidepath . . .*
>
> *Slightly right of course . . .*
>
> *Correcting . . .*
>
> *Slightly above glidepath . . .*
>
> *200 feet above landing threshold . . .*
>
> *You should have the runway in sight (fat chance!) . . .*
>
> *Approaching landing minimums . . .*
>
> *Still slightly right of course . . .*
>
> *Slightly right of course . . .*
>
> *100 feet above landing threshold . . .*
>
> *Now below GCA minimums . . .*
>
> *You should have the runway in sight . . .*
>
> *Right of course . . .*
>
> ***Right of course!"***

X-The First Missed Approach

At maybe 100 feet I have ground contact and **NO RUNWAY** . . . I am maybe 40 yards to the *right* of the runway, but descending into the helicopter revetment area . . . FULL POWER, PULL UP, GEAR UP, FLAPS TO APPROACH . . . THEN FLAPS FULL UP. Damn!

As I pitch back up into the raining blackness there are the flashes of mortar rounds almost right under me, hitting in the helicopter revetment area and being my only illumination in the few seconds I could see anything.

X-Fuel is becoming the Issue

I have overstayed my welcome and no longer have enough fuel to divert across Laos to Ubon. I screwed up. I should not have risked even the first approach and just diverted over Laos to Ubon for the night and gotten laid probably as the side benefit. That is to say nothing of getting some real food and a real bed. However, it is too late now.

I am radar vectored around for another approach and am talking to Spud Operations about getting some lights turned on. No deal. Air Force controllers running the airfield will not turn them on even for a moment while taking incoming, even as the attack is just 82 mm mortars. Just mortars? Like it is nothing to be landing at a blacked out runway that is actively under attack with explosions (small as they were mortars, not rockets that night) and treat it like it is simply an anomaly.

How adapted to the insane we had all become in no time at all?

Spud Operations said they would put two trucks out on the end of the runway and at the last second turn on their headlights for my runway alignment, regardless of what the controllers wanted. The GCA controllers were in their reinforced bunker. All right, that *sounds* okay.

I am radar vectored around again and back onto a long final for another GCA approach. This one would not end well either, though the GCA approach itself is okay. While descending through the clouds, we see random mortar flashes, while .50 caliber tracers from our perimeter defense guns are still ricocheting up through the clouds—

> "On glidepath . . .
>
> On course . . .
>
> 200 feet above landing threshold . . .
>
> Continue . . .
>
> Slightly right of course . . .
>
> Approaching landing threshold."

It is raining hard, and my wet windshield is obscuring what I can see and then . . . *right at breakout . . . on short final* . . . two of our unit trucks are showing their headlights . . . **Right at me**—not down the runway. I am blinded. FULL POWER, PULL UP, GEAR UP, FLAPS TO APPROACH . . . FLAPS UP . . .

FUEL LOW red light is now brightly glowing on the warning panel. I am in ***Emergency Low Fuel*** state with maybe 15-20 minutes of fuel, depending on my flight attitude. Damn, I could have been drinking Thai beer, in a real bed, with real food and maybe some companionship.

X-This is The Last One - It's Now Land, Crash or Eject

Have the guys turn the trucks around and when signaled on short final, get out and run because this Mohawk is going to be on the ground, hopefully on a runway—but maybe not. There are no second or third chances now. The runway is not long enough, even in daylight, on a dry runway, to take chances of a longer delayed landing and to come in even a bit short is going to put you into the minefields right at the end of the runway. These are tactical runways, to be sure.

At that point, my only other alternative is to roll to the east, go a few miles towards the coast, but not over it, and both of us eject and wait for the Cobra gunship cover and a Dustoff pickup. Not a good plan either, but one used by many in Vietnam by the Army, Air Force, Navy, and Marines. Better that, risking an ejection and a hopefully quick pick up, than an uncontrolled crash.

By the time I am approaching the GCA final controller, I am at least 10-minutes into the **FUEL LOW** light. My TO and I both know this is the final approach, to be sure. We unfasten our ejection seat survival packs, as we do not want to risk a low-altitude ejection and be dragging out the survival pack from under our ejection seats that go out with us on a *normal ejection*.

Ejection seat harnesses are tightened up. The GCA final controller is back with us. Completely cool, calm and professional like this is a daily routine just before a coffee break. Good thing I do not have to acknowledge anything because *my voice would be way too shaky by now.*

We descend into the wet darkness, again; the red **LOW FUEL** light is glowing; the three green landing gear lights are showing, flaps are to the approach setting, the inboard hydraulic ailerons are out—and we are landing in only seconds—*one way or the other.*

Like a Romulan Starship uncloaking to smite Captain Kirk, we materialize out of the rain and darkness.

Coming out of the bottom of the clouds on short final, maybe a bit higher ceiling cover, but still less than the 200 feet (!!) that would be comfortable, if not itself risky . . . and now there are the two trucks with their lights shining down the runway as they should be.

I *impacted* the blackened, wet runway, with a thud and then pulled the levers to reverse idle. Usually, I might use full reverse—not being certain how much runway

I still had leased in front of me—but the Mohawk had an ugly habit that sometimes one prop would reverse just before the other, and that brief delay would cause the aircraft to swerve; though this is usually handled safely. But it is black out, with no runway lights, a very wet runway, and raining heavily—I would not know which way the aircraft would jerk. Better if I simply go to reverse idle, brakes, and in the seconds it took to ensure both props were in reverse, together, I could stop the aircraft.

I said never again would I pass up the chance to divert to Ubon, but I would, with maybe more risk later on.

1-13 / ONE ENGINE, AT NIGHT, IN THE A SHAU VALLEY, DAMAGED WITH A HUNG DROP TANK

Event Note: We black candle-smoked *Bomber* into our Spud Club's ceiling tiles, like many other events before and after, when on this night I dragged my crippled IR aircraft out of the *A Shau Valley*, (The Valley of Death)—on one engine, and with a nearly full fuel load in a hung drop tank on the dead engine side (the worst side) that I could not shake off.

1/ It Was All Too Real

I am on my second combat tour and at this time the 245th SAC had left the country, and the 131st had taken over their missions in I Corps, on top of our North Vietnam, Steel Tiger and Barrel Roll missions. My single-aircraft night IR mission is working a dozen or so targets along small rivers and trails in the north end of the *A Shau Valley* just to the south of the then closed Marine base at Khe Sanh. Anything that is down into a valley, especially the *Valley of Death*, is very high risk. At times, the valley would be so narrow, and you are well below the bordering ridges, that making a turn, with no night visibility, was impossible. Many years before the advent of life-saving NVGs (Night Vision Goggles) you descended blindly into the targets and figured to have a way out—maybe, maybe not.

Once you dropped into the valley there is no radar coverage to know where you were so without a high SLAR aircraft working with you, like in Steel Tiger in Laos or the PDJ in northern Laos, you were *alone* and *invisible*. We kept a radio notice with the Air Force EC-130 C&C capsule, *Moonbeam,* as to our approximate location. I am too low for any other communications with anyone other than *Moonbeam.*

The *standard fuel management* for flying a Mohawk mission is to start the transfer of fuel from the wing drop tanks to the main fuselage tank shortly after takeoff and continue it until the drop tanks were empty. One did not want to get up into North Vietnam and find out that you were not able to get to your drop tank fuel to transfer.

The IR and VR aircraft fuel handling were a bit different due to our maneuvering and especially the IR night aircraft to accommodate a lost engine on a mission. While enroute, we would take a few minutes to make sure we could transfer fuel from the drop tanks and then turn that off and continue to draw down the main fuselage fuel tank until we felt *we had just enough fuel to get home* or to Thailand if we lost an engine. The logic is that if we lost an engine, we wanted to be as light as possible and that meant we could jettison the external drop tanks, carrying about 2,100 pounds of jet fuel, and just drag the fuselage fuel away.

On this fateful night, I had just started my IR mission working strip targets to the south of Khe Sanh when a rapid series of bright flashes and explosions hit the right side.

The Mohawk shuddered and jerked hard to the left and right as I vigorously peddle-walked the rudders for control. I had a **#2 FIRE** light showing in the engine fire extinguisher T-handle. We were taking a steady stream of .30 cal gunfire from the valley and nearby mountain sides, but nothing more—*yet.*

This is surely an "Ah, shit . . ." moment.

It is the right engine, shaking, and then there were several more flashes and small explosions. I pulled back the right throttle with a bit of care, as many a pilot has shut down the wrong engine in an emergency—

Idle Foot - Idle Engine

That is how to be sure you had the right engine. When I throttled back, the flashes and small shaking explosions stopped. The anti-aircraft fire continued, but the shaking stopped.

I pulled the #2 ENG fire handle and fired both extinguishers into the right engine.

It is maybe only five seconds now, with things happening rapidly, but also while time seems to *stand still*.

I confirmed I had ahold of the external stores jettison T-handle that is just below the throttles on the power quadrant and then looked out my darkened left window as I pulled the handle and watched my nearly full left-side drop tank tumble away to the jungle. With the heavy wing fuel gone I had a chance now.

I had assumed that the right drop tank was successfully jettisoned.

My left leg is jerking as I have full rudder peddle into the left side, and the aircraft still had control problems pulling hard to the right, to the dead engine side.

Damn!

Before I went to fuel off on the right engine I again slowly advanced the right throttle just to *be certain* and, as expected, it started to flash and fire again. What I figured then is that I had a fuel controller failure, perhaps mechanical or maybe from taking hits on the right engine, but either way I had effectively lost the engine and had to shut it down before it exploded into pieces. This violent failure is unlike my other, more or less, routine engine failures where the engine itself failed, or the prop is out of control, but not shuddering like it now is.

The fuel controller failure had induced a severe internal compressor stall situation, and the flashes and small explosions coming out of the front of the engine were internal explosive fires shooting forward from inside the engine. If the engine is not shut down *immediately,* it could start to come apart—and that would be a cause to eject—right into the Valley of Death!

Maybe just ten-to-fifteen seconds now—though it seemed longer, much longer. So many things now are happening all at the same time.

I am still losing altitude and confused by my left leg and rudder shuddering. For reassurance, I glanced *again* out to the left wing and made sure my drop tank was gone.

While the anti-aircraft gunfire is *critical*, the immediacy is always control of the aircraft.

Ahead and slightly to the left could see the starry outline of a saddle back low area at the south end of the valley but I am still below the lowest part of the ridge. I am not going to make it out now, not on this pass anyway.

Moonbeam had relayed my troubles to Spud Operations, and they were preparing another Mohawk to get out to me, but that would be maybe, at best, another 35-minutes. Across the runway at Phu Bai, a light helicopter fire team is getting ready for a rescue and recovery if I made it back to Phu Bai and could not land or if I had to punch out into the *A Shau Valley* if it came to that.

Within minutes, we would have a pair of Cobra gunships, an OH-6 LOACH, and a medical Dustoff Huey all part of a rescue and pickup team in this area. In other regions, in the DMZ or further north or anywhere to the west in Laos it would be the Air Force and the Jolly Green Giants with some A1 *Skyraiders* carrying CS gas to help with a recovery.

I made a reversing turn back to the right and lost a bit more of my very precious altitude in the turn. I am struggling with the controls and uncertain why, now on one engine and light without the drop tank fuel—why is this Mohawk not wanting to fly? Unfortunately, I had only started the mission so I effectively still had nearly full fuselage fuel—but my fuel drop tanks were gone—*right*?

We took more light ground fire while turning back to the north and did so in two more turns and runs but never suffered any hits, just that I am low and staggeringly slow by then. Thankfully, there was no flak in the *A Sha Valley*.

By this time, I had turned back to the south for a third time to try to get enough altitude to clear the ridgeline that I could see silhouetted against a near moonless but starry night. Had I overhead clouds and no stars, my only option would be to eject as we were otherwise blind and inside a valley whose sides were higher than we were going to be able to climb out of on one engine: if we could not *see* those ridges, then ejection is the only answer.

Ah, shit . . .

The loss of an engine meant that the electrical *Emergency Bus* is not powering the IR system, so I had no look-down capability to be sure we were even still in the valley and not about to hit the ridgelines, as several of our guys had done before.

I came around again, turning to the bad engine and held my own, but still struggling.

We are maybe only ten to twelve minutes into this by now. It seemed both much longer and shorter all at the same time if that makes any sense at all.

I started back down the valley and continued to draw .30 cal fire while luckily no .51 cal gunfire or it would have been all over very quickly.

I picked up a couple of hundred feet altitude going back to the south but trying to hold the Mohawk straight in just a bare minimum climb is almost impossible now. Something else is wrong, very wrong.

As I approached the saddle back outline again, my left foot is pressed so hard on the rudder my knee is shaking. My TO leans forward in his seat, looks out to his side and yells to me: *"Jettison the drop tanks!"* **What!?** I had—but *his tank* is still hanging there under the wing on the dead engine side—*the worst side*.

I pulled the stores jettison again, several times and went ahead and armed the electronic firing of the stores for that hard point, but to no avail. I tried shaking the Mohawk and jamming the rudder again with my twisting, but the right drop tank is hung in place and dragging down that side. Had it been the hung tank on the good engine side I might have handled that, but a dead engine and a hanging fuel tank on the same side is about to do us in.

We turned around *again* and went north for another try to get more altitude. The bad guys came off their break and sat down at the guns and started firing at this slow, lumbering Mohawk that they could only barely see an outline of—but wait, he will turn around and come back south again. Am thinking I now know how the little moving ducks at a carnival shooting gallery operate. We just move slowly one way, and then back again, until . . . PING. The shooter finally knocks you down.

*Me thinks **I** am the little floating duck in the shooting gallery that night . . !*

Right then, what is worrying me more is what killed Jim Shereck. When he and I were working a SLAR/IR combo mission in Steel Tiger North, near Tchepone, he took a .51 cal hit to his left engine, lost that engine and less than an hour later the other engine started a runaway propeller overspeed—and he had to shut that engine down too. That was bad enough, but as you read in this book, when he went to eject—his seat failed, and he tumbled through the night locked to an ejection seat from which he could not separate. Here I am on one engine, struggling badly, and needing every bit of power I could get, even to an overspeed or over boost situation. *I had no other options*.

The next run on the southern pass had me pressing all the power I had. Against my better judgment, I not only had full engine power on the left engine, but I still pushed the prop to max RPM. If I am going to take apart the good engine, then maybe I could at least be out of the *A Shau Valley*.

I turned the radar altimeter down from the regular 400 feet warning of impending terrain impact and gave it 200 feet. If we were down to just 200 feet of clearance and sinking, we would have only seconds to eject.

1/ It Was All Too Real

By this pass, with only the starry outline of the Saddleback visible, we barely slid out of the valley and descended east toward the coastal plains south of Phu Bai.

By now the Spud chase aircraft is in the air and being vectored toward me. I had cleared the ridgeline, while only seeing it as an outline against the starry night, and am letting down towards the distant lights that I could see at Hue, with the Phu Bai airfield just to the south of that. But I am not home safe yet—I had a hung drop tank full of jet fuel that would likely explode if it came off on a landing and hit the runway beside me, and I would need to make a night, single-engine GCA approach to Phu Bai, and maybe under gunfire there too.

Ah, shit . . .

I flew towards Phu Bai as our chase aircraft came up to see if there is any other damage. Checking for damage would be difficult in the darkness, but it was still nice to have another of our Mohawks up there with me.

Over the next fifteen minutes of so, watching the fuel level in the drop tank, I determined that I am able to transfer fuel from the hanging tank. So the basic idea now is to empty the tank, taking away the landing explosion scenario, and go into Phu Bai on one engine. Because the electronic jettison *squid* had already failed on the hung tank, there is no way to know if a touchdown itself would be enough force to drop the tank and cause a cascading crash on the runway. I would rather take my chance on that versus the *point to the coast and punch out* idea.

Plan B is that if I could not shake the drop tank into falling off the wing, *and* if it is not transferring fuel, that with a helicopter recovery team with us I would trim as best I could and point the aircraft out toward the ocean and when close, but not too close to the beach, we would eject making sure we did not come down in the water and either drown or become shark food.

Recently a helicopter crew crashed in the same area when they tried to maneuver under the weather and get into Phu Bai by flying in from the ocean. They crashed, and the dreadful part is that only one person survived, and the sharks ate several of the others that were floating, alive, by the wreckage.

In the meantime, now with the luxury of being near Phu Bai, and the helicopter team standing by for a quick pick up if we did eject, I started to try other things to get the drop tank to shake off. I slammed the rudders while jerking on the elevators and sometimes rolling, but careful to not go over on my back, and do anything to shake the tank. Nothing worked. Over and over I tried.

With the fuel transfer coming out the hung tank it would be empty in about 60 minutes, and I would attempt a landing. *If* the tank tumbled off during the runway impact, it would have nothing to explode. I would just make a longer landing so as not to touch down too hard and then hope for the best.

The Phu Bai airfield crash crew is out, but the runway lights were kept off for now due to mortar attacks that kept happening. I would get a GCA radar approach, and the runway lights would come on just before touchdown—*I hoped.*

Then, as things happen unexpectedly, I am done with my attempts to shake the tank and am just killing time, and I feel the control stick jump back and forth and *presto*, the hung tank is gone, on its own. Losing the hanging tank is great news though I still had to do a nighttime GCA, on one engine, though better in this configuration than the unpredictable control drag of that full fuel drop tank.

The CGA and landing and recovery are uneventful; I cleared the runway, shut down and let maintenance come out and put a hook on and tow me to the parking ramp, our standard routine in any emergency recovery.

It is later that night at our *Spud Club*, a bit drunk to be sure that using a candle the word *Bomber* is smoked into the ceiling tiles with so many other words and phrases all related to something, good, bad or really ugly.

The next day a helicopter and ground team went out and found the drop tank and make sure no one was injured or killed by this drop tank falling on them.

1-14 / Staff Officer Got More Than He Expected Flying With Me Over Laos to Vientiane

One day in early 1972, after we had moved, *fled*, south to the Marble Mountain Army Airfield by DaNang, that I get assigned to take a colonel from our battalion staff from Marble Mountain to attend a meeting or briefing being given at the US Embassy in Vientiane, Laos. The meeting, of course, would have dealt with our 2- or 3-aircraft-a-night (2 IR, 1 SLAR) missions in the CIA's Secret War in Northern Laos / the Plain of Jars that we flew out of Udorn RTAFB.

It was forbidden to fly our Mohawks into Vientiane, least someone that is blind, deaf, and kept in solitary confinement for several years did not know we had a significant military presence in Laos that may have *potentially* been beyond the *two persons* that were allowed—just two CIA associates from a past agreement. So the rule was, no US military aircraft on the ground in Laos, especially at Vientiane or the CIA/Air America main base at Lima Site-20a (Long Tieng). *Fat chance for that.*

It is early morning and daylight when we left Marble Mountain and flew northwest over Laos to our CIA flight operations at Udorn RTAFB. In daylight, at least at the altitude I am flying, at about 12,000 feet, there would be little risk of anti-aircraft fire or heavy flak, except perhaps for a possible radar guided 57 mm. I flew to the south of Tchepone, *dirty, deadly, Tchepone*, as it was known, in the northern part of Steel Tiger North and I expected no anti-aircraft fire at that time of day and altitude. Had we come by very much lower, and looking like we were doing a recon or photo work, in daylight, in that area, it is easily fatal—but not just overflying at altitude. So, no gunfire, no anti-aircraft, and certainly no 23/37/57 mm flak. None.

The colonel is not impressed about our tales of anti-aircraft fire in Laos. Here we were, in daylight, flying near to *our allegedly most dangerous area*, by Tchepone, and there were clearly no threats at all. I would have been wasting my time with the explanations of why the sky is *not* full of flak.

By mid-morning I had dropped the colonel off in Udorn where we had a non-US military (read Air America) helicopter set to fly him to Vientiane for the meeting. My expectation is that he would come back late in the day and stay in Udorn that night, for a variety of reasons. Admittedly maybe some good reasons like perhaps, real food, shopping, getting laid, as the case often was, and if for no other good reason is that I did not want to fly back across Laos at night by the time the nightly fireworks would have started, but I am not so lucky.

As it was, it is late in the day when this colonel got back and *insisted* that he had to get back to Marble Mountain that night. What? Why? He is insistent, and I had no choices. He did take the time to eat at the Air Force officer's club and thus pushed our departure back towards the early evening.

I got him into the Mohawk and departed on a different route home. Mind you that we did not file any flight plans, we just launched and went where we wanted to and, if in radar control range, would simply advise them of the general direction and altitude. This *calling in the blind* usually made for some interesting ATC situations. No matter where you were flying—and another good reason not to fly on any *fixed* altitude, like say 10,000-feet—as it would be better to fly at, say, 9,750 feet, or 10,210 feet, just so that pilots that *like to fly at some perfect altitude*, on an autopilot, are not likely to suddenly become the fly in the windshield.

Flying back over the same more-or-less direct route, the one near Tchepone from that morning was never an option. I would stay in Thailand and fly southeast going down by Ubon and then eastward, staying not far north of the Cambodian border, and then back northeastward, across *the Trail* in Steel Tiger South and then into South Vietnam in the Central Highlands and toward Pleiku and up toward DaNang, to Marble Mountain.

This flight would end up being somewhat of a game changer for us in the 131st.

I am down southeast past Ubon and into Laos. All the aircraft's position lights are out, and the radios are starting to run hot and heavy. All the regular players for Steel Tiger South had by then checked in with the nightly *GameMaster*: Moonbeam. There is, besides Moonbeam, the Air Force EC-130 C&C aircraft, an AC-130 *Spectre* gunship, some *faster-mover* strike aircraft, and our SLAR and IR aircraft that were working *the Trail* in coordination with the *Spectre* gunship. The anti-aircraft fire is light to nonexistent while we were still west of *the Trail*, blackened out, and at about 12,000 feet.

By then, we were moving eastward and getting above *the Trail*, the *Lightshow* has begun . . . in earnest to be sure—and it is **Showtime**.

Why they would be firing at me, at 12,000 feet no less, is probably explained by a nearly full moon, and that we were thus clearly visible to the gunners on the ground—or, looking up and finding us, they perhaps thought I am one of the *Spectre* gunships and worthy of shooting.

First, there is some .51 cal basketball sized tracers coming up. Those, as mentioned many times in this book, are *very dangerous*. Such a high-velocity round that they did not have to guess on hitting us by leading the aircraft, they could start shooting and then walk the tracers right onto you—but that is okay. At this altitude, if I can see the tracers coming up I can avoid them.

Next started the 23 & 37 mm flak, but not much of it, and thankfully none of the radar directed 57 mm fire, at least not down in this part of Laos. I had maybe six to ten guns tagged and working on me with no more than three or four guns working on me at once; *not a real threat in my view* so long as I could see the tracers coming up, up much slower than the .51 cals to be sure. No big deal—*none at all.*

Just to keep on the safe side I did need to see the flak tracers that were drifting up as the gunners unloaded a clip, usually of six to eight rounds, at us. One needed maybe two seconds, at most, to know if you were in danger.

If in those two seconds, the tracer streams are staying in the same relative position—*then you have trouble.* It means the relationship between you and tracer heads of the flak shells are staying connected, and you need to turn away, now. If in the two seconds, sometimes you are judging three, or four or more streams coming up at once, you see, or maybe more you *sense* a divergence in your view of the streams, then you are probably okay—but you have to see the stuff coming up to know what to do.

It would be the red tracer streams coming up from your right, your blind side if you did not have a TO or another pilot in that seat, or from behind; that would be what could take you down, not the stuff you can easily see. The whole idea is, not like a .51 cal. that can actually shoot *at you*, but with the flak, the threat is to fill the sky up and let you fly into some of it.

Again, this is just a half-dozen flak guns and maybe, at most, twenty to thirty streams of flak total. Maybe just over a hundred plus airbursts, maybe two hundred. Sounds like a lot, but it is not. Not like the Navy and Air Force faced up by Hanoi or Haiphong to be sure with usually over a hundred guns firing upward just to fill the sky with flak and see what might be hit.

As I scoped out the flak streams I had rolled slightly to the left twice, maybe quickly over to 90-degrees, wing up position, and right back, and had caught sight of multiple streams coming up, but I felt we were okay. Then I rolled about 120-degrees over on my right side, not fully upside down, but enough so I could see out of that side and through the canopy above the right ejection seat and not get blindsided.

Usually, the very able TOs, sitting in the right ejection seat, would be calling the shots on that side of the aircraft, the blind side. As I rolled up on my right side the second time this colonel snaps back in his seat and swings his arm over at me and hits me in the chest—hard in the chest as it was—while he was yelling at me. He was not even using the press-to-talk helmet intercom—*just yelling, not to me, but at me.*

Asshole . . .

He had lost it, which I understood. The colonel was not a pilot and did not fully appreciate that I had to roll up on that side to see the flak. Did he think I am just going to fly along and hope and wish that someone on *that side* are not going to shoot me down?

For a few seconds, he is flapping around and yelling. I grabbed his arm the second time in just seconds as it had come at me. I calmed him down and explained that I had to turn to that side every few seconds to keep it clear. He is shook, and scared, and not expecting this—which to me is almost *nothing*, but it is impressive the first time one experiences going into a sky of flak and machine gun fire.

Oh, by the way, this is not even enough anti-aircraft fire to even be calling or reporting. A half dozen guns at most in just one area and we were already past their effective location and moving toward the South Vietnamese border.

He is then all over the FM radio trying to call back to Marble Mountain. We were still too far away, but he is trying so—I reached down and clicked off his FM radio audio input to my helmet so I could not hear what he is saying. He kept this up over the next hour and had apparently had made contact when we were closer, but with my side of the FM radio cut off, I did not hear what he was saying when he did finally make contact nearer to Marble Mountain.

We landed at Marble Mountain sometime before midnight, and as I taxied into the protective revetments, I could see there are two battalion staff vehicles and other senior officers waiting at my parking spot—including my own CO. What is going on? Why is my CO there—*at this time of night?*

So I get parked, and there is this gaggle of staff officers, at this very late hour, on the colonel's side of the Mohawk, and he crawls out and does not even say thanks to me. I had fully expected to be by then eating real food and fine liquor in my room back at our Paradise Hotel location in Udorn—not, back in Vietnam.

The battalion officers disappeared into the night, while my CO comes over, nearly breathless, wanting to know what had happened? What happened? He is so anxious, but why?

Well , . . well, let me think now? I did get him to the embassy meeting on time, but it was the colonel's idea to come back that night, not mine.

Not that? Huh?

The CO is pressing, right now, with the staff vehicles disappearing off the flight line. What happened out there tonight—in Laos?

It seems that we were nearly shot down over Laos from massive anti-aircraft fire and flak everywhere—*simply everywhere*. We had but barely escaped with our lives that night while under this heavy attack on us.

What?

Seems that when I had my monitoring of his FM radio turned off he had been calling his staff and is so excited—*and I understand that*—and had called for others and here were these officers out late at night meeting us—and they had gotten my CO up to be there too.

I had to think for a few seconds. Oh, yeah, there was *some* **minor gunfire,** some moderate flak, a .51 cal or two, but gosh, nothing even worth reporting, nothing *in our world worth reporting anyway*!

Within a few days, word comes down that the battalion felt that any of the pilots that flew missions in Laos had to be awarded at least a DFC, or a Silver Star. I had those plus multiple Bronze Stars for valor, with clusters, and more Air Medals. I had a *staggering* 35 awards of the Air Medal when I left.

I am not sure I ever saw that colonel again. Within days, I am back in my room at the Paradise Hotel where all we had to do for that good living is to spend a few hours each night flying near suicidal, low-level, night IR mission against some heavy anti-aircraft fire and flak in the Plain of Jars and the Chinese border. The tradeoffs were just fine.

The irony is that one does get used to the most intense of things, as any ground fighter would know, or the other pilots, that it becomes while concerning, but just not a significant issue. One's perspective of nearly *everything* gets warped fast in a combat zone.

If it is ever an issue, then your fear factor is not under control, and you were a hazard to yourself, and anyone that might be on a mission with you, in the aircraft or working with a support aircraft. Soldiers of all times have protected themselves this way, unconsciously, so that the most bizarre, or dangerous things, or events or sights, they soon become *the norm*.

The fact that this stuff becomes *the norm* is what is scary.

1-15 / LANDING GEAR SUCKS UP BEFORE TAKEOFF

Bill, not his real name *for good reason*, but we all know who is sitting at the run-up runway area getting ready for takeoff with a new SLAR mission TO in the right seat on that guy's very first combat mission, a simple SLAR flight up RP-1 to North Vietnam.

While waiting in sequence for takeoff the cockpit conversation, the experienced pilot and the new-to-country TO, were talking about aircraft things and somehow this got onto the topic of what would happen if you accidentally moved the landing gear lever to the *retract position* with the plane still on the ground? Surely this question would have been asked in the TO's Mohawk sensor school and in-flight training at Ft. Huachuca, Arizona, just months before? Would you think?

Well, nothing, because of the *squat switch*. Here, let me show you. The purpose of a *squat switch* is that with weight on the landing gear or some helicopter skids, the electrical circuits to things like weapons, external stores jettison and other things would be disabled. In the Mohawk, and most airplanes, the *squat switch* ensures that the gear retraction circuit does not connect, and the gear could not, *theoretically anyway*, be hydraulically retracted on the ground.

I am certain the—

Oh, shit . . .

. . Could be heard all the way back to the maintenance ramp that day. Bill, moved the gear handle forward to the retract position and IMMEDIATELY the Mohawk used its waiting 3,000 pounds of hydraulic pressure and sucked up the landing gear.

The Mohawk plopped down onto the run-up area: the propellers are grinding into the asphalt.

Oops . . . Ah, shit . . .

There were a number of other instances, not with us, but others arming the guns and rockets on the helicopters as they too had a squat switch on the gear struts, on most I am told, to be sure the guns and rockets do not fire while the aircraft is on skids—and those have gone wrong too, sometimes with fatal results.

Well, one less Mohawk that day, embarrassingly sitting on its belly at the end of the runway for everyone to point at and snicker.

Frankly, it could have happened to any of us, but names are changed to protect the guilty.

1-16 / OVERFLYING THE NVA ARTILLERY IN NORTH VIETNAM FOR US NAVY PRECISION FIRING

It is in mid-1972, just weeks before I medevac'd out, and that two of us, my dear friend and great IR pilot, Capt. Roger Thiel, known as *Round Ranger,* and I are tasked to go into southern North Vietnam to fly IR passes over NVA heavy artillery sites for precision marking while our Navy is firing into the targets. Roger, like so many Mohawk pilots, would later perish in a Mohawk crash, and again, an ejection at the last minute that was, as usual, outside the safe ejection seat profile envelope and fatal to both of them.

This is another suicide mission, perhaps more so than any of the others we thought we should never have gone on, this is in the top four on our list.

It was part of the NVA's 1972 Spring Easter Offensive (the start of the final stroke to run us out of South Vietnam), and the NVA were now coming down the open coastal highways, through Quang Tri, and about to move on to Hue. The issue is no longer the *Arc Light* (B-52) bombing on *the Trail* in Laos, but more so now, out in the open and bombing along the coast on Highway 1.

Ah, shit . . .

A critical issue is that more Soviet SA-2 SAM sites had moved southward and with them came more radar fired 57 mm, 85 mm and now the 100 mm flak guns. With our working skies now mostly closed to much of the air power we otherwise had, the ability to attack the truck and tank traffic was shifting over to the Navy and their offshore artillery.

At the time, the Navy had moved ships closer to the southern end of the North Vietnamese coast, to the north of the DMZ, with three heavy cruisers and some 38 destroyers, to attack the road traffic. This road traffic used to be out of the range of Navy guns because the trucks and tanks were usually far to the west, moving through the jungles north of Khe Sanh and, of course, usually down *the Trail*. The problem now is that the NVA had some heavy artillery of their own to fire back at the Navy ships that were in the range of the NVA long guns.

To spot the NVA artillery so that the Navy could fire at *them*, the Air Force put up several FAC aircraft in the daylight and lost several of them—in rapid order. And more of these brave guys would be lost very soon—some of the staggering numbers of *339* Air Force O-1/O-2/OV-10s lost in Vietnam, with *251* of them to direct combat shoot downs and crashes.

So it is decided *somewhere* that putting up an IR Mohawk to overfly the outbound NVA artillery sites like had been done in the PDJ on a 57 mm gun site, just one I might add, was something we could do. The run in the PDJ, with four Air America T-28s with me to attack the gun and radar site, is very different from dozens of heavy flak, and now multiple SAM sites, in this very region.

What was planned is that when the NVA outbound artillery firing started the Mohawks would already be in the very close area, obviously with our borrowed *Starship cloaking device hiding us*. When the NVA coastal artillery begins to fire back at the Navy ships, we would overfly their big guns, get an instant, right-to-the-meter location of the firing guns; then pass that data back to the Navy in real time and watch as the Navy directly hit the NVA artillery before they could move the guns just a bit down the road every few minutes and thus not be hit by the precision firing from the Navy ships.

Y-G-B-S-M
(see the Wild Weasel emblem and what that means)

It was clear that using just one Mohawk, that it would never survive getting up to our best IR altitude of just about 700 feet and running over the firing artillery; but maybe *two IR aircraft* each at about 350-400 feet could do this, in a parallel run, get the images, and drop back down (this is near the coast and mountains are not an issue) while the Navy, probably within five minutes, is responding. *Then*, to fly back to this hornet's nest protected by a lot of guns, and do this over again several times.

The OV-1D model's SLAR system has a large screen that the TO could start and stop so they could spend a few seconds looking at an image and coordinate with a ground map, then scroll the image forward, or backward.

*S-U-I-C-I-D-E and **we did know** what those letters meant.*

Roger and I went out and twice practiced this off the coast just south of Marble Mountain. We figured that we would have to come in low across the North Vietnam beaches, at probably less than 100 feet, and then change course at least twice and sort of meander around for a few minutes while the Navy kicks the nest and gets the NVA guns firing back out toward them.

Surely this is from someone's drunken movie script . . .

Hundreds are dying every day, so time is critical. We decided to go the next night. This mission now is one of only maybe two or three times that I wrote a letter to my parents and put it under my pillow before I left.

We had our choice, as usual, of the very, very best of the IR TOs, not that they were not all great, but this is surely going to be a bit hairy, and we needed TOs that could mark and plot the hot gun sites within seconds. And then run the data through the INS for precision, and get the data immediately relayed back to the Navy—all we figured within two or three minutes at most—and then be ready to go back to the sites a few minutes later, after the Navy had fired on the coordinates—when everyone within a mile would be really pissed and looking to shoot down another aircraft.

We had a *long* Intel mission briefing that night, going over the very latest, within the past hours, Intel on guns, missiles, the latest *Safe Letters*, a rescue plan, of sorts, and some other things.

If you had to go down anyplace, then North Vietnam is the place. We lost most of our guys in Laos and knew by my first tour that no one is being taken alive, or they all disappeared and even after the war, *none came back*. **None at all came back from being lost in Laos.** If you were shot down over North Vietnam, taking you as a prisoner of war is very important, and the NVA were not likely to outright kill you. The North Vietnamese were usually timely in identifying the crewmembers of the aircraft they had shot down. So that is a plus, the only possible plus. We are assured there would be Navy rescue helicopters in the air while we flew this mission so that a rescue might only be minutes away, either over land or out over the water.

Roger and I headed north, some miles off the coast, and made contact with Red Crown, Deep Sea and the Navy controllers for the warships.

We wondered if maybe there is a fly-by planned for us so they could toss flowers out to the suicide flight crews?

It is dark, very dark. I am hanging down and under Roger's right wing, tucked in relatively tight as we usually were. When flying like that, day or night, you see only one thing, **just one thing,** and that is your focus mark. No outside peeking is allowed as you are constantly jockeying not only the pilot's flight control stick but also the constant small motion of the throttles.

On cue, the Navy gave the word and in the blackness we dropped down to about a hundred feet and headed toward the coast. We had practiced some of this in *daylight*, something that in retrospect was a mistake in planning because about the time we were coming up on the coast, Roger made a course correction. Then, suddenly lacking any horizon, we had a mixture of stars blending with the many ground lights, mostly small fires or lights from homes, and what must have been just feet from the waves my TO yells something, I look up, and we in a descending left turn headed right into the water—

"PULL UP!"

"PULL UP!"

I pulled up and to the right and in doing so lost sight of Roger's blackened aircraft. We both headed back out over the ocean and had to have the Navy find us on radar and put us back together off the coast and behind the Navy ships. We were a bit shaken, as expected. Forming aircraft up in a formation at night—without turning on our position lights—is another challenge we had not anticipated in our practice work the past days.

The next time, maybe fifteen minutes later, we decided there are to be no diversionary course changes, just get onto the planned course, track with the INS, be down just above the water, and make *no turns,* or at least not until we have to climb for the first IR run—so maybe five minutes at most.

We never made it that night. Roger and I skimmed inbound across the coast of North Vietnam just like Doolittle's Raiders coming up on Japan's coast some thirty years earlier; only we are much lower *and* in the dark. Once inland we had no anti-aircraft fire, and the NVA are not firing back at the Navy ships. There were no targets to run the IR pass. Naturally, *we objected to that*, so we dallied around for a long, *a very, very long* 5-8 minutes until the reserve power of our *Starship Cloaking Devices* is run out and then we headed back to the coast, out over the ocean, and back down to Marble Mountain.

Surely, any well-deserved awards we would have received for this mission, all four of us, would have been given *posthumously*.

1-17 / FOUR IR FLIGHTS ONE NIGHT WHILE US MARINES ARE TRAPPED INSIDE QUANG TRI CITY

During the early days of the 1972 Easter Offensive the NVA, around May 1st through the 4th, during which the NVA army had crossed the DMZ at the bridges of Dong Ha, taken most of the northern end of I Corps and overran Quang Tri City. From the west, the NVA had moved more armor and artillery across Highway 9 (a dirt road), just below the DMZ, through Khe Sanh, and joined up with the forces that had driven across the DMZ. Thousands of NVA died in massive Arc Light strikes, but still they kept coming. Clearly MACV had not anticipated that the NVA are going to violate the DMZ agreements and boldly move their tanks, trucks and other armor down the coastal roads and right across the bridges at Dong Ha, in the east end of the DMZ. Oh really? Violate an agreement?

The irony of this is that two of us had spent many nights over the past two weeks running specific IR targets into and just north of the DMZ. These missions were showing hundreds of tanks and other armored vehicles massed to the north of the DMZ—and indeed not coming through the jungles. So someone, *somewhere,* who is making up our IR missions knew the tanks were coming this time on roads, *fast,* and not through the jungles—but they must have kept that bit of Intel a secret.

The NVA came in massive force with hundreds of tanks and armored vehicles across the still standing bridge at Dong Ho, in the DMZ and along the coastal highway just a few miles inland from the ocean.

Quang Tri City then fell within days, if not just hours.

By May 1, 1972, there is quickly organized an emergency helicopter evacuation of the remaining 132 combat survivors at Quang Tri City, including some 80 US soldiers and Marines.

On May 2nd, 1972, Quang Tri City fell, but not everyone had gotten out.

There were, as I recall, **seven rescue, attack and support helicopters that were shot down in just days** on the few miles' path from the coast inland to Quang Tri City—plus all the other aircraft shot down in that area not linked to the Marine's rescue. There were aircraft down *everywhere* and most we figured were shot down using the newly introduced heat-seeking, *game-changing*, SA-7 shoulder-fired missiles.

For several days now my nightly IR flights were diverted to see what we could do to help the rescue, mostly by trying to find whoever from the downed helicopters may be alive on the ground and on the run. To put more helicopters in then, during those couple days, would have been suicidal, but our Mohawk—whisper quiet as it is, and coming at low-level—could do just that while another helicopter would have been added to the downed list.

With the US Marines trapped and seven helicopters already down, a decision is made to clear a flight path, literally from the coast over to the edge of Quang Tri City, and to do so with round-the-clock aerial and naval bombardment. For nearly two days anything inside this pathway was bombed. What we had to do over several nights, two of us, is to be in this kill zone for a few minutes at a time trying to find as many of the crewmembers from the seven downed helicopters as we could.

When we did find someone, to then do misguiding maneuvers, like had been done with the Wild Weasel crew downed in the PDJ, to make the searching ground forces, the NVA, and VC, think that whom we found is *over there*, or *over there*, or maybe *over there* or anywhere but where we actually knew they were at on the ground.

X-After Quang Tri City Falls

It was on May 3rd, after the sudden fall of Quang Tri City, that the Marines who were still alive are rescued—but many others remained missing from the downed helicopters. By now the NVA had put a large armored convoy onto Highway 1 and headed south the mere 30 miles, to overrun Hue, and by then, whatever remained at our Phu Bai airfield—which was not much.

By this time, with multiple night missions back-to-back in the same night, my heart problems, the *atrial fibrillation* that would later be at about 445-beats per minute on an emergency EKG in the ER at Marble Mountain in mid-August, is beginning to be a *significant problem* for me. I covered this up for months and months; now my episodes were sometimes 2-3 hours long.

I would pull in and shut down the engines; the ground crew, now maybe five guys, not the usual two, would hastily start to refuel me, clean the windshields and bring me coffee. Relief tubes were needed, of course.

I flew *four* back-to-back IR missions one of those nights, with about 13 hours of seat time and never got out of *my* Mohawk. One TOs flew with me twice and two other great guys once each. They would be plotting the next mission IR targets while I am in the air and would come out with the latest marked up maps and reload the IR film; all as I am being refuel, and while I stayed strapped to my ejection seat.

I am the unit SIP and earlier in the day I used that to erase other names off the schedule board; this is now multiple nights of really focused and intense missions and only two of us, me and Round Ranger—*were totally engaged in the rescues*. It is just that I had not planned on four flights, maybe two, but as the night wore on and the targeting was rich we decided to press this until near daylight when the IR would not be of any further use—to say nothing of them being able to shoot our ass out of the breaking dawn.

To our saving grace, to a point, we encountered very little ground fire, working in this recovery path from the coast into Quang Tri. The SA-7 threat is our immediate nagging fear, but mostly we were fast, *quiet*, low, very low, and the heavy guns and all the flak was farther to the west and south, away from the coast. So it was the .30 cal guns, mostly, that we encountered and the *sparklers*, the AK-47s.

With a new TO in the right seat, the crew chief pointing his lighted wand at an engine, and swinging his other hand I would press the *start buttons* and begin another flight.

I had come back from the last of the mission flights, *the fourth of the night*, got out of the cockpit and collapsed on the blackened PSP ramp, down on my knees—*again*. The ground crews knew I was in trouble, but did not say anything, as neither did the TOs, whom I suspected feared that if *I* am not flying, they were going to have to fly with *someone else*. Better then the devil you know, than the one you will not be sure of.

I was already long off the reservation—and would be more so in the following weeks.

1-18 / THERE WERE NVA ARMORED VEHICLES ON HIGHWAY 1 AND A RESULTING 131ST CREWMEMBER MUTINY

I think this one is not recorded in our official 131st company journals if they even existed. It is on the night of May 2nd or 3rd, 1972, at Marble Mountain during the tank invasion of the Easter Offensive in the spring of 1972. This is right during the story just before this, during the same nights.

By February 1972, the 131st had hastily fled from Phu Bai south to Marble Mountain.

I had already flown back-to-back IR missions on this night, and things had been some of the worst ever. There were supposedly some 23 aircraft shot down in the first 24-hours of this tank invasion, and this is because, for the first time, the NVA had brought with them the Soviet shoulder-fired SA-7 heat-seeking missiles. While not large, they were extremely deadly as the heat-sensing sent this right up your tailpipe and exploded. They were also running the larger track-mounted 57/85/100 mm flak guns and quad-.51s; danger beyond even the SAM missile issues.

This is still the first night, and we did not know all this for sure.

I am the unit SIP at the time, with the other two IPs under me, so I got to call the shots a lot on who could, or would, fly what types of missions. The actual IR mission pilots were assigned by Captain Thiel, from a small pool of qualified IR pilots.

On this night, one of the IR TOs came running to my hooch, near breathless, and told me I needed to get over to Spud Operations *right now!* Not being a *complete fool* I did grab two beers from my hooch cooler to have in my hands and headed over there.

There were supposedly some *71* NVA *armored vehicles* on Highway 1 south of Quang Tri City moving towards Hue. The importance here is the number, **an exact number**, meant that someone, probably a ground guy hiding beside the highway, had already counted *71 armored vehicles.*

On the top of all this armor were more machine guns including, .30 cals, surely some heavy .51 cals, and probably one or more of the deadly never-to-get near quad-.51's. This is a lot of lethal, dedicated firepower, but worse now we knew were these SA-7s.

It is then our Commanding Officer, whom I never saw or heard of him *flying a combat mission*, even an RP-1 SLAR flight, (but he might have, *maybe*) *had that night* ordered that an IR aircraft be sent up to make a single run down Highway 1 so they, whoever *they were* at that time, had photo (IR) evidence of what types of armor there is. This mission sounded like a good idea, in theory, to know how many are tanks, anti-aircraft guns or others, all of which we *could determine* with a single IR run down the roadway.

Making matters worse, the Air Force had already lost back-to-back two of their OV-10 *Covey* FACs trying just this a few hours earlier. They were shot down either by the SA-7s or the heavy anti-aircraft fire. These were part of the 23-aircraft shot down during those first 24 hours.

We heard that the IR TOs apparently refused to go on this *suicide mission*. And this *is* pure suicide—and for what? They needed a count, yes, and *it would be extremely valuable to know exactly what types of armor is on the road*, but no way could a Mohawk make that flight *and* survive.

At best, we would have to be at 600-700 feet and would live about 12-18 seconds—*if we were lucky*. We could go in lower as I had done in the PDJ on the 57 mm radar run, but even if we dropped to say 200-300 feet and passed over them, we would not make it. At that altitude, with the props pulled all the way back to the 1,275 RPM low-end mechanical stop versus the usual 1,450 rpm (in running silent mode) or the mission max of 1,600 rpm would make the pass-over whisper quiet.

But now they knew we probably would be coming. We had run many low-level camera runs on the Soviet SAM SA-2 sites in the North, and other places like this, but in those cases we were coming from over the jungle to over a SAM site clearing and then gone. Highway 1 going south of Quang Tri is on the open plains just inland from the coast—so there would be *no sneaking up on them*. They would see us coming, visually or on radar, and would be all on the edge and firing. **It was suicidal.**

The two just opened beer cans in my hands felt a bit comforting right then.

I had run multiple IR missions during the taking of Quang Tri City, just in the last nights, this night included, so I knew the area, and some of the threat, but this is moving too fast for all of us to make good decisions that were not—*suicidal*.

Anyway, the CO, *the non-combat flying one*, had ordered the flight to go—while the TO's were in a justified action and *apparently* refusing to go. Then the CO *ordered* two of the pilots to suit up and go as pilot and TO. I am not sure the CO would not ultimately have simply been shot dead within the next 2-4 minutes but for the issue of the TOs coming to the rescue and *apparently* even refusing to get an IR aircraft ready, even as they were not going to fly in it.

The IR TOs, in this somewhat crowded briefing room that night, had apparently said that they would *not load the IR system film* and would not make active any of the systems—*nor help anyone else that tried to*. Period. No pilot knew—*or claimed to know*—just how to do any of this complex electronic stuff and the loading and handling of the IR film.

As a note here, the then TO's senior enlisted section leader, who had responsibility for all TO assignments, wrote and told me he did not recall a *"mutiny"* as such that night so that reference is perhaps a bit strong as the events unfolded in our very tense operations office.

This refusal action worked that night. The standoff ended with the CO storming out uttering some threats about what he is going to do.

Did that including sending someone to Vietnam to fly Mohawks *on for the sure near suicidal mission?* My objection to this CO, even refusing to give him a checkride renewal (he got one from one of the other IPs that worked under me) led to his call to have me tossed out of the Army in one of the OERs. So be it.

1-19 / MY LAST FLIGHT AND I AM IN TROUBLE

Obviously, I did not know that this was to be my last flight in Vietnam. After collapsing beside my Mohawk just the night before, after multiple IR flights on the same night—*and not the first time*—our operations officer directed that I am *not to fly a combat mission this coming night*; I slept in and got up a bit past noon, worn out still, but what I thought was okay. I am off the schedule for that day and night and would pick things up the next night. It was not to happen that way.

The commanders wanted no one else killed in the war, which I do understand, but only in a retrospective view, and some of us, not many mind you, were still fighting in this *got to win* fruitless situation. I think there were only two or three other second tour Mohawk pilots in the unit at the time, a commissioned officer with other duties so he did not fly much, other than perhaps an occasional RP-1 SLAR mission and two others working very hard.

I had flown over 500 combat missions by then, *probably a record*, and most of them were flying the *Kiss of Death* missions, night IR missions in Laos and now back into North Vietnam with Roger and the Navy warships we supported.

So night-after-night, it is me, and usually Gary, another great warrant officer, and Captain Roger Thiel (Round Ranger), *our actually flying IR missions section pilot*, going into real combat. Just us, and we had an air of arrogance to go with it to be sure. Meanwhile, it seemed that other commissioned officers were just going up on the RP-1 SLAR missions, no real combat of any sort, and no real risk. Good guys, working all day on other duties so no time to plan so as to run an IR or VR mission, but that did leave just a few of us, mostly the IR warrant officers, to go into the deep combat missions.

I am not one to be complaining as I had tried to stay on at the end of my first tour, just a year before, went back to the states, almost directly to the Mohawk IP school and then right back to Vietnam; back to the 131st only months after leaving. So this is my doing. I am inevitably stuck in this *sole survivor guilt trip mode* to be sure.

Making matters worse is by now months of covering up my serious heart condition, one that would, or could have, led to a stroke or heart attack and if discovered, I would not be flying again, *ever*, as a pilot.

By August 1972, the 131st is packing up to move over to DaNang AFB and from there, just a few weeks later, packing up and moving to Ft. Hood, Texas. No one wanted to be the last one dead in Vietnam, and in all consideration of the commissioned officers, no one wanted to *send out anyone* to get killed in what is now surely a fruitless and apparently lost war effort.

Defense Secretary Robert McNamara would later say we knew by 1968 that the war was lost; before another 31,715 Americans are killed. So much for Peace with Honor!

Being grounded for just this one night, I am concerned with who would be taking the IR aircraft up into I Corps, considering the intense anti-aircraft fire, the new SA-7 missiles and especially what had happened with the Marines near Quang Tri

City. I had felt heavily invested in the Marine rescue and wanted to stay back up there, but my heart issue is starting and stopping, and when started, is going on for hours now.

Ultimately, the core of the heart issue was the food and lack thereof, triggering electronic imbalances in my heart. Having flown several more nearly all night back-to-back IR missions without getting out of the Mohawk during the quick turns. I had thus *again,* missed breakfast or lunch, a troubling routine leaving me eating only out of cans, or if lucky, or to have found some C-rations for nourishment. When C-rations are a *plus*, you get the idea of how bad other things are.

By early that afternoon I am in Spud Operations to see how the war is going. I am off the schedule, but even now not by my choice. There is a need for an IR equipment test flight, so I grabbed that up just to get back up in the air that day. *Stupidity and recklessness surely know no bounds.*

I took an IR sensor technician, not one of the mission TOs, to go on this mere 45-minute, local area flight to test and evaluate some maintenance issues on the aircraft's IR system.

I fly out to the southwest, over the jungle, to run some IR test strips over a variety of random ground targets. I would never be more than maybe 20 miles from DaNang and am only out that far so as to stay clear of DaNang's recovering and launching traffic on what is a heavy strike day in northern I Corps and the DMZ.

Things seemed to be going okay with the aircraft and the IR system. There were no grounding issues on either one of them.

The Mohawk's UHF radio has a constant Guard frequency monitor on 243 MHz that is always on and is not selectable, just there. That is how you got the SAM and MiG calls all day and night long.

The VHF radio had the same always ON Guard frequency running on 121.5 MHz. SAM and MiG calls on Guard were coming into our cockpit on both the UHF and VHF radios at the same time and usually overlapping with other radio calls on whatever frequency we were working for ATC or mission control work, such as with Red Crown or Deep Sea.

On this day, with what are surely dozens of aircraft in the air, the radios were running nonstop, SAM calls, and downed aircraft. No MiGs as I recall, but there were continuous calls from Deep Sea and Red Crown on Guard, mostly stacking aircraft on recoveries.

It had not been long now since we lost some 23 aircraft, downed in just 24-hours in I Corps to our north: Quang Tri City is gone, of course, and our old home of Phu Bai is all but gone—surrounded and being heavily bombarded by mortars and tanks.

How the hell had all this gone south so fast for us?

The subconscious mind can play funny and often dangerous tricks on the conscious mind, and this started to play itself out that afternoon—*of my last flight of the war.*

Whether it was the lack of sleep, or a lack of food, or my sometimes hours on end of heart issues, or the stress I cannot know—but in just a few minutes, with both the UHF and VHF radio Guard channels continuously running on top of the regular now nonstop ATC calls from DaNang and in all this my mind, *on its own,* slipped off the tracks. Not actually off track, it is that my mind jumped over to *an entirely new event track,* one that it is making up on the go with the inputs from the radios. I am now a player, of sorts, in the new program. Just that it is not real—*not a bit of it.*

One minute I am running this routine, noncombat, no-brainer IR test flight near DaNang—and the next minute I am *up north, on a combat mission*, a combat mission somewhere north of the Hai Van Pass into North Vietnam. My mind had suddenly and comprehensively created an entirely new script for me.

I am running some combat mission; my mind is saying. I am listening to the constant emergency calls, the Maydays even. I am *there. Someplace,* but wherever, I am *there.*

To get home, my mind had programmed in, in mere seconds, this great new plan and a need to get off the targets (?), make a low-level run to the coast (?), past the ridgelines as close as possible (?), get past the guns and SAM threats (?), then drop down to the coastal region and make it out over the South China Sea and get back to South Vietnam (?) and then south to DaNang. I had to. I had to make that dangerous run. I had lost it, completely—*and did not know it.*

But I was never more than a few miles from DaNang, which is right outside the windows all this time. In my subconscious mind, there is a struggle going on, something saying that *no*, I am not in combat but that something else is going on. Which one is real? I did not know, *but the well-honed survival instinct from over 500 combat missions is running ahead of things and would follow **that** script.*

I told the right-seat IR tech guy—*now surely wide-eyed and scared at things I am saying*—that he needs to watch close, and we will make it past the mountains, but we should be okay.

What?

He is scared, and rightfully so may I add.

The radios on Guard are still going nonstop. We are right in the middle of this battle, but about to make a run to the coast.

1/ It Was All Too Real

The TO is surely even more scared now.

With DaNang still in the right side of my windshield and only ten minutes away, I dive down and towards safety, to get to the coast and out over open water. My mind has me somewhere far north, in the middle of this battle that is running on the radios, and I know I can make it back okay.

The TO is justifiably scared now and asking me things, but my responses are only as the question might be about *this combat mission* we are on. Whatever he is speaking in my headset is going through some mental filter, the words then rearranged in my mind, and related only to his efforts to be sure we can make it to the coast and head back to South Vietnam, which is actually right beneath us.

I am but a few miles northwest of DaNang by then, but it is completely invisible to me. Gone. I think maybe DaNang approach control may have called me, perhaps even yelling at me, about coming down through his controlled airspace, but I am not paying any attention to his frantic calls as they surely are for someone else—because I am a hundred miles north of him, at least.

I flew east and passed over to the coast just a few miles north of DaNang and continued out over the water, maybe five miles or more before I started to climb and take a look around.

The IR guy by now, for several minutes, had been making rather frantic calls on the FM radio back to Spud Operations, that something is *seriously wrong* here, he told them—*something with me.*

When out over the South China Sea, I climbed to about a thousand feet and turned south, to head back home; however, home, MMAAF, is only maybe ten miles away; just very few minutes at most. Something I knew is wrong, but I did not know what it was. Surely Marble Mountain is, what, almost an hour south of me. It *has* to be.

I brought up Marble Mountain tower on the UHF and without even asking had a landing clearance, for they were waiting for me, or waiting to see what the hell is going on with me.

I am shaking even as I landed. I could not be there, *not at Marble Mountain*—not that quickly. It had only been a few minutes since the race to the coast in North Vietnam and turning to the south, but now, just a couple minutes later, *in another reality,* I am now landing. Where is the time? Where am I?

I taxied in, slowly, and am met by maybe six or more of the ground guys at my parking revetment.

I am still in a daze. Confused. The IR guy jumped I think from the plane and went straight away to Spud Operations and did not even take any of the IR stuff. He had been talking to them for maybe the past twenty minutes about me.

I got out, on my own, and am down *again* on my knees, the second time in the last 12 hours that I had collapsed when getting out of my Mohawk.

I am in a daze. I went right to my hooch, skipping the trip to Spud Operations. I still had on my ejection seat harness and survival vest. Within maybe just two or three minutes our Operations Officer and another of the pilots are in my hooch.

"What the hell happened to you?"

I did not have a clue what was going on—none at all. Worse, now my heart is racing again, one of the valves almost entirely closed, and running well into the three or four hundred beats range I figured. My chest hurt, my neck hurt, and I was mentally off the block in this other reality and trying to pull myself back. It is still, now ten minutes later, that I seemed like I am in a dream state watching myself, listening to some babble from me.

Out there, about an hour before, my mind had completely jumped off the program track, the real one, and was running on this other track that was playing out because of the radio chatter. I *had seamlessly stepped* over and picked that up without missing a beat. I somehow *knew* something was not right; DaNang was right outside my window, not a hundred miles to the south, but it was all so real; after over 500 combat missions I was in *full combat survival mode* running on this mental autopilot.

Within an hour, I would never see my room or these guys ever again; by the next night, I was in the military hospital at Clark AFB in the Philippines.

X-*I am found on the Ground on the MMAAF Airfield Perimeter Road*

I decided that I needed some fresh air. My heart is pounding. My chest is shaking so hard my suit is moving. I had not eaten a regular meal or barely slept the past 24-hours, and over 8 of those hours, I was strapped into my ejection seat, not even leaving the aircraft while it was refueled last night and then turned back out on the next mission. Drinking coffee that was brought out to my cockpit, and using the relief tube, and then pressing the start button—I knew I needed to be back in the battle.

I am very weak now, and my heart was running fast in *atrial fibrillations*. I could not run, of course, but I felt I needed this walk around the airfield's perimeter road to get my head straight. I was hurting bad, really bad, physically and mentally too now. I am down to maybe just 160 pounds, soaking wet; I had lost so much weight from missing meals by flying all night, almost every night.

Somewhere on this walk, with my heart shaking hard, not beating, I went down: first onto my knees like I had twice while getting out of my Mohawk in the last fourteen hours, and then down completely. I think I had stayed at least partially conscious, but I am not sure. I do not remember getting picked up, but I do remember going in and out of consciousness on a hospital gurney, now at the Army field hospital next to our runway.

Several doctors or medics are working around me, very excited, probably scaring me even more. Someone is working on my chest, but then I don't remember what happened for what must have been some hours—or is it just a few minutes?

I drifted in and out of consciousness that afternoon and evening. I do remember, *I think*, to briefly awakening, on a gurney, semi-conscience in an operating room, with a lot of excited chatter; people are asking me questions that I did not understand. What I *do recall* is a large needle going into my chest, into my heart, adrenaline I think, a direct injection—and then someone is pressing on my chest, doing CPR—and then my consciousness is gone again.

Many years later I am watching John Travolta's **Pulp Fiction** movie. When he and Samuel Jackson have the drug guy apparently dead on the living room floor they mark his chest with a magic marker and plug an adrenaline needle into his heart—*that was me! JFC!*

One of my two major heart valves is almost entirely closed. Over several hours, the doctors had not been able to slow down my *atrial fibrillation*—as it had been probably dozens of times during the past months that I hid so I could keep flying. A long, long, EKG tape appeared almost solid black from the recording marks they had my fibrillating heartbeat. Actually, it was my *shaking* heart as little blood is moving through a mostly closed valve, shaking, but not really beating at about 445 beats per minute!

Failing other means to stop this before I had a stroke or a full on heart attack, my heart was stopped momentarily to let the closed heart valve relax, to open on its own; then this injection is directly into my heart to start it beating again. I had come back, just barely semiconscious, for only seconds. The typical arterial fibrillation has a heart-shaking in the 250-600 bpm range, so I am, and had been over and over, deep into this stroke inducing condition, usually with a 90% closed heart valve. And this had led to several collapses by my Mohawk, including two in the last three days alone.

The underlying heart medical issue, perhaps even more severe and stroke inducing, was PAT (Paroxysmal Atrial Tachycardia) that comes on instantly, from one beat-to-the-next, closes the heart valve nearly all the way; the heart jumps into arterial fibrillation and stops most of the blood flow. The heart is not *beating* at that point, but *shaking*, and shaking so hard that people could see my flight suit moving—and then it ends just as suddenly, from one beat-to-the-next. That is what is more troubling because the sudden opening of my heart valve, often after several hours, would cause a rush of blood and I would, or maybe had, passed out or fainted for a few seconds several times, which might explain being down on the ground.

And it was painful too, often severely hurting up through my upper chest and neck—while I am trying to fly night IR combat. But I would not quit; I was staying for the duration, being the only one of five of us that had come to the 131st at the same time over a year earlier. They were all gone, one still fighting for his life and the others dead, or MIA in Laos.

The next time I am awake is sometime the following morning, missing maybe 14-hours or more of time from a much needed drug-induced sleep—the first real sleep in many, many days, if not weeks. This Army field hospital also had food, real food, not a C-ration box from World War II, to eat through.

In my hospital room is a Marine, who had earlier been part of the ground forces in Quang Tri City that I had spent several nights a couple months earlier, over and over, running missions to help rescue.

Hours later, just before I am to be helicoptered over to DaNang AFB for the medical flight Clark AFB in the Philippines—*we lost our last Mohawk and crewmember*—right near to the Marble Mountain runway in a massive explosion, failed ejections, and more death at our doorstep.

See Chapter 3 for details on the last deadly crash, just as I am within two hours of being medevac'd to the Philippines.

X-The Follow-Up

I stayed in the Army medical and hospital system for several months. Several times I was reminded that I had dodged a bullet in regards a stroke, especially as I was flying and covering this up. As astronaut Neil Armstrong had gone to the moon with atrial fibrillation, and if under the control for a year, just like a heart attack, if the underlying heart PAT can be controlled, then I could go back to flying after several years, which I did for many more decades. Today it would take a year of constant heart monitoring ever to fly again.

I arrived at Ft. Rucker after several weeks in the Air Force medical evac system: at time a series of Pacific and domestic hospitals from the Philippines, to Guam, to Hawaii, to a hospital at Travis AFB in California, later in a hospital at Scott AFB in Illinois and ending my Air Force medical evac in a hospital at Maxwell AFB at Montgomery, Alabama. I was now just 90-miles north of my final destination of Lyster Army Hospital at Ft. Rucker, Alabama. From there I was medevac'd by an Army helicopter to nearby Ft. Rucker.

I am stuck, now weeks into the medical system; my only worldly belongings being pajamas, a robe, slippers and a little shaving kit. That was it! Everything else is gone, never to be seen again.

1/ It Was All Too Real

I was checked into the Maxwell AFB hospital about noon, on this Friday, and being only an hour or so from Ft. Rucker, I assumed, hoped, that I should continue to Ft. Rucker yet that same day. But no, a doctor came by and told me they had medical movements to Ft. Rucker only on Thursdays; that I would be staying at Maxwell until the following Thursday! No way could I let this happen.

I got access to a phone and for several hours I made calls all over Ft. Rucker trying to find someone that could help get me out of this hospital and to Ft. Rucker. I had trained at Ft. Rucker three times: first in primary Army flight school, then the Mohawk pilot course, and now less than a year before, at the Mohawk Instructor Pilot course; so I knew some people there, or at least some offices might know of me?

It seemed to do no good. I never made a *direct connection* with anyone at Ft. Rucker.

As it is, the Air Force is never sure what an Army warrant officer is? A pilot? A combat pilot?

It was now nearly 9 p.m. that Friday, my arrival day at Maxwell, that an Air Force doctor—and not a very nice one either—comes to my bed and starts with the *"I don't know who the hell you are . . . but there is going to be a helicopter on the pad in 10 minutes, and you will be on it."* And then he stormed out. Mad at me, why?

On this storming night, with lightning in the background, an Army medical Huey is sitting on the hospital's pad; its blades are turning in the light rain. I got onboard, and we headed for Lyster Army Hospital, just an hour away. I never knew whom I had apparently connected with at Ft. Rucker, with my calls, but someone, with some pull, called the hospital and told them one of the guys, *me*, is sitting just an hour away.

How different the medical system seemed to be between the Army and the Air Force hospitals. The Air Force is nearly completely segregated between the officer corps and the *others*: the NCO cadre—who really run things in all the Services—and the enlisted men. Within a few minutes of checking into the Army hospital, I am in a room with three other NCO and enlisted soldiers, all with local illness or injuries. The sergeant in the bed next to mine immediately offered me a beer—*beer!* The nurses kept a large bedpan full of ice, and the guys and their friends kept it stocked with beer. I had arrived! These were *my men, my Army.*

The next day, an Army LTC cardiologist—*gave me back my life, my flying career.* When we met, he had the 445 bpm EKG tape—nearly solid black as it was—as he sat with me for some time and we had a long talk. He was, himself, a combat doctor with a tour in Vietnam, and I think a son that had, or was then, serving a tour Vietnam.

The doctor told me the details of how this deadly heart situation had happened to me—already with my personal history of arterial fibrillation from childhood that I had covered up my previous hospitalization as a teenager—to be an Army pilot.

That in Vietnam condition—*critically severe the past months*—this was triggered to a more intense level likely by a lack of sleep, self-inflicted fatigue, and a lack of food, *fresh food*, the right food. And, that the EKG tape he is fingering would be the evidence of the ending of my flying career.

Other than a heart valve replacement, there is no treatment—nor any residual means of detecting this other than *during an actual episode*.

As I am sitting there, still in only pajamas and a robe, he listened to me tell my story as just a few weeks new—*old by then really*—22-year old combat pilot that had flown over 500 combat missions during almost back-to-back Vietnam tours. Month-after-month, mission-after-mission, I was over and over on the verge of heart failure or a stroke. I was mentally in a severe *sole-survivor-mode*—and <u>completely off the reservation</u>. I was determined to stay to the end—whatever the end might be for my friends and me—and for the hundreds of thousands already dead in another senseless war.

> *If there is any saving grace, it is that I was not some Marine*
> *commander with this mindset and leading his men to death with him.*

The doctor sat there and listened. He knew what had happened and now, back in the states with regular food and other issues workable that can trigger this heart condition, that my risks for continued problems were small—*but not gone*. And, as he pointed out, most people outgrow this condition by their 20's, or 30's so even if this continued, it would be less of an issue and then eventually gone for good. Because this heart condition cannot be detected *except during an episode,* that how I wanted to deal with this would now be up to me.

He spoke in his fatherly way, as he is fingering the long EKG tape and looking in my medical folder and back at me. Finally, without more explanations, he told me that *the tape is the only evidence of atrial fibrillation*—and that from what he read in the medical report, hasty as it was as I was medevac'd out of Vietnam within mere hours of being found on that road—there was no cardiologist (really?) at the field hospital and that, <u>lacking the tape he is rolling in his fingers</u>, it looked like some medics or doctors *had simply jumped to conclusions in the rush to get me out.*

If the tape is not in this medical folder?

The doctor then laid the EKG tape—*my life as it was*—back into my medical folder, handed it to me and said that when *I am done reviewing this*, that I should give the folder back to the records people.

He gave me back my life, my career.

1/ It Was All Too Real

The EKG tape, of course, disappeared from my medical folder that day: The doctor met with me only once more for another fatherly-type of chat. I owed him my life. He told me that perhaps it is that the Army owed me more than I could have given.

At just sixteen, I had been in an emergency room with this heart condition in Fargo, North Dakota. I covered this information up so I could go into the Army as a pilot. As it was, from the ER doctors, I knew some of how to deal with what had usually just been a few minutes of heart valve closures, to cover it up, and usually how to stop it within just minutes—but it had gotten so much worse the past months. For whatever reasons, I *wanted* to stay in Vietnam; I think in retrospect of the past years, because of a nagging case of survivor's guilt.

Over the following years, I did have dozens of more incidents, but they were never as deep nor as long—usually only a few minutes—not the 1-3 hours each I had in my last months in Vietnam.

After some months of recovery at Ft. Rucker, including a few weeks of medical leave with my family, the Army Warrant Officer Branch offered me a new flight assignment to keep me on active duty, starting with a tour flying Mohawks in Germany—which I probably should have taken. But, my last flight in Vietnam had shaken me a bit. I knew I needed a break from almost three years of combat focused training, a full combat tour, right back to training for only a few months, and immediately back to Vietnam, just months later to the 131st again—until I am found lying on a dirt road along a nameless runway in a faraway land.

My fun meter had clearly been maxed out by then . . .

Some weeks later I left the Army, cashed out on a Friday afternoon—and did not even end up in a jail cell for, what, at least five hours—and spent my first night out of the Army in jail in Marietta, Georgia. That's another story, for later.

It would be decades of more flying: CIA-front companies, until I owned one of my own, more charter jet operations around the world, more CIA, more FAA, more Mohawk flying, more Special Forces command pilot, more close encounters with a jail cell—*or worse.*

Then, in my mid-50's, the FBI at my back several times, working at times for the State Department, or the FBI on projects or investigations—it is that one day my FBI main guy brings me in whom would be my CIA *handler* of some years.

And so started the **Rest of the Story**.

1-20 / DaNang Graves Registration - Unreal

It was the 1980's, and I had an individual Army Reserve (IRR) flying assignment to Ft. Hood, Texas, where the remains of the 131st now existed at Gray Army Air Field.

That first night at the BOQ's bar I met a Special Forces officer with a deeply moving story from Phu Bai and DaNang that I will recount as best I can here as it

has a flavor of the intensity of the war in I Corps.

This man had done multiple Special Forces tours in Vietnam and is accustomed to the very personal, hands-on, violence and killing, mostly from ambushes and things he recounted.

> *He took another drink and was already a bit drunk anyway. We both were that night.*

On his third Special Forces tour (13 months in those years, not the six to seven months now) his Vietnamese Army counterpart, his partner on the previous tours, and a close friend to be sure—had been killed in an ambush near to Phu Bai: his body taken to the 85th Evac Hospital for *processing*.

There were days when bodies brought to Phu Bai, mostly Americans, were not just in Huey helicopters: during Lam Son 719 large Army CH-47 Chinooks were sling-loading in Army deuce and a half trucks in which the back cargo boxes—*are filled entirely with just bodies*—dozens on each load that had been picked up on the battlefield. I was there. I saw it on the Phu Bai airfield ramps: truck bodies full of just bodies! Mostly these were some of the staggering 10,000 plus RVN soldiers that were dead or dying, but too a lot of the hundreds of dead Army aircrew members and other support troops we had supplied to this losing battle.

This Special Forces officer, deeply bereaved as he was over this, decided that he would personally transport the body of his friend from Phu Bai down to the man's home village near Chu Lai, some miles to the south of DaNang.

He showed up in the morning at the 85th Evac expecting to find his friend in a body bag to transport, but instead he found that—because he was a Vietnamese soldier—they had done nothing to his body, and worse, they had merely tossed his contorted body into a cooler full of dozens of other bodies—without bothering to straighten them out.

The Special Forces officer demanded that his friend be taken out and fixed, straightened up, so he could be taken away in his jeep. The 85th staff did not see it that way, and as he recounted, he then pulled out his pistol, put it to the head of a doctor and demanded that, *right now,* they take his friend and get him ready.

It was dicey, as the body is severely contorted and twisted from *rigor mortis* and straightening him out would be a problem—especially I would imagine, with a severely bereaved SF officer standing there with a gun threatening to kill a doctor. But it was done; only now it was getting late.

In all fairness, the 85th was running hard as fast as they could; while the still living needed the attention that the already dead did not.

I took another drink as I thought *this* was the story. It was not. *The* story he was getting to—was much worse.

Anyway, late in that day the SF officer left Phu Bai with a jeep: his friend in the back in a body bag. He headed south, through the dangerous Hai Van Pass south of Phu Bai and down into DaNang. As it was so late—and he could not get to Chu Lai yet that day because of the delays—he decided he had to leave the body of his friend at the Army's Graves Registration facility at DaNang: the *processing facility* that prepared to be sent home the remains of the American dead.

As he and I gulped another drink that night at the BOQ bar, he recounted how very late in that day, too late to still be driving, he had arrived at the main graves registration facility in DaNang, and told them of the situation and that he had to leave his friend's body there overnight. They agreed—but what happened next he said has never left him—*ever*.

I imagine a man such as this, a Special Forces combat officer that had undoubtedly killed many, probably many of them by hand or with a knife as they often did in ambushes, would be prepared for anything related to the killings—*or so he thought too*—but it was not to be. An Army pilot, even in a gunship, usually kills from afar, (except maybe the Cobra guys) and one seldom sees what they have done to someone. We never did. We never looked in the face of someone we killed—*never*.

As you may know, or not, the bodies or other remains of our military dead are not to be viewed by *anyone*. I think this includes the funeral homes when bodies are returned to the States. No pictures may be taken of our war dead. In many cases, this is because not only of extreme carnage but that there may only be a single fragment or pieces of the individual, *if that*, in the casket.

To be frank, though, this policy—besides justifiably protecting the families—has heavy political overtones. If society sees what the battlefield dead have suffered, and then, we might have fewer wars, and in turn, of course, fewer billionaire arms suppliers. All the other rhetoric aside: wars and weapons sales are mostly about jobs and personal political power.

This protection of the dignity of the remains is why a body is usually accompanied by a volunteer soldier to a person's home city, a funeral home, even along with the airlines, and to a funeral. An excellent, and true movie, based on this process is *Taking Chance*, starring Kevin Bacon.

Bodies are *prepared*, as insensitive a word as that may seem, at a graves registration facility and then shipped home in mass airlifts—*another reason to end war*—and then once they arrive in the US, in sealed and locked metal boxes, the remains are put into caskets at a funeral home. However, there is a constant personal military escort of the remains to be sure this is not violated. No one must ever see, or know; mostly I think to spare the family.

In this case, the SF officer went into the central area of this graves registration facility and is confronted with an awful sight. In this vast, cold room, he said the walls had what he thought were surely several hundred openings with bodies, four hundred he thought, most of them with the body remains in them, on moveable trays. Hundreds he thought.

Worse yet, was that in the room is a long row of over a dozen stainless steel metal tables awash in blood where the bodies, sometimes dozens coming in at a time, were taken and *processed*, straightened and perhaps embalmed.

This event, he said that night, was, after all, the war he had lived through and all the killing involved with—that this was the most emotional thing he had experienced in his years.

To me perhaps, I reflected that in our day-to-day life in a war we are usually wearing a mask: a mask not only to project to others, or more so to hide to others, what is within us—our personal fears and insecurities. At that moment, this man whom I am sure had seen and touched more of the horrific realities of life and war than I had—that this event had stripped from him of his protective mask—*perhaps forever.*

In the case of some of my friends lost in the war, there were surely only pieces, *if any*, ever recovered, or nothing, nothing at all. To this day, the US military has teams still recovering remains of fallen or lost military people going back to the Korean War. Often they are working through newly located aircraft crash sites that were long hidden in the jungles of Southeast Asia.

OV-1A w/Rockets & Machine Guns

OV-1D w/Upgraded SLAR

Chapter 2

FLYING IN THE CIA'S SECRET WAR IN NORTHERN LAOS

NOTE: For about eight years the 20th ASTA/131st kept several aircraft at the Udorn Royal Thai Air Force Base, in northern Thailand, flying nightly IR & SLAR missions in the Plain of Jars in Northern Laos. These were flown far north, up against the Chinese border in real-time, nightly attacks on Chinese and NVA trucks and tanks.

For the best background information and fact about this secret war is the CIA's website on the subject-

CIA Publication: CIA Air Operations in Laos, 1955-1972

2-1 / SOME BACKGROUND HERE

This book is not just about the war in northern Laos, or as it was known then, the *CIA's Secret War in Northern Laos*. This CIA war, as deadly to the players as was the war in Vietnam, was fought primarily as a proxy using thousands of members of the Hmong tribe members, an ancient Asian ethnic group located in northern Laos, who paid an awful price in blood for working with us.

Many years before, it was President Kennedy that had put down the gauntlet that Laos is to be protected and defended and kept for the West least the communist forces spread rapidly down through Laos and into Thailand, and who knows where else this would go? Laos was one of the kingpins then in the misguided idea of having the political dominos start falling resulting in a complete communist sweep of Southeast Asia. Of course, even as North Vietnam won, none of that ever did happen, *but millions needlessly died just for the idea of it.*

Bear in mind that this was not so many years—about nine is all—since the Korean War, and the issue of the Chinese entering the war in greater Southeast Asia was a real concern.

There was a treaty signed with the leading players, including I understand, with the Chinese and Russians, that the US would not have military forces on the ground in Laos and that we would not have any more than just *two* CIA people actively involved in Laos. Of course, we could thus fund as many private armies as was wanted; as we have done again in the Middle East wars. These private armies and air forces offer a faux deniability and are unaccountable for most actions, including war crimes. But still, good men, mostly, fighting for what seems like different reasons; some for the adventure as I was there for, but probably then and now, often for the money. And whether driven by greed, or just the need to survive, money is often at the root of these things. The more money in play, the more outrageous things can become.

This war in northern Laos played out differently than in the rest of Laos. The *southern* Laotian war, in what was to us, Steel Tiger North (Tchepone) and Steel Tiger South down to a point at the border with Cambodia was part of the bigger Vietnam War, and this in northern Laos, was only a part of that.

The CIA's not-so-Secret War was only partially the interdiction of supplies and equipment moving out of China and across the north end of the Plain of Jars: the CIA's apparent main focus was to combat the indigenous Pathet Lao forces, whom were supported by the NVA, to take over the north end of Laos and to move down then past the CIA base at Long Tieng (Lima Site-20a) and take the Laotian capital at Vientiane, thus effectively taking over the government of Laos.

Our focus, with the Mohawks, was then two-fold: first, to help in the hunter/killer teams to destroy as many of the trucks and tanks moving across the north of the PDJ and onward toward North Vietnam or diverting to *the Trail*. Our second focus, for us and the gunships each night, is the attacking of Pathet Lao forces in the PDJ and any area north of Vientiane. During the dry season in this area we worked both missions, but during the wet season the PDJ work was much less, and our focus is on the vehicle traffic moving across the north of the PDJ.

Most of southern Laos, Steel Tiger, was an open gun season, and we bombed everywhere—endlessly in the attempt to interrupt the traffic of supplies on *the Trail*. In northern Laos, there is still the indigenous civilian population to protect, so except for a very short period, the B-52s were kept out of northern Laos. The war in the north of Laos was an operational area (AO) called the *Barrel Roll*.

I still have a black Spud Party Suit patch that has a set of eyes peeking above the rim of a wooden barrel, and the caption is *Over 130 Missions—In the Bottom of the Barrel* referring to having flown down into the PDJ, mostly flying IR missions, at the bottom of the Barrel Roll.

The secondary part of war operations in northern Laos was to use various gunships as the main attacking force. We had the Air America (CIA) T-28 Trojans, mostly in the daytime and at night, the Air Force AC-119 *Stinger* and the Laotian AC-47 *Spooky* gunships. All of this was supplemented with various *fast-movers* to interdict, attack and destroy, trucks and tanks that came out of China and moved across the northern part of the Plain of Jars (PDJ). These vehicles would move past *Ban Ban*, and into what was known as the *Fish's Mouth* region of northwestern North Vietnam, or from the PDJ filtering down toward the CIA base at Long Tieng, otherwise known as *Lima Site-20a*, then the most secret site in the world and a location that is not even shown on a map.

Another member of the 131st, Richard Curry, wrote a fine book titled *Whispering Death* about our flight operations there from the view of the TOs. His book is very detailed, while this book is not.

The best, most concise, and clear account of what was going on comes from the CIA's website on the subject.

> *"Laotian independence suited the policy of the United States, so long as the government remained noncommunist."*
>
> — *CIA Website*

2-2 / How We Ran Our Mohawk Missions in Northern Laos

Each afternoon we, or at least one of the pilots, would mission brief in person with the USAF EC-130 Command & Control crew, *Alley Cat*. Alley Cat was the call sign in the northern Laos mission area at night for 12-hours and then replaced in the daytime by another EC-130, call sign *Cricket*. We generally did not brief with the Cricket C&C crews.

The briefings were in a large room with several tiers of seating facing a wall covered with an assortment of large maps and images. The briefers would go over the recent events in the PDJ area and what might be coming up. Keeping in mind; we were told *only the information needed to know to run our mission that night*, **nothing more** for fear if we were shot down and captured that we might have tactical information of significant value to the opposing forces. The briefings usually would run less than an hour and then we might go back to our hotel, the Paradise Hotel in downtown Udorn, and take a nap.

Each night we would launch a SLAR/IR ship combo mission the same as the two combo missions we flew each night in southern Laos in Steel Tiger North and South.

The SLAR ship would launch towards the PDJ about 30-minutes ahead of the IR aircraft to a location at the north end of the PDJ from which they would start running either a back-and-forth track across the north end of the PDJ or a box pattern. The SLAR film was being read-out for real-time plotted targets—versus our 24/7 SLAR missions flown on the RP-1 missions along the coast of North Vietnam that were read out hours later for traffic counts.

The TOs primarily ran the SLAR missions—and we had the very best of the TOs stationed in Udorn. The TO would start to plot the black dots on the SLAR film as it slowly moved upward across a light table, the SLAR system. A single SLAR pass would only show that there were *Movers* someplace, usually on a known road or trail, but not their direction or speed. It would take a second pass, or a side view if making a box pattern, for the TO to determine the direction of the *Movers* and an estimated speed.

The IR aircraft, one or two of them, but usually one IR aircraft dedicated to going down on the SLAR *Movers* for identification would show up about 30-minutes after the SLAR ship arrived to be sure there were targets to go and check. The SLAR TO would code in the coordinates on a daily changing secret coding wheel and pass that over to Alley Cat and the IR ship's TO.

Within a few minutes Alley Cat, only them knowing the secrets of what was going on in the PDJ, would determine if the IR ship should take a pass at the *Movers* ahead of directing either the AC-119 *Stinger* gunship or the Laotian AC-47 *Spooky* gunship from Vientiane, to go and attack. The AC-119 aircraft were based at Nakhon Phanom (NKP), an Air Force base located in the very northeast border of Thailand and Laos. The C-123 *Candlestick* aircraft are also operated out of NKP.

Alley Cat did not want to risk putting the gunships into an area of the heavy anti-aircraft fire unless these were rich targets—and not just elephants or people moving rice on bicycles, both of which were commonly showing on the SLAR as *Movers*.

The IR aircraft goes on down, finds the road or trail and makes one or more passes over the targets at just 600-700 feet above the road/trail to see what shows on the IR screens. Again, this is about 90% the success of the TOs in determining targets and location to avoid hitting the mountains.

As we would do in Steel Tiger, the IR ship would also be scouting for the anti-aircraft fire, and sometimes turning the aircraft's beacon and position lights on, going *Christmas Tree* as it was called, to see if we could draw out the anti-aircraft weapons ahead of risking the overhead gunships.

The AC-47 *Spooky* gunships would stay further south in the PDJ and usually did not venture up along the northern end, near Ban Ban, for example, because of the heavy anti-aircraft fire. When *Spooky* started firing their triple mini-guns, there is a solid red streaking of thousands of tracer rounds coming down from their aircraft making them an easily found target in the night sky.

The AC-119 *Stinger* gunships did not fire tracers; also like their larger counterparts in Steel Tiger, the AC-130 *Spectre* gunships, and thus they were a bit harder to see in the sky except when they would start to *sparkle* down upon the targets with the machine guns or the 20/40 mm explosive guns.

Stinger could mostly handle the 23 & 37 mm flak because it came up pretty slow, even if there were hundreds of rounds, and this usually gave them time to maneuver away from the stream of tracers. However, if a .51 cal came up firing—and there was a quad-.51 from time-to-time—then even *Stinger* had to move away from those guns. Thus was the importance of seeing if the low and slow flying Mohawk IR ships could draw fire ahead of the larger and slow-moving gunships showing up overhead.

The story about the 57 mm guns is important because they did not shoot tracers, were radar pointed, and thus the high gunships (and our SLAR ship) could not actually dodge the flak because they could not see it coming. When it started exploding around them (big explosions!), it was not possible to know which way to turn. Thus, the determination of trying to draw out the anti-aircraft fire was an important task for the few 20/21-year old's, like George, and me, that were ~~stupid~~ daring enough to agree to run the low IR missions.

In northern Laos we did not work with any *fast-movers* on night bombing runs like we did all night long in Steel Tiger. Other than my story about attacking a radar-controlled .57 mm gun with four Air America T-28s, I do not recall other fixed-wing assets in the area at night.

Alley Cat would run separate aircraft communications on distinct secure UHF frequencies so we would *usually* only be hearing contact with Alley Cat and not their contact with the *Stinger* and *Spooky* gunships—usually. So, other than what we might have picked up at the Alley Cat afternoon crew briefing at Udorn, we would not have the big picture of the night's activities in the Barrel Roll or the PDJ.

After *Stinger* or *Spooky* would attack, the IR ship might go back and make some more low-level runs to determine if anything was burning. But, in the meantime, the IR ship was off making runs on the steady flow of *Movers* being called down from the SLAR ship.

Another Mohawk IR ship may be part of the nightly missions when specifically targeted for fixed, or strip targets. The IR film is then later read out back at our base. We did the same in Steel Tiger wherein we had the SLAR/IR combo and sometimes another Spud IR ship working the advance targets.

The greatest risk was obvious the SLAR/IR combo because the IR pilot did not have the luxury to have spent some hours of mission planning going target-by-target with reviews of the terrain and known anti-aircraft threats. The IR guys were doing this on the fly, so to speak, to get the *Movers* from the SLAR ship, pull up the bigger map by a red cockpit light, make some quick checking and decisions, and then proceed to the *Movers*. Not only not much planning in that process but also you were going towards trucks and tanks that usually had some anti-aircraft protection.

If we had a maintenance issue on one of the IR aircraft at Udorn, then the SLAR/IR combo IR aircraft would do dual mission work. Or, sometimes we did not have enough spot or strip IR targets to put up a second dedicated IR aircraft and one aircraft would do dual missions that night. ***Very, very, very dangerous work.***

X-Survival and Down Aircraft Rescues

The 20th ASTA/131st SAC had, before my time, lost some Mohawks in this area from a variety of threats. The rescues at that point were being run mostly, or perhaps all, by Air America helicopters, whom also did a lot of the rescues deep into North Vietnam. This scenario naturally involved having other clandestine jungle bases near the north end of the PDJ for purposes of refueling. Again, another good reason that our briefings were very limited in scope. We did not need to know where these bases were or what aircraft or call signs were used.

X-Our Personal Survival Stuff

We wore our over ground survival vests (we had different vests for missions on RP-1 off the coast of North Vietnam) as we did in North Vietnam and Steel Tiger. Basically, with the personal side arm (.38 cal pistol), we had a second pistol on the vest, another large knife and two smaller ones, two survival radios and four radio batteries plus the medical and signaling stuff.

Tucked down into our flight suits was our serial-numbered personal *Blood Chits* and around our neck were usually 1-3 solid gold *Baht Chains*, supposedly helpful to barter for help, but I doubt it would work.

2-3 / WHO'S DAMN PLAN WAS THIS ANYWAY?

It was to be a no-brainer mission that night. Not two hours of low-level night IR, dodging anti-aircraft fire and hoping a mountainside does not suddenly materialize in my windshield; just a single IR pass, *just one*, down and along a small road near a mountain—and then go home and get laid. Just one IR pass on this mission—perhaps 15-minutes at most at risk.

X-And the Rest of the Story

I am now coming up at the six-mile point, with less than two minutes from my target, a radar aimed Soviet AZP S-60 57 mm gun, or two, that had shown up in the PDJ just in the past few weeks. Two minutes, or less, to a decision I had not yet made.

"Spud 22, Candlestick is at the IP."

It is Alley Cat, the EC-130 C&C aircraft calling in the blind that *Candlestick*, the Air Force C-123 *Provider* flare aircraft is starting a run on the first IP point so as to beginning to lay a line of flares several miles to my right and slightly ahead of me. The timing of the flare drops, the big canister-type flares they could kick out of the cargo bay, were being laid in a row on the other side of the high mountain ridges just off to my right. Hopefully, the timing of the flare drop would illuminate the ridgelines from behind, with the flares themselves already below the ridges, so, if I needed it, in about two minutes, then I did not have to pull up and turn to the right and face directly into a line of glowing flares. I trusted they knew what they were doing, and the timing would be right on. It was.

It is dark, with a new moon, as we had planned on, with a clear and starry night sky as you can only see when one is away from the artificial lights of civilization. Ahead, and to my left, towards the lake, is a number of anti-aircraft guns; a few heavy .51 cals, a small basket of 23 & 37 mm guns, but our target, that night, on this run, is the radar that is directing the fire of a 57 mm gun, or two, as the case maybe was.

Air Force C-123 flare ships, call sign Candlestick flying out of NKP

That is less than two minutes from now, and I had not made *that* decision yet.

Ah, shit . . .

There is a steady stream of tracers racing from the front left, towards and then past us. First the .51 cal's, *troubling*, and now several streams of glowing 23 & 37 mm with the explosions mostly above me, to my right, and behind me. I had never seen any of these guns, neither here nor in Steel Tiger, lower the aiming down toward a low aircraft like on my IR pass tonight. I am just a few hundred feet above a road and backed close, *too close*, to a rising mountain on my right side. But they *could* point the barrels down to about a -5 degree level as they were doing this night.

Air America T-28 Trojan from Lima Site-20a, Long Tieng, used in the PDJ

This is the only time in my two years that I recall having any of the Air America guys flying combat missions at night. To hit this radar site, this 57 mm gun, it had to be the T-28s, not any *fast-movers,* and it had to be before they would drag the weapon a few hundreds of yards further down the road. To put a *Stinger* or *Spooky* gunship overhead was also too dangerous.

The T-28s could have come up from the Air America group with us at Udorn RTAFB, or from Lima Site-20a. We had briefed this mission in Udorn, so I suspect the T-28s came from there rather than Long Tieng.

The T-28s were expected to hit this radar gun within two minutes after we made the call, in only seconds it would be now, from my TO, as to exactly where in this enclave near the mountain, at the turn in the road, would be the gun and radar. The T-28s would not see the details, but we would with the IR screen, and we could make the call from a point we had set, and rehearsed over the past days, as to where from our reference point the radar and gun were showing on our IR screen. It is all up to the TO to make this work, and keep us alive at the same time—and I had one of the very best of our guys in the right seat doing just that.

The exploding flashes from the nearby flak were so heavy now, so close, that I reached to the left and turned my canopy left-side rear-facing mirror away, so the flashes did not blind me, and then up to the same small mirror just above my overhead eyebrow panel that had allowed me to look backward through the Plexiglas canopy toward the tail. I still had a tail—*which is one of the very few good signs at that point.*

Less than two minutes to go . . .

Decades later, in the first *Star Wars* movie where Luke is making a run on the Battlestar, and he turns his eye-level guidance away and goes with his gut feeling, is just what this is like. I could not dodge anything in the darkness, at this low altitude, and risk missing the road on the IR screen, so I am stuck, like some World War II B-17 waddling high over Germany, flying straight, level, and not maneuvering at all to avoid the gunfire.

That last two minutes, or less, I had to be 100% focused on the road below us, which I could not see except in the IR screen in front of the TO, and not be swerving or dodging anything that seemed to be coming at us. Time stood still and is moving a thousand miles an hour, all seemingly at the same time.

I am low, very low, flying at just about 100-150 feet above the road and with my butt loosened from the ejection seat harness so I can move a few inches over onto the radio panel and get my own limited view of the IR screen: to be sure we are on the road, have not lost it with an evasive maneuver, and are on track to the target point—and still be able to use my left hand to make control changes though the pilot's stick.

This one—one unique mission—was for the promised three days of getting laid in Bangkok? I am already living on and off with a young Thai woman at my place, my room at the Paradise Hotel in downtown Udorn—*courtesy of the CIA funding* that kept our pilot group off the Udorn AFB base and living on the Thai economy, just as the Air America guys did over at the nearby Charoen Hotel.

Damn, there is enough gunfire coming at or past us that our arrival is no longer a secret. I had my propellers pulled back to the mechanically minimum setting, about 1,275 RPM, versus our normal operational speed of 1,450 RPM, or our climb-out power settings of 1,600 RPM, or the too-often used, **Ah, Shit . . . prop setting** of just over 1,723 RPM. The slow propeller speed, the 1,450 RPM anyway, usually made our arrival and passing over someone nearly silent, thus the *Whispering Death* term sometimes given to the Mohawk overflight.

Whispering Death might be what the bad guys called us, but from our viewpoint, the Mohawk held the more widely used term of the Army's *Widow Maker*, and for good reason—tonight being just another one of them.

It was these damn noisy, giant Wright radial engines on the Air America T-28s that are making enough noise so as to be heard for miles and miles. The gunfire is actually pointed at them—just that we are directly in that line of fire. The NVA gunners, from off to my left that could see, or not, or hear the T-28s, are leading them with the flak, thus putting that stuff coming mostly right at me—sometimes a bit above me, but it is a sky full of racing, flaming basketballs coming across the court at us that night.

Who the hell's plan is this?

—And not to say that at my very low altitude there were not a lot of *sparklers*, the usual ground gunfire from the guys with the AK-47s whom could see *us* coming; but at such a low altitude and my speed, they usually did not have the time to take aim—so they would just point upward and shoot—which pretty near brought me down at Pleiku in the opening story of this book.

Am coming up on just three miles—

About one minute from the target.

—And now is the time to pull up to the mission run altitude for our IR, at about 600-700 feet above the road. Low to be sure, at night, in near total darkness and against the mountains. We could get better lateral coverage of the road and the target from a slightly higher altitude, but we would not survive it because more of the anti-aircraft fire would come our way. There was already too much of that.

I did not need three days getting laid in Bangkok . . .

I did not need another DFC . . .

And I did not need to be there that night.

However, someone had to do it, and I liked the adrenaline drug high that came with missions of this type—I liked it *a lot*, and so too did many others.

X-How This Mission Came to Be

We never had an SA-2 SAM missile threat in the PDJ, so that was always off the table, and there were none of them inside of Laos, ever, that we knew of?

There is a single, maybe two, we thought, radar targeted Soviet AZP S-60 radar guided 57 mm guns. Hopefully, this is right on my nose, or I have done this crazy mission for nothing that night. Maybe there is just one radar system for several of the guns.

About this time, to try to stop an NVA advance across the PDJ in this dry season, there was a decision to run some of the B-52 *Arc Light* strikes into the Barrel Roll, just to be sure we *permanently* and *forever* wiped out all the heritage of that lovely and otherwise peaceful nation with hundreds of thousands of craters—the horrible destructive outcome of which you can see on Google Earth.

The Soviet AZP S-60 could fire an explosive projectile up to 60,000 feet and could bring down our high bombers. They never did, I don't think, and we only ran a short time of changing the PDJ landscape, but it is thought this is why they brought in the larger, radar guided guns. We were facing the outcome, specifically for the SLAR aircraft, but also the AC-119 *Stinger* and the AC-47 *Spooky* gunships that one of them would be brought down from an unseen gun that you could not defend yourself from.

A decision had been made to attack the radar and gun site directly, at night. The 57 mm guns are on a trailer (later the NVA introduced the really deadly 57 mm onto a tracked vehicle during the 1972 Easter Offensive), and easily moved in just minutes, so knowing where they were, *exactly where they were*, an hour ago, or even fifteen minutes ago so as to put in a *fast-mover,* an Air Force bomber, would not work at all. They would be gone, if only a hundred yards gone, but gone.

The decision is we would put an IR aircraft into the area, near almost exactly where the gun(s) were firing from, and use the ECM's radar detection on the Mohawk to come right at the radar gun, sort of like the Wild Weasel aircraft did on a SAM site, and from that point run the Mohawk IR aircraft over the radar paint and we would know, *in seconds*, exactly as it is, where the radar and gun were at that very moment. The IR image would show that, at least to a very good IR TO, and we had the best in the 131st. Precision bombing of gun sites is difficult because if they know they are found, they can move the guns within minutes just far enough away that other than a B-52 strike, they were safe.

I might mention here, as I did in my SAM story, about the Wild Weasel aircraft and the letters at the bottom of their unit patch, the **Y-G-B-S-M**, meaning, as they put it, **You-Gotta-Be-Shitting-Me**. Nothing about dodging the radar or the SAM, you are making yourself the bait.

This plan is only going to work if we hit the radar *and* the gun; the radar really being the most important, but only if we hit it almost immediately. That could only be done if the IR aircraft, only seconds after passing over the ground spot, gave an exact pinpoint of the radar. This is why the Air America T-28s were close on my tail.

The Udorn Alley Cat group decided on this mission and they coordinated it with everyone, especially the T-28s out of Udorn and flown by the Air America guys, or sometimes our Air Force guys dressed up to be civilians, as the case may be, and with the AC-119 *Stinger* and C-123 *Candlestick* flights out of NKP.

We met several times over a week doing planning on this and going over the coordination that would be needed, the timing being critical, and how to pull this all off.

Somewhere in this is where the three nights getting laid in Bangkok came into the picture. Then there is the talk of a DFC, the Distinguished Flying Cross, but I already had one of them and more in the works, so that is not of enough interest, but what won out is—this is *your mission* and—*good luck.*

So it was that, over the next week or so, we met the Air America guys in the afternoon's Alley Cat Barrel Roll AO briefing at Udorn to work out the details.

There were a number of anti-aircraft guns directly to the west of where the road turned and where the radar is suspected to be. The only known ZPU-4, the quad-.51 cal is there for sure and probably 6-10 of the 23 & 37 mm guns. This is really not a lot by the standards the Air Force and Navy pilots faced over Hanoi and Haiphong, but this is a lot of flak for us, and because we are not part of a group attack, all of those would be firing in our direction that night.

One minute or less now . . .

I have a nose ECM radar paint on me, sort of like a homing beacon as it was.

Am up to about 700 feet above a jungle road we are hoping to follow to the radar and gun-firing site.

We had met up with the four Air America T-28s at a point about 20-miles to the south of the target to get some coordination on how to be sure they were far enough behind me so that my TO could make a very quick, and accurate, call as to where the radar is placed and give the T-28s time to make any last minute adjustments and bomb and strafe that particular point in the dark.

This is going to be tough in the dark. We had to wait for a new moon, so there would as much darkness as possible, which is useful for hiding from the gunners, but that also meant that the mountains, of which this radar site is almost backup up against and firing out to the northwest, into the PDJ area, is our real threat.

The idea then is that I would, and separately from the T-28s, would decide that after my quick pass over the site whether to swing to the left, directly toward the most concentration of anti-aircraft and flak in the PDJ AO or to pull up to the right and climb over the ridges. That is where the *Candlestick* aircraft came into the plan. A swing to the left would be toward the low ground, and I could be back down at 100 feet, in total darkness, and pass right over and through the area of the most anti-aircraft fire and be too low for them to hit me—*or not.*

I grouped with the invisible T-28s, (I never actually saw them) and spent a few minutes on practicing joining up, which took longer than we had planned. I went down to the 100 to 150-foot level, picked up the road on the IR screen—*stayed on the road*—and moved towards the radar. The T-28s would be no closer than two to three miles, maybe a bit more, on my tail giving my TO the time he needed for the IR image plot and call back to the Air America guys.

The decision to go to the left or to the right after flying directly over the radar (it is in a curved area, so we had to turn) would be an individual thing and based on the anti-aircraft fire we were taking then.

If we were to pull up against the mountain to the right, we would be blind, completely blind facing these ridges. My radar altimeter would be set to 400 feet and my TO, if we pulled to the right, would have his left hand on the T-handle for the wing stores jettison and without command would jettison the wing stores, the fuel drop tanks, without any command from me, just do it if the RA light came on and then decide, *in only milliseconds*, whether to eject. Some guys did, most did not, and thus the list of lost 131st IR aircraft.

To pull off this timed and coordinated run we set up two IPs (Initial Points for coordination): one is the 6-minute (IP-1) point so Candlestick could time any turn he is holding in to be exactly over the final IP at three minutes from our expected pass over the radar. They were, of course, right on time and point.

I am less than a mile now from the radar and gun . . .

The anti-aircraft fire, while undoubtedly being pointed toward the Air America T-28s, is mostly toward the noise I think from their radial engines. The anti-aircraft fire from my left side is already more than we had hoped for. There are multiple streams of racing .51 cal fire coming across in front or near me, then bouncing off and upward from hitting the mountains on my near right side. The multiple 23/37 mm guns too had been pointed downward and were firing nearly horizontal at us. That too is hitting and exploding into the mountains on my right and a lot of it also above and behind me. It was *Showtime*.

Maybe 30-seconds now . .

Am at the 700-foot level above the road, *sparklers* are on us from below, and I am holding as straight a flight line as possible so as I did not want to risk any maneuver that might not have the IR facing directly down when we are over the radar target.

We are radar-painted on the ECM scope on my pilot's glareshield,
but the 57 mm is not going to lower its barrel to fire point-blank at
us. I hoped anyway.

There is much radio chatter from and between the T-28s, excited, like schoolboys at a frat party. The psychology of what we did.

"On the target . . .

On the target . . .

Steady . . .

Over the target!"

Break right and climb. The decision is at the very last moment, to be sure, but there is so much gunfire from my left that no way am I going to risk turning into that and having to work my way out of it.

My TO had pressed STOP on the IR cockpit display, found what is needed on the electronic image, and in just seconds is calling out to the T-28s the displacement from the corner point we had set as the marker. They would hit the target on the first pass in about 30-60 seconds and then come back around for more attacks before the radar and gun could be moved out-of-sight.

The gunners to my left had evidently expected us to pull up to the left, for in the new moon, in the blackness, one would not try to climb over an invisible mountain to my right side and behind the radar and gun area. As I pulled up to the right, now full throttle, full propeller, my TO's hand is already down on the external stores jettison. I looked to the left and saw the waves of gunfire and flak tracers arcing upward, expecting to find us moving over them, not be turning to the right and up the mountain side.

Candlestick is right on point-and-time with the canister flares. Their on target and on time flare drop is providing enough illumination to see the high ridge, but not to see how close I am coming on my side. The radar altimeter that had only briefly jumped up to about 1,000 feet as I came up to the right and is now back in the 500 to 600-foot point, dangerously close to a mountain we are trying to out climb—*but cannot even see.*

About 600-800 calories of heart muscle exercise were in play now, which is a positive thing because I am sure all the blood is gone from our brains right then.

The adrenalin is flowing heavily in our veins after that single run.

We were pumped up! Going home!

A low-level, high-speed pass over the heart-shaped pool at the Paradise Hotel is now less than an hour away.

2-4 / SPECIAL FORCES LOST ON POW RECOVERY MISSION

How many guys, ours and the Thai and Laotian Army too, did we lose that week on this mission? Who knows - the war was a secret - right? Such is why there are many errors of facts in the post-Vietnam War books—mine included.

What we did know is that for over a week before this night there were many blackened Huey helicopters, Thai I think, flown by (?) that late at night are refueling in the grassy area between the runways and ramp at Udorn. I believe it was, which we would only learn of much later, they were going on a POW rescue mission near Ban Ban, in the north of the PDJ or just down the road from there and inside the Fish's Mouth area of northwest North Vietnam.

Regardless of from where, they must have had *balls they moved around in wheelbarrows* to go on this sort of mission: to basically just drop into a suspected POW site, and then everyone jumps out, guns firing, from inside the compound mind you, shoot whom you can, rescue whom you can, and jump back into any of the still flyable helicopters. This is how the Air Force conducted several very brave, very, very dangerous rescue attempts already. The idea I think was to create sudden and violent chaos inside these camps, then snatch whomever they could and get out.

Apparently these were part of the forces. I suspected it would have been Air America helicopters operating out of the CIA base at Long Tieng, but in later conversations, I think it was Thai Army helicopters probably with American *Army Special Forces* advisors and many Thai soldiers.

On this night, I am running my IR mission up near Ban Ban to the north end of the PDJ. That afternoon, at the Alley Cat Barrel Roll AO briefing, there is mention of having the IR aircraft watching for *other things*. Of course, we did not know, and would not be told, what to be looking for or what is going on. Apparently, by then a sizable number of our forces had already been lost, the helicopters shot down or gone, and these guys are on the run in the jungles trying to get back to someplace to be rescued from.

Not until that night, on my tactical FM radio, would it be clear that there are a number of American guys leading this brave effort.

Anyway, early in my IR mission I could see what looked like a firefight with a lot of mortar fire, and other machine gun fire, from an area that was not on our regular, *go check the tanks and truck* mission work. I called Alley Cat, as perhaps this was some of the *other stuff* to be on the lookout for that they had briefed us on that afternoon.

I worked my way over to the firefight to see what is going on. As I got near the ground fighting Alley Cat gave me an FM frequency to use and see if I could make contact with anyone—*and with whom would that be?*

Surprisingly, an American came up on the radio, rattled to be sure, with explosions and gunfire clearly in the background.

He told me there were about 75 men on the ground with him. At the time, I was sure he said there were *75 Americans* on the ground with him, so this might well have been an all American Special Forces POW rescue mission that had gone wrong—but 75 of them? That would be much of the forces they put in that were now left to fight their way out of the bad guy land and move south into the PDJ itself. Or, my speculation is that perhaps these ground forces had been inserted days before the raid to cause a diversionary attack and give the drop-in helicopters a better chance of getting out?

I passed the Intel up to Alley Cat, and was asked if I could get more information, or do any help for them? In the background, Alley Cat is already pulling up more attack aircraft, *fast-movers* as they had to be because of the flak, and probably a group of helicopters that are already staged someplace nearby.

I was picking up some .51 cal anti-aircraft fire only, but I am staying too low to be at risk of the flak, but the .51 cal is, *as always*, the real danger.

For the next forty minutes or so I made repeated flights, first blacked out of course, but then later with my lights on, going *Christmas Tree* as it might be called, to misdirect any of the anti-aircraft fire and determine what the overall anti-aircraft fire is going to be. Down in Steel Tiger, in southern Laos, this turning on the position lights to intentionally get the gunners to fire on you so the follow-on attack aircraft might know what they faced is not unusual. So it was that night. Making yourself bait while trolling for anti-aircraft fire, with your position lights on, *is surely somewhere* in the back appendix of our combat tactics book—*someplace I am sure*.

From my calls with the American on the ground, and my repeated low-level passes over the fighting, I am not sure which of the firing groups the good guys are, and which are the bad guys? I could divert fire, get a call on the anti-aircraft for the *fast-movers,* and at least give some moral support that someone is on site with them.

The only immediate aircraft anywhere in the AO is a Laotian AC-47 *Spooky* gunship, the ones with the three rapid firing mini-guns. When they fired on ground forces they would give a call a few seconds before; it was simply—

"*Spooky fire now.*"

Not real descriptive as to where that might be to be sure.

Then, out of the blackened skies would come this solid streak of red tracers created from the firing of all three mini-guns at once. Some of the tracer rounds are colliding in flight and flipping off in different directions while the other ones are piling up on the ground and bouncing up from there. Firing the mini-guns would take maybe just 6-10 seconds in a steady stream, and when they stopped firing this streaking, solid red tracer stream went *zip*, down from the aircraft to the ground. Neat—but it does make hiding from the ground gunners impossible.

The other gunships, the Air Force AC-130 *Spectre* and the AC-119 *Stingers*, had mini-guns and rapid firing 40 mm exploding rounds, like the flak guns, but they did not have tracers so they could start to fire on a ground target and all we would see from below was the *sparkles* from the aircraft, if you could see it, and the impacts on the ground. Thus, while the Air Force gunships could not easily be seen, or thus fired upon by anti-aircraft fire, the *Spooky* aircraft was an easy target to see. Only the *Stinger* gunships worked in the Barrel Roll, and the *Spectre* gunships stayed in Steel Tiger North and South.

So it was that Alley Cat started to push *Spooky* to get over to where I am and lay down mini-gun fire until a *Stinger* and some *fast-movers* could get there for more help. But *Spooky* wanted nothing to do with it—*Spooky* kept refusing to get anywhere near the location where the Americans are on the ground. Alley Cat kept pushing, needing to get help on the scene. From afar Spooky could see the flak and heavy machinegun fire I am drawing up, trolling as it was, so we would know before the slow moving gunships got there just what the overall anti-aircraft threat situation is—

"Spooky no can go . . ."

Alley Cat would insist some more, then more—

"Oh, Spooky no can go . . .

Spooky think maybe has anti-aircraft fire . . ."

"Spooky no can fight anti-aircraft fire!"

That was the end.

Shortly thereafter Spooky was RTB to Vientiane and gone.

AC-47 Spooky Gunships with Triple Mini-Guns

I stayed on my mock attacks for about another hour until I am in a *bingo fuel* state and had to go. By then fast-movers were coming in with bombs and a *Stinger* gunship is on site laying down fire as best they could.

As is the case in war, I never heard any more about this. If they got out, got rescued, who they were or what happened?

2-5 / WILD WEASEL MISSED THE TANKER AND IS DOWN IN THE PDJ

Many of the air strikes in North Vietnam had the support of the specially equipped aircraft, such as the Air Force's F-105 or F-4G aircraft, carrying what was called a *Wild Weasel* electronics and missile package and used to attack the SA-2 SAM sites. Discussions about the missions and use of the Wild Weasels are in several areas of this book so I will pass on this, but here is my only direct interface with a downed crew.

KC-135s were available in many *Anchor Orbits*

When it came for Dan and me, it was the first stage booster separation that caught our eye . . . coming from the wrong SAM site!

Soviet SA-2 SAM missiles used in North Vietnam.

It is during the wet season in the PDJ, and I am up on an IR mission, to the best I could, considering the inclement weather for getting down under the clouds and run the truck and tank traffic out of China. A single aircraft, deep into bad guy land. Deep, deep into bad guy land and all alone.

There are continuously Air Force KC-135 tankers up on various orbits, *Anchors* they were called, that provided fueling to aircraft going outbound and returning from Thailand—this being NKP, Udorn, Takhli, Utopao and other bases. The jets, fighters, and other bombers would go up, get fuel and go on their mission and then plug into the tanker on the way back. The refueling tankers also provided the near constant support of the 555th TFG F-4 Phantoms out of Udorn that had the *MiGCAP* role up in the Barrel Roll.

It is storming on this night, and heavy thunderstorms had spread across the area. Our SLAR aircraft is mostly in the weather just tracking *Movers,* and I am in an IR aircraft, low, but not doing much because getting under the overcast and heavy rain is tough, *if not suicidal deadly.*

I was following some of the conversations with Alley Cat that are now running on UHF Guard and not their regular frequencies, of which they surely had many working frequencies. So something is up, plus UHF Guard is not a secured and coded radio frequency as we had on other frequencies.

An Air Force F-105 *Wild Weasel* coming out of that night's North Vietnam air strikes and headed back to Takhli had been trying to connect with fueling probes extended from one of the unseen KC-135 tankers and was not successful. The heavy weather and darkness and clouds and rough air and this guy could not make a good connection to get fuel.

He is now flamed out and about to eject over the PDJ area.

Ah, shit . . .

Alley Cat did not have any radar information on my whereabouts, as I am too low, but he did have a general area of the trajectory of the aircraft as these guys were punching out.

Scared, scared, and scared, to be sure.

I headed toward the best-guessed parachute area while I am still underneath the weather. Within about 20-minutes I had made direct contact with one of the pilots and *surprise*, he is sounding shook up, but basically okay, and the two of them had landed close enough together to be already getting teamed up.

The worry is not really the enemy, as just the same in Steel Tiger. If you did not land on a road or camp, then these guys are not going off into the jungle to try to find you. From that point, these guys are probably okay. It is the creatures that lived in the jungle that always had us on edge, the snakes, *especially the Cobras*, the other snakes, *tigers* and more. The guys were physically okay, and an Air America helicopter was already coming, most likely out of Lima Site-20a for a nighttime recovery. Air America guys did most, if not all, of the rescues in the PDJ and many of them over into North Vietnam too.

What I could do to help, besides being close enough to talk to them for some moral support, is that I set up an orbit and multiple fly-bys at a point about a mile away, enough to let anyone on the ground *think* that I was looking *over there*, for these guys, and to stay away from flying over the top of the real site. A diversion that is usually used to get the ground searchers, if any and I doubt there were any in this case, away from where the downed guys really are.

2-6 / GEORGE FOLLOWS THE CRIPPLED AC-119 STINGER GUNSHIP TO NKP

CW2 George Rogalla was my best friend in flight school and fellow 131st warrant officer, whom some weeks later switched missions with me one afternoon and with his TO that night, they hit a mountain ridgeline in Laos—*and perished.*

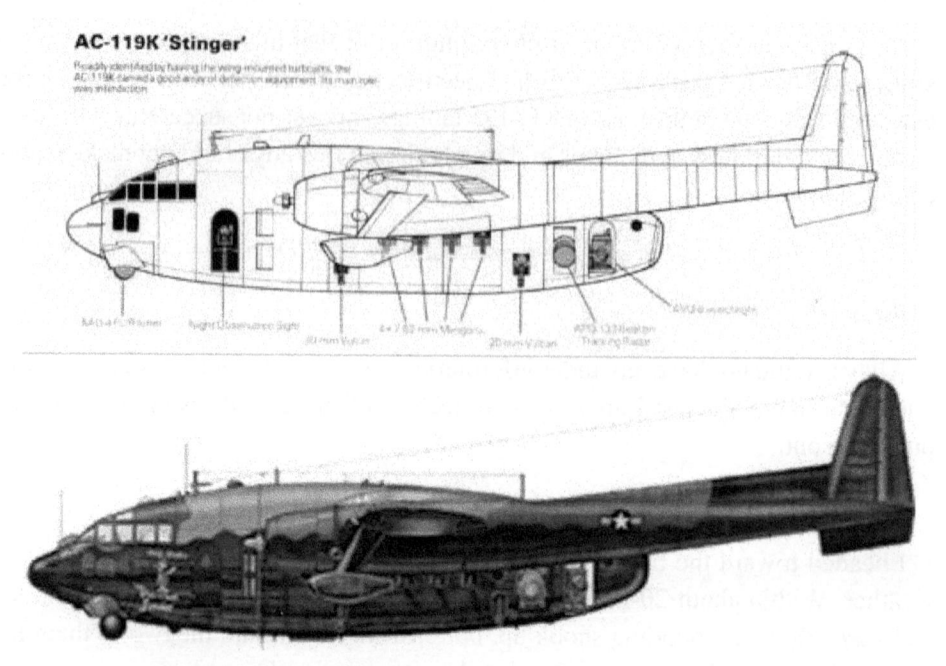

Air Force AC-119 Stinger Gunships from NKP flown in the PDJ

On this night, George is running an IR aircraft in the PDJ when the Barrel Roll AC-119 *Stinger* gunship is hit by anti-aircraft fire and lost an engine, amongst other issues.

The crippled aircraft had now turned toward NKP and George, being nearby and with both aircraft in ATC radar range, got a fix on *Stinger* and moved his Mohawk up on the aircraft to provide whatever support he might be able to help with, especially if the plane is going down and the crew would be bailing out over the jungle.

Other than moral support there is little he could do but stay right with the aircraft. *Stinger* is losing altitude and headed toward a bad ending in the jungle below. That is when the crew started to strip out everything they could and throw it into the jungle—the guns, equipment, ammunition and anything they could rip out. A similar scene was later part of the movie *Memphis Bell* as that B-17 was limping back to England. So it was this night coming out of the PDJ and trying to get back to NKP.

The aircraft is still getting lower and lower. More things were thrown out; everything that could be ripped from inside the plane was going out the doors.

Still, the aircraft was going down . . .

The lights of NKP are in sight by now. Not just the city and airfield, but the runway is visible.

Still the aircraft is going down . . .

At some point, the aircraft commander had to make a tough decision. If the crew is to bail out they would need to do so very soon, or the aircraft would be too low for the parachutes to deploy, so it is soon, very soon, going to be to bail out or risk riding the plane to a crash site.

Still the aircraft is going down . . .

There are rescue helicopters already in the air from NKP; now only a few minutes away. Someone finally made the decision, with the lights of the runway not so many miles off the nose, to go ahead and bailout, which all but two of them did, or perhaps only the pilot as he stayed, determined to drag this crippled aircraft to the parallel row of runway lights, now so close, so very close.

Out went the other crewmembers—watching, as they drifted down to a dangerous and uncertain future of risks in the jungle, mostly the issues of snakes—*as their crippled aircraft safely touched down on the runway at NKP.*

Ah, shit . . .

2-7 / FLIGHT OPERATIONS AT LONG TIENG (LIMA SITE 20A)

It was that the strategically placed village of Long Tieng, northeast of the Laotian capital of Vientiane and southwest of the Plain of Jars (PDJ) became the gold rush boom town to support the air operations in the PDJ. Invisibly, Long Tieng became the second largest city from the CIA/Air America Base (Lima Site 20a) in Laos as massive numbers of troops, of various loyalties, CIA supported contractors, and more poured into the crude base with a small and rough runway.

At one time it was discussed with us to move our Mohawk operations from Udorn to the jungle airfield, but clearly the rough airfield did not have the support ability to cover the sophisticated and technical needs of the Mohawk. To say nothing of the fact we lived off base at Udorn, in civilian style at the Paradise Hotel. Like we would agree to move from *there* to a hooch up in the jungles? Another suggestion to move to Vientiane met a similar and well-deserved fate.

The CIA base airfield was thus designated as *Lima Site-20a*, somewhat suggesting that, as it was known as *-20a* it was perhaps a smaller satellite of another small location to the northwest, known as Lima Site-20—a minor and little deception at the time.

CIA/Air America Airfield at Long Tieng / Lima Site-20a

The city and Lima Site-20a were removed from all maps. The location had become invisible. The most secret airfield in the world.

The runway was enlarged and lengthened and by 1967, this otherwise invisible village and its airport supported as many as 400 flight operations a day in a mix of all sorts of aircraft.

The Air America fixed-wing aircraft included the two-engine C-123 *Provider* transports, some with wing-mounted additional CJ610 small jet engines for boosted jet-assisted takeoffs (JATO), and T-28 *Trojans*, radial engine ground attack aircraft, and an assortment of smaller planes including the single-engine STOL aircraft like the Pilatus Porter and Helio Couriers. Later many of the T-28s not flown by the Laotians would come from our base at Udorn and flown by a mixture of Air America and perhaps some active duty USAF pilots.

The 1990 Mel Gibson movie *Air America* was made, very loosely, on this base and the CIA and Air America operation—not including an elephant drop.

C-123 Provider Aircraft used by the US Air Force and Air America

Keep in mind that throughout this book, and our time in the war zone, that there were many things, *obvious things maybe*, that we knew no details about. Aircraft, call signs, missions, weapons and more were on a *need-to-know* basis and other than the call signs and planes for each mission nothing was disclosed to anyone for concern that if someone is downed they could give things up to the enemy. Let this explain, to a point, why there may be so many errors in these war books.

2-8 / DURING THE SIEGE ON THE CIA BASE AT LONG TIENG (LIMA SITE-20A)

It was over a decade after the war, as my ultimate Army career did not end until I had some 27-years of service mostly flying Mohawks in both the US and Argentina armies, that I learned that when Captain Al Musil's (my Phu Bai hooch mate) stuff was gone through, after he and CW2 Jack Brunson (my flight schoolmate) had been shot down (MIA) in Laos on May 31, 1971, that in his belongs was a nomination for a Silver Star for me that had originated from the US Embassy in Vientiane, along with a lot of other awards and decorations not yet completed a number of us. Just the way it was.

Captain Musil was our 131st Intel officer and being a non-pilot officer the commander had made him the awards officer, probably to avoid some biases. As always, accounts of mission events, either foolishness, utter stupidity, *for which I had excelled in*, or the bravery of so many went unreported because we flew mostly single-aircraft missions.

This particular mission, for whom the award was recommended, was really undeserving as it was no more mission bravery than all our guys were doing on a nightly basis all over Laos. It was just that what happened on this night was right in the face of the US Embassy in Vientiane, MACV in Saigon, as it was, and got floated up the line. It was also one of the very few missions that ultimately I pulled back from and went home—completely due to there being too much anti-aircraft fire.

> *It is perhaps also that I am the pilot that had made the run on the 57 mm gun site with the four Air America T-28s recounted in this chapter.*

In 1971, the NVA and Pathet Lao had taken over the PDJ in the dry season for the first time in many years and then continued their push to overrun Long Tieng, and surely from there to stage for continuing south to Vientiane. Thus, this became a complete and total war effort to protect and keep LS-20a—*at all costs*.

For several deadly and bloody weeks, the base had come under siege from the mountains surrounding the airfield. Flight operations were hugely disrupted, and many aircraft are either destroyed on the ground or shot down from the large numbers of anti-aircraft weapons that had been pulled into position over the preceding months and set up to the north and east of the airfield. Many flight crewmembers, including Air America pilots, were killed trying to hold LS-20a.

Finally, the battle is *apparently* over, and the NVA and Pathet Lao had retreated back up towards the PDJ, which they now firmly held, and would continue to hold. Long Tieng had been saved—*maybe*.

X-How an Otherwise Routine Mission Becomes Something Else Completely

We were running the nightly IR missions out of Udorn in support of the breaking of the siege at Long Tieng, looking for where the bad guys are in the nearby mountains. In those missions we are not drawing much anti-aircraft fire, at night anyway, as I think the bad guys were holding off shooting at us at night as we posed no immediate threat, plus firing on us would have brought more detailed gun locations that *Spooky* or *Stinger* could attack. The anti-aircraft fire, even during the siege, is relatively light. All the while we are backing this up with our regular PDJ SLAR and another IR aircraft up there watching for the traffic that was working toward, or away from, LS-20a.

With the siege *seemingly broken*, and the NVA and Pathet Lao *supposedly* in retreat back up into the PDJ, my mission that night is simply to keep running IR on the mountains around LS-20a and see if there were any significant residual forces that could be identified on the IR system. And also to run the roads and trails from those mountains back up toward the PDJ. Not working in a SLAR/IR hunter/killer team in real-time, this is more using the IR film to be read-out back at Udorn a few hours later with a possible count of vehicle traffic given to the powers to be.

I had spent about an hour in the target area while running a couple of strip runs on the roads and then moved over to begin several small box patterns that had probably ten individual strip legs. This allowed me to stay above the mountain ridges and not worry about hitting a mountain.

A piece of cake . . .

About an hour into this mission, and with the strip targets done, I decided to move over a few miles off from the target area from where the NVA and Pathet Lao had retreated from—retreated back up into the PDJ it was assumed—and take a needed smoke break.

I set my aircraft into a holding orbit over just one area, an area of *no significance* or intelligence interest that was some miles northeast of Long Tieng, and lit up a smoke. I just needed a bit of a break before dropping back down, and it was best if I kept myself away from where the few remaining anti-aircraft guns might start shooting at me. Just take a few minutes, smoke just one cigarette, get my nerves settled down and then go back over to the assigned IR strip targets.

Of course, the smoke breaks would hurt my night vision, which I really needed, but it did wonders for my nerves.

I orbited, smoking, paying no attention at all to anything really when out of the blackness below me several flak guns opened up on me. What? From where? Then several more clips of flak tracers started snaking up towards me. There should be no guns here, this was not part of any targeting area and yet here was 23 & 37 mm with some heavy .51 cal machinegun fire.

Why? I called Alley Cat and said I had stumbled onto some flak that was not where I was targeted, that I had been just dallying around smoking a cigarette, to the east of my target area by maybe 6 miles or so, where there should *not* be any guns, but there were—*and many them.*

With no real direction in mind, I went first one direction for a minute or so and then turned and went another way, just flying around.

Up came more and more flak . . .

Something was up. I updated Alley Cat, who seemed very excited, and told them I was going to run a box pattern over here, not where I was supposed to be that night, and see what was going on.

We hastily programmed in an IR box pattern above the mountains, so no valley work was involved, that was about 15 x 10 miles just to be sure we had coverage of this area and then started on the first leg—*and all hell broke loose.*

On the first strip run, I was drawing fire from at least six guns, maybe more; their clip-after-clip of tracers arching up from the jungle from where there was not supposed to be anyone—*and still the gunfire kept up.*

We finished the first leg and had taken several hundred rounds of flak on that run alone, did a course reversal, and started back on leg two of what I had plotted out as 5-6 legs.

More gunfire and more flak . . .

Lots of it and heavily concentrated.

By the third leg of my quickly setup IR box, the flak was the heaviest I had seen in Laos, Tchepone aside.

It was the fourth run that I finally had to abort and get out. This would maybe only the second or third time in my two years of combat that I had aborted any part of a mission solely due to anti-aircraft fire. If you quit running targets and went home, you, or your buddy, would just have to go back out there, and you did not want to be the one sending your friend out to run targets you had run away from due to the gunfire.

On this fourth run, we took fire from 9-12 of the 23 & 37 mm flak guns and at one point, at one time, I had at least six guns rapidly sending up clip after clip of the tracers. Hundreds of rounds of tracers were crisscrossing the sky as the gunners fired a clip, shoved in another clip, and had that one coming up before the first ones had burst—and more of them repeatedly.

This was looking dangerously like something from an episode of the old *Twelve O'Clock High* TV series.

I had repeatedly rolled to the left, then rolled to the right, and at one point rolled all the way over in a rapid aileron roll. There was no way to divert from the streams of flak tracers, no way to run the 2-second check to decide if the flak streams were going to merge with you. There was just too much flak and no way could I dodge it. Turning left or right did not matter. It was the exact type of flak fire that would bring an aircraft down, just fill the sky with this stuff and their target—*me*—would have to run into some of it, and it only took one, or even just airbursts very close, to bring us down.

I aborted the box runs. I got off that run, with maybe 400 or more rounds of flak on just that one run alone and decided I had to go home. Overall we figured we had taken more than 2,000 rounds of 23 & 37 mm flak fire—a total that is at least equal to my top two other missions *combined.*

Alley Cat is running wild by now, calling over the AO *Stinger* and *Spooky* aircraft, though—*Spooky* would not get anywhere close to the anti-aircraft fire, and had backed off and is going to head for home.

What had happened, and in retrospect and after hearing about the embassy designation for the Silver Star, which of course I never saw, is that when the siege on Long Tieng had stopped, it was assumed, *wrongly*, that the NVA and Pathet Lao had pulled back up on the trails into the PDJ from where they came from. But in fact, while some had as decoys perhaps, the rest of the force, including all this anti-aircraft stuff, had been moving laterally to the east, to launch a massive renewed siege on Long Tieng.

What had happened to me, we think, is that when I went off my regular IR target runs to have a smoke break I had stayed in a circling pattern so as not to drift too far away; and the bad guys must have thought they were found, discovered and that is am why I am apparently orbiting above them. Nothing could have been farther from the truth. It was just blind luck.

> *The terms of Luck, Fate, and Shit Happens are really all too true in combat.*

If the gunners had done nothing, ignored me as they should have, these forces would have been attacking Long Tieng within a day, and from where they were not expected.

By the time I am moving down past Vientiane and headed toward Udorn I could hear Alley Cat already talking to the inbound *fast-movers.*

Through the night and into the next day the bad guys took a heavy pounding and were broken up by our ground forces.

> *My accidental flying in a circle had blown the whole game for them.*

Okay, so maybe I *did* deserve the Silver Star, but all of us that flew any Mohawk VR or IR missions, for any of the Mohawk units, had done equally or much more daring things than to just be stumbling onto a chance to make a combat difference. And that includes the TOs also.

2-9 / THE MONTH OF THE WHITE ELEPHANTS

There had come a period when we were, for lack of better description, looking for elephants. For many nights, the SLAR ship was finding solid reflective *Movers,* but when the IR ship would go down on the targets, getting a proper ID for the *Stinger* or *Spooky* gunships, we would not find the tanks or trucks we were expecting to find on the IR screens.

Over a period of weeks then I would go in and attend the afternoon Alley Cat AO briefing and on the big walls the guys were putting up these White Elephants symbols; Representing the areas mostly in the northern part of the PDJ where we were getting good SLAR paintings, but no real targets to attack.

Within a couple weeks it sunk in that in fact maybe we were dealing with elephants. After all, an afternoon in Udorn would hardly pass without a number of elephants being seen moving down the streets. In northern Thailand, and up into Laos, elephants are used for logging, so the idea of the Chinese or NVA or others using elephants to move supplies was not so unusual. The trick then was to get the SLAR ship to find these *Movers*, the assumed elephants, and then for the IR ship to get low enough to determine they were in fact, elephants moving equipment.

Having done so on many nights we faced the tough decision whether to move the *Stinger* or *Spooky* gunships on to the elephant targets. The irony of this is that none of us had any sense of remorse, mostly, about raining down death and destruction on these otherwise peaceful people we were killing every night, yet the very idea of killing the elephants is strangely troubling.

2-10 / GEORGE AND I FLYING OUT OF UDORN

For some months, George Rogalla and I had lived at the *Paradise Hotel* in Udorn. We flew dozens of missions, night-after-night, into the Barrel Roll, the Plain of Jars as it was, in the *CIA's Secret War in Northern Laos*.

One morning we were awakened at our hotel and found we are *ordered* to the Udorn base commander's office right now—but not for some awards ceremony to be sure, which of course we certainly deserved on a near daily basis in our view. It was common for us, for George and me anyway, separately in our Mohawks coming back from high-stress flights in the PDJ to unwind with a high-speed, low-level pass over the main street of Udorn, which was approximately aligned with what would be our downwind leg to landing.

On some really high adrenaline drug fueled nights we would turn off the aircraft position lights and drop down to just a couple hundred feet and scream past the late night street traffic. Then pass low and fast over the heart-shaped pool at our hotel, the Paradise Hotel, where we lived and where our ground crew hung out waiting for us to come back. As we came over the pool, we would flash our landing light (otherwise retracted up into the bottom of the left wing) onto the area so our ground crews knew we were back and that they should be heading over to the airfield to bring us in and get parked and serviced. Then we would pull up, throw out the landing gear and flaps, and turn for a close in landing.

On at least one other night, the adrenaline flowing thick in our veins, George and I had snuck up on the Udorn control tower at about 220 knots, in the blackness, with our position lights out, and showed them our belly side. It was actually a bit more than that as we had come screaming across the airfield, our lights off of course, low across this huge airfield, talking to the tower controller like we were in the pattern, and then just at the last seconds we pulled up, nearly right at the tower, and I rolled up on my right ride and George on the left at maybe fifty feet to the side of the control tower cab—as close as we could come and not hit the tower. Apparently, *they failed to appreciate our skill*, or how emotionally high we were on this drug induced bit of playing, reckless, as it might seem. Many have died to do even less stupid things I am sure.

It is one night shortly before we lost George that the two of us had made our passes down the streets of Udorn, fresh off a night of gunfire—and mountains we could not see waiting to take our lives and infinitely more deadly than the enemy gunners ever were. We were perhaps just a *wee bit low* on that 220-knot pass. What we heard was something like George being about even on the first floor of the hotel; so hot and fast and close over the top of the pool that people fell out of their poolside chairs—*maybe 35 feet up* at most, or less. I am *way up high* and out of the way, *surely no lower* than the second floor and staggered slightly back, maybe sixty feet, from his right wing and sort of crunched closer to the hotel structure than even I was okay with.

Anyway, the next morning we are ushered to the Air Force's Udorn base commander's office. It seems that a gaggle of Air Force officers (planning on getting laid really) were having a late night poolside party and were *shocked* at what we did. Surely they were not the poolside regulars, or they would not be so surprised to find a pair of Mohawks sweeping past so low, so silent, and fast one could toss their drink up and have it mixed in our wake.

We got our collective butts chewed on a bit that day. Would they punish us and send us to Southeast Asia—and make us fly near suicidal, low-level night missions in the mountains of Laos while every type of anti-aircraft gun that could be built are nightly using us for target practice? Surely not!

2-11 / Just Where the Hell Did I Snag a Cable on a Night IR Flight in the Mountains

The Mohawks we did not lose in combat by hitting a mountainside, which is way too many as you read here, had at times hit trees. Hitting a tree on a low-level, high-speed VR camera run while evading some anti-aircraft fire might be understandable. You were skimming along a ridgeline at 220 knots, swerved to avoid something and went through the upper level of a tree, and survived—if you did not hit something real solid.

However, a number of the IR pilots, myself included, had hit or clipped trees at night—trees *that we obviously did not see.* One of the IR warrant officers came back with all of his lower antenna stripped off; resulting from a really hard hit on a tree somewhere, somewhere he had not seen. I had lost a single antenna, and some upper tree branch scrapings, going over a ridgeline one night, a ridgeline I had clearly misjudged my clearance of. We had been lucky.

One night I came back out of an IR mission in the PDJ, back to Udorn and our protective revetment and before I had gotten out of the cockpit my crew chief is starting to unravel about 150 feet of light twisted cable that is wrapped around the inboard side of my left wing, back to the tail and whipped around the horizontal stabilizer while the remainder was dragged into the revetment.

Where did the cable come from? Who knows? Our original assumption was that I had simply snagged the bottom of a weather balloon and had then broken away the suspended weather-recording package. Sounded reasonable, as you are not going to be able to see these anyway, but after we had turned the cable over to the Air Force, a few days later they were asking me where I had been?

The cable line was not from a weather balloon. They were not sure, but they thought that the light cable was perhaps attached to something like a helium balloon that itself was used to raise up a long-wire HF radio antenna from some bad guy radio that was located on a ridgeline that I had passed over a bit too low. This was *troubling*, to be sure, as I did not recall having come that close, that night, to going across a ridgeline that I would have been low enough to snag this cable.

> *We were too often just a moment from living or dying—and never knowing it.*

2-12 / THUNDERSTORMS WERE WAY TOO HEAVY

There is no way you could not fly a mission, or at least launch it in inclement weather, no matter what the weather is in the target area. Even during the wet season in the Barrel Roll, or the worse monsoon rains in Vietnam or in Steel Tiger, and you had an IR flight to fly *you had to launch,* get onto the target areas, make a suicidal let down, or two, to try to get under the clouds, in complete and total zero visibility and then try to figure out where you are or jump back up in maybe a mere minute, or two at the most, have a smoke break to get your nerves settled and go down again. At least twice—*and then you could go home.*

Well, this is one of the nights I am heading into the PDJ, and there are heavy, really heavy thunderstorms, at Udorn, and later, up into the PDJ. The story in this chapter about the Wild Weasel guys punching out after not being able to plug into a tanker to refuel was about this type heavy weather.

This night I knew was not going to go well. It is storming, thundering, and with heavy lightning and intense rain; and I am thinking, what the hell am I doing heading out in this weather?

Oh, right, because I had volunteered for this . . .

I taxied into position on the runway at Udorn. The tower had me switch over to the departure controller while still sitting there, powered up and holding the brakes.

No one else was foolish enough to be going in or out, so I had the runway and the time to myself.

More lightning that is absolutely blinding us even as we sat there.

I checked in with the departure controller, and he gave a very troubling briefing about the thunderstorms. I had to get out, so I waited for maybe ten minutes or so while the controller was surveying the storm cells sweeping through.

Finally, a decision is made. I would take off and *immediately* make a left turn; ATC would try to guide me through the worst of the storm cells and then on northward toward where the weather is better. The problem with radar and thunderstorm cells is that while you might find a route initially between storm cells, you could not see or know what is on the other side of these. Is there yet another narrow path (and the Mohawk did not have its own weather radar) or did you now have to go right into a cell, risking the hail, the turbulence, and the chance breaking up an airplane—to say nothing of being sick in the cockpit? It is best not to eat much before a night launch in such inclement weather.

I had the cockpit lights turned up to the maximum position, as the lightning is bright and intense, blinding even and wrapped up in heavy rain and winds. I let the brakes go, throttles to the max, and would make a jerk up and off the runway so that the high and gusting winds did not cause me to slide on my gear if I made a normal rotation. Just get up to speed holding onto the runway slightly longer than normal, and then jerk up, gear retraction, and get away from the runway.

That worked fine, and I was near immediately climbing into the weather, but the lightning now is so intense, not so much the turbulence, which this Mohawk could handle, but the near constant flashing is blinding. I remember that I had to reach up and turn on the cockpit emergency lighting that included two bright white spotlights just above and to the side of the top of each ejection seat. So here I am, in a cockpit with full intensity white floodlights trying to be sure I can see the instruments.

And doing this mission for what reason?

2-13 / THE MiGCAP MISSIONS

I do not recall any time there was an active MiG threat in the PDJ, but we did have constant MiGCAP cover provided by the F-4 Phantoms from the 555th (Triple Nickel) TFS also located at Udorn. There were always KC-135 tankers somewhere in their *anchors* (we could hear some of the related ATC) that not only kept the F-4s mission fueled, but often just having them sit with the tankers until needed. The tankers were also there for refueling Wild Weasels or other attack aircraft that came out of strikes in North Vietnam and were going to or from Udorn or Takhli AFB.

2-14 / IR Aircraft Getting Down in the Rainy Season

During the rainy season, the SLAR aircraft is always on high station at night watching the truck traffic, but the use of the IR is limited and much scarier. While the SLAR aircraft were okay at altitude, until the radar firing 57 mm came into play, the IR aircraft still had to attempt to get down into the PDJ to run targets.

This is scary, really scary to do. The issue is that the PDJ is surrounded by mountains that are several thousand feet higher than our usual target area. While the mountains were our great IR killer in Steel Tiger, they were more along a line of which we could run a strip target and pull up. In the PDJ, we are going round and round in this area and could not go in a straight line for too far before we had to get reoriented again.

This is how an IR TO in the right seat kept us alive—it is nearly all in their hands to keep us oriented and run the IR system and watch for the anti-aircraft fire.

In the area of the PDJ we had only limited radar placement ability, so getting a radar position fix over the center of the PDJ was tough. Our backup is to get a TACAN fix to put us over the center of the PDJ, but then that too was a bit iffy. We did a combination fix of the weak, and not really accurate TACAN and the Air Force ATC radar, decided we are over a workable area, and then started descending into the scariest part of all our flying—gunfire issues aside.

The Doppler navigation system on the OV-1C was basically worthless for orientation. When we got the OV-1D, with the Litton INS, we had a better chance. We ran a constant analysis on each of the INS systems, knew which one is the most accurate, and could use, with some reservations, the INS to get us into the middle of the PDJ in weather and drop down under the clouds and find a road intersection to orient us.

The TOs had to be not just good, *but the absolute best*. Period. Usually, I would start from the eastern or southeastern part of what I am hoping is the mountains of the PDJ and make a descent into the clouds. Blind. Completely blind and heart beating fast!

Insane.

I had the radar altimeter set first to 1,000 feet, waited for the red light, and then reset it to about 600 feet. I needed to get to the base of the clouds and determine where we were—and do that in no more than about 2-3 minutes.

Under the clouds, at night, with virtually zero visibility, sometimes in the rain, and we had to know—*to absolutely know*—where we are. That is why the TO, *and he alone,* determined life or death. In the OV-1C, the IR screens were small, and the terrain is moving fast on them. The OV-1D IR is a lot better, but still it is an issue that once we were under the clouds, we needed to determine *exactly* where we were—*and do it fast.*

If we can determine where we have come out under the clouds, then from there the TO could guide us with his expert knowledge of the roads to where we needed to be, which is usually up towards Ban Ban. Ban Ban was right on the road route out of China and from there we could go to the northwest to China. More than a few times the IR film readout has us well beyond our Visa limits (!)—or to the southeast and into the Fish's Mouth region of North Vietnam northwest from Hanoi.

If we knew where we are, we are okay, for a few minutes anyway. Even if the high SLAR aircraft is passing targets, this is not workable because the gunships had to see the ground to fire, so the IR aircraft's only mission at that point is to identify the *Movers* from the SLAR planes and let the Intel people have that information after we got back.

Having said all this—

If we got under the clouds and could not fix where we are, or we did not get under the clouds, and the radar altimeter was blinking at the 600-foot point—then it was FULL POWER, PROPS FORWARD, PULL UP and climb back above the invisible mountain ridge levels, still while in the clouds.

Scared. *Scared a lot.* Time for a cigarette, or two, and then maneuver around with the weak TACAN and questionable radar fix, and do this all again.

On one particular night, I had positioned myself over what I figured is near the center of the PDJ. I had the *seemingly good fortune* to find a big hole down through which I could see ground fires, the field burning type, under the clouds; So I figured I had a good ceiling down below the cloud base.

However, down in the PDJ are a couple of NVA gunners sitting at a .51 cal and slapping each other and pointing up at the *sucker hole* above them as some idiot (me) had rolled my Mohawk over on its back and pulled the aircraft's nose down into this opening. The over-the-back roll was better at keeping Positive-G's rather than pushing over the nose into a Negative-G situation.

Soon my good fortune of finding this hole and being able to see ground burning fields below seemed just what I needed that night until, now in a near vertical dive through this hole—the hole starts to fill up with steady streams of racing .51 cal tracers coming up through the hole—at me! A major mistake and a nearly deadly miscalculation in judgment I had made to use this hole as my way down to the PDJ that night.

Twice was usually my limit. Twice riding this blind, at night, in the clouds, in the rain, descent *into stupidity* was enough for a single night, and then it was time to go home, back to the Paradise Hotel. To my then Thai girlfriend, of the week anyway.

2-15 / Life at Udorn

Because of the nature of the CIA operations we were tasked to support, for over six years, the 131st few pilot officers were housed at the Paradise Hotel in Udorn. Nearby, the Air America people lived at the Charoen Hotel, which was just a bit nicer than the Paradise.

This was a young single man's living dream to be sure. I was twenty, as was George, and some of the others; all but one or two were also single, and no older than their mid-twenties. Night-after-night you flew these combat missions in the PDJ, came back with the adrenaline flowing heavily in our veins and looking for what young men everywhere looked for, mostly for some female companionship. To that end, the hotels had a cadre of young women that you could choose from, like a meat market *I hate to admit.* The girls would be in a room with a glass window and wearing a large number on their chest, so you could simply say *Number 6*, and you had your date, right then.

The girls had to be VD-checked every week at the Udorn AFB medical clinic and have a current clean VD-card to get access to any part of the hotel, even the pool area.

Of course, there was often sex; we were in our twenties, but it was not just that, nor certainly not always *that*. These girls, most of them probably less than twenty, and surely from poor families, were making a living for their whole families. But they were also keeping their dignity in the process. We would go to dinners a few times a week, and to some of the nightclubs in the city (not on the AFB), and on sightseeing trips and these girls were always, *always*, dignified, polite, and polished in their nature. From time-to-time, some of us had more-or-less full-time girlfriends that lived most of the week with us at the hotel.

The local food, there and in Ubon of course, was great; unlike in Vietnam. We had Kobe steaks with great regularity, so tender you could cut through it without a knife—and good wine to go with it.

Of course, you might well be dead tomorrow night, so life did live a bit on the edge for the pilots.

On the base we also had Air Force officer's quarters at the transit BOQ, so on some nights, coming back from very late missions and completely, and totally, wiped out, we might just stay on the base, go to the officer's club, eat a dinner at midnight or later and then just stay at the BOQ for the night.

X-Cobra Snakes Were Everywhere

Thailand is famous for the cobra snakes and the mongoose animals that would spar with or fight the snakes. What makes the cobra so very dangerous is they are supposedly the only snakes that act like an animal—and may for days in the jungle stalk its prey to get a kill. Otherwise, snakes would not be much of a danger unless you stepped on one or surprised it, but not so the cobra. We feared *that snake* more than the enemy when discussing what would happen if we were downed in the jungle.

Cobras were everywhere on the airfield at Udorn

One day I am on the airbase, in the back of a jeep heading to our Mohawk revetment, and suddenly the driver stops, backs up, jumps out and grabs a wooden Coke case and steps into the ditch. He is smashing some small snakes, Cobras, and killing them with this crate. I wondered just where did he think mom and dad Cobra might be right then?

In another case, one of the Air Force ground guys was found dead in a revetment from multiple Cobra bites, repeatedly attacked—*though only the first strike was needed.*

On some nights, we would refuel the Mohawks away from the revetments and next to a grassy area. Not unusual to step a few feet in front of the aircraft, into the grassy area to take a last-minute pee and then get into the aircraft. One night, after doing just that, one of the Thai security guys were out on the grass, no more than twenty feet from my Mohawk, and he comes walking back with this large dead cobra draped over the barrel of his rifle.

No more peeing in the grass for any of us . . .

X-*The Udorn Air Force Officer's Club*

These guys knew how to party hard, and most I suspect were as drugged up on adrenaline as we were coming out of a combat mission. The Air Force built them a club, probably about the same time as the BOQs and the golf course—and then later something about a runway and hangars.

I am there one night when two of the guys got a bit stuck—in a jeep. They had driven up the front steps and were trying to drive through the front doors of the club. My kind of guys! There would be these, for lack of words we called them *Spud Guns*, the six steel beer cans speed-taped together and used to fire a flaming tennis ball at some opponent.

I have seen half dozen tables laid down while a bunch of drunken Air Force guys was fighting it out with the flaming Spud Guns. They would have fit in just fine at our dirty little officer's Spud Club at Phu Bai.

2-16 / ALLEY CAT CAPSULE CREWS

The Air Force's 7th ACCS operated the Airborne Command, Control & Communications aircraft operated out of Udorn flying modified C-130 aircraft designated as the EC-130. The EC-130 aircraft flew with a self-contained control capsule inserted into the back of the plane that held the guys working the radios, maps and current Intel for the AO.

The EC-130 with Command & Control capsules in the back.

There were two sets of controllers for each AO, one for daytime and one for nighttime operations over Laos. Controlling the Barrel Roll, the PDJ and Steel Tiger North the daytime call sign was Cricket and at night, it was Alley Cat. Running control operations over Steel Tiger South, during the daytime the Call Sign was Hillsboro, and at night, it was Moonbeam.

Because we worked very close on a near minute-by-minute function with the Alley Cat crews in the PDJ, we often attended their daily afternoon intelligence and planning briefings, giving us a chance to know personally the guys we were talking with each night and to go over issues we were having with targets in the PDJ.

Once in a while some of us attended the one-over-the-world intelligence briefings that covered more of the world threat issues than just the Southeast Asia war. Those were interesting indeed, to see what all was going on in other parts of the world and how that might have an impact on what was going on even with us.

These EC-130 C&C capsule crews were responsible for the big picture in each of these AOs. The gunships could not act on attacks, usually on the *Movers* our SLAR aircraft had found and our IR aircraft had gone down and examined, without being cleared by the capsule crew to do so, in case they were attacking friendlies or other issues.

AC-119 *Stinger* Gunship from NKP firing the mini-guns.

Much more impressive at night, though . . .

CHINA
Cao Bang
Sa Pa
Lao Cai
Bac Ha
Mai Chau
HANOI
Halong Bay
Ninh Binh
Luang Prabang
LAOS
Vinh
VIETNAM
VIENTIANE
Vinh Moc
DMZ
Hue
Danang
Hoi An
THAILAND
My Son
My Lai
Kon Tum
Pleiku
Angkor Wat
Battambang
Siem Reap
Buon Ma Thuot
CAMBODIA
Nha Trang
Phnom Penh
Dalat
Sihanoukville
Kampot
Cu Chi
Mui Ne
Chau Doc
SAIGON
(Ho Chi Minh City)
Phu Quoc Island
Can Tho
Vinh Long
The Mekong Delta

Chapter 3

THESE ENDED REALLY BAD

US Embassy evacuation from Saigon – April 29, 1975

In this chapter, I pulled together what I had from my personal experiences and tried to tie-up as many of the loose ends from historical records, of which there are precious few. These ended badly, mostly as fatal events of just missing from a mission. Some I have great details of, with some errors I am certain, but as realistic as I could make them.

There are many reasons the Mohawk is called the *Army's Widow Maker* and here are just a few of them.

3-1 / EJECTION SEAT FAILURE AT PHU BAI - (1-FATAL)

4 March 1971 / Captain James Shereck (31)

OV-1B #64-14240

Event Note: At night, in the monsoons, with one engine shot out over Laos, the other engine coming apart and then the ejection seat failed.

We all *really* liked Jim. At 31, he was older than most of us and had already served time in the Navy and then went over to the Army and went to Vietnam first as a young warrant officer helicopter pilot; did a combat tour in that, went back to the states, got himself a fixed-wing transition and then into Mohawk school and was now in our unit as a captain. A true combat officer and a man of impeccable character and skill.

We all valued Jim's experience and his ever calm and professional mannerisms, something that most of us early 20's kids sorely lacked. Jim had a wife and kids back home too, something few of us had either of.

It was March 1971 and the disaster of Lam Son 719 is still playing out. The cool, ever raining Northeast Monsoons were in full force. Jim was out on a night SLAR/IR combo flight, with me as the low IR aircraft in Laos, in Steel Tiger North toward the anti-aircraft and flak-filled night skies near to Tchepone—*deadly* Tchepone.

Usually, two SLAR aircraft were running box patterns with one each in Steel Tiger North and South. They are flying at around 10,000 feet, well above any small automatic weapons, but routinely in the range of the 23 & 37 mm weapons, and the radar guided larger 57 mm flak that is exploding around your aircraft without showing a glowing tracer line from where it is coming. And there are the all too frequent .51 cal heavy machine guns to deal with, as it was on this night.

I had completed my IR targets for the night. Jim was still feeding SLAR *Movers* to Moonbeam to pass along to the AC-130 *Spectre* gunship that was in the box. I had turned back to Phu Bai and was maybe 35-minutes ahead of him. He was okay when I left, but there were the never-ending gunfire and flak coverage over that area to deal with.

Jim took at least one hit from a .51 cal that came up through the left engine's oil tank area. From the cockpit window with a flashlight, Jim could see oil spilling out even as the engine was still running. He made the right decision to shut down the engine, jettison the external fuel tanks and head back to Phu Bai. This was not a good scenario; it was night, in monsoon weather, and a crippled single-engine aircraft without any escort. When he got to Phu Bai, he knew there would be just *one approach chance* to make this work. Turning west to dryer Thailand might have been better that night, hindsight always being so clear and precise.

Having lost half of what power he had, and still carrying a heavy internal fuel load, the remaining right engine was being pushed to its limits pulling Jim and his TO home that fateful night.

My IR mission over; I was back to Phu Bai and inside Spud Operations doing my mission debriefing when Jim called in with the troubles. He was cool, calm, and professional.

The Phu Bai crash crew was put on standby. Runway lights were still kept blackened to lessen the aiming of what was near nightly heavy mortar fire from outside the wire. Monsoon time gave the VC and NVA good cover, and it was always difficult to return perimeter fire or get the gunships up to patrol around the outside of the wire, so it was that the field would stay darkened and whatever rescue vehicles we had would be crawling around by the very dimmest of lighting. We had been taking incoming mortar fire on and off that night so the runway lights were out, not that anyone could see the runway location in the rain.

The Army Phu Bai approach controllers picked up Jim and started to vector him to fly over the top of Phu Bai and then he would go wide for a long, extended, easy flying, straight in GCA approach. Just what you always wanted to do; at night, in the monsoon rain, a very low ceiling, on one engine, and a talk-down GCA approach to a blackened runway. He is being vectored over the top of Phu Bai, now just below 8,000 feet and then would go outbound on the radar approach, come around and maybe have a long, five miles or more, stabilized final approach while letting down for a single-engine, straight-in recovery. It would be tough, deadly even in the best of circumstances—and there is no chance for a go-around or missed approach.

Across the runway, a Pink Fire Team, two AH-1 Cobras, and an OH-6 Loach were already cranking their blades in case there is to be a night recovery from an ejection, but in these wet monsoons, even a helicopter is going to have trouble finding someone that is down near our airport. In the cockpits of the Cobras and Loach were most likely just 19-, 20-, and 21-year old warrant officers just like I was—kids at war. Their blades were turning, the rocket arming pins were ready to be pulled, and the pilots were flexing the moveable long barrel machine guns of the Cobras, flexing for a fight if need be.

By then there were maybe six or seven of us in the Spud Operations office. Jim is giving us updates on the flight situation. He is, as always, cool, calm and professional. He is clearly in charge and taking this in stride.

While still some miles out from the overhead vector Jim comes up with the shocking news that the right engine, the good one, had a runaway propeller that immediately endangered the aircraft.

Ah shit . .

Having run the good engine hard coming back from Laos, the propeller controller now failed, and the prop immediately went to an overspeed condition, an urgent and critical situation that may cause the engine itself to start coming apart in pieces. An engine shut down is not optional; it has to be done *immediately*. There is no choice; Jim had to shut the right engine down.

The silence would have been *deafening*. No engines are turning. No power. No hydraulics. The dimmed battery power is only enough for lighting the cockpit, the instruments unpowered and rolling. Jim now had just limited controls and is encased in solid rain and storms. This is going to be a tough one.

Jim is still cool, calm, and professional. He shut down and secured the right engine and would try to restart the left engine with the oil hole in it, and try to nurse it back to life for as many minutes as he could. At the time, Jim is being vectored to come directly over top of Phu Bai. If he did not have the bullet damaged left engine running online by the time he passed five thousand feet, a minimum ejection altitude for a right-side up, but sinking ejection profile, then they would eject, wherever they might be.

A 571st Dustoff helicopter from next door is already cranking and across the runway, the Pink Fire Team is getting ready to pull pitch and supply cover and support for any rescue needed if the Mohawk crew ejected. Even with the airfield blacked out that night, and occasional incoming mortar fire, the crash crew, and others were mobilizing in the rainy darkness.

Jim is talking through what he is doing. He now had both engines out, is shot up, and descending into Phu Bai—with the airfield under fire. *Damn tough.*

He is not successful in getting the left engine back online and as calm as could be he said that at five thousand feet they would go out—eject. As it was, the five-thousand-foot mark is nearly right over top of the Phu Bai airfield itself.

The significance of the five-thousand-foot marker was a supposed Martin-Baker J5 ejection seat limitation on making a manual seat separation in case of a seat malfunction. After leaving the aircraft supposed this would be the time one would need to make a manual body twist-and-roll motion to pull yourself away from a non-functional seat separation and still get your personal parachute deployment—or so the training videos had told us it would work out. Martin-Baker lied—it was then and always had been impossible to make a timely manual seat separation after leaving the aircraft. Jim would prove that to be the case.

Jim did not get the left engine alive again: he is talking clear, calm and professional and at five thousand feet they both ejected nearly simultaneously. As it was, *they were right overhead Phu Bai*: the doomed Mohawk starts its deadly downward spiral to the airfield. Ironically, there were now at least eight to ten of us in Spud Operations that knew that a 20,000-pound Mohawk, still half loaded with fuel, is coming down on top of us—*along with the two crewmembers*. And one would go and hide—*where*? The lucky ones would be the guys that *did not know* that a Mohawk was coming down on top of us that night.

Where do you run? Where would you hide? It is pouring rain. Visibly is nothing. The raining cloud ceiling is at most a couple of hundred feet. Anything coming out of the sky is going to do what it is going to do, and no one could watch it. Surely the issue of ignorance being bliss had some meaning that fateful night.

As fate is the hunter (and it truly is in war), anything that could go wrong did go wrong. Both engines are out, in weather that you could not possibly have made a damaged aircraft approach in. To top it off, when Jim's seat rode the ejection seat rail out of the cockpit a series of explosive pancake charges fired and pushed the seat and Jim up through the Plexiglas canopy into the stormy night.

Then the seat separation failed!

No one could image the hell Jim went through after the ejection. The standard seat ejection sequence would have the seat riding up a fixed rail as the result of three sequencing pancake explosive charges built into the ejection seat back rails. As the seat came up, and usually through the overhead canopy, a timer would delay a few seconds to be sure the seat is away from the aircraft and then out would come first a stabilizing drogue chute about five feet across, and that would have fired, stabilized the seat, and then pulled out a larger chute. The seat, with the crewmember still attached, would have ridden down until the aircraft is below 15,000 feet, designed so that you did not have a seat separation at such a high altitude that you lacked oxygen, though your personal mask is linked to a 10-minute oxygen bottle attached to the ejection seat itself.

When ejecting below 15,000 feet, a barostatic device should trigger the final seat separation; then breaking away from the seat leaving the crewmember with their personal full-sized parachute to come down with. There is a sensing unit that determines the 15,000-foot pressure level, approximately, and if the ejection were already below that point the entire sequence would have taken place, and the crewmember is hanging under his chute within about three-to-four seconds.

It never happened as it should have been.

As Jim's seat came up the ejection seat rail and out through the canopy, a tube broke that would have deployed the initial drogue chute to pull the other chutes out. With the broken drogue chute rod Jim is left trapped in his seat. There was never any sequencing of seat stabilization nor separation of the man from the seat.

Our stateside ejection seat training had videos of controlled ejections including how someone would make a manual twist-and-roll maneuver to separate yourself from the seat and then you can manually pull the parachute ripcord. What went wrong then, that Jim failed to pull away from his broken seat?

The TO lived but is hurt badly. *Incredibly*, he initially impacted on the roof of the Phu Bai airport control tower, then immediately bounced off that and plunged over the side for a long, long drop; usually deadly in itself, to the concrete ramp nearly fifty feet below. What saved his life is that the parachute cords and chute canopy got tangled with the antenna and structure at the top of the control tower, and he is left dangling, severely injured, barely just feet from the concrete. He lived.

Jim, unfortunately, is still in his seat when he impacted about two hundred yards away, bouncing and crashing into the helicopter hot medevac pad at the 85th Evac

Hospital. He had been decapitated in the impact and was obviously alive all the way down while trying desperately to roll manually out of the seat. It cannot be done: We were lied to.

Within a few days, an expert from the Martin-Baker seat people arrived in Phu Bai and started going over what had happened and what had failed. With some five thousand feet of falling time, two minutes for sure, why could Jim not execute a procedure we had practiced many times in the ejection seat simulator and would take only a few seconds? Because it simply cannot be done is the answer.

In the Martin-Baker training films that we had watched in flight school, in the Mohawk school, a guy had himself made over two dozen video filmed in-flight ejections testing all aspects of the seat and chutes. However, according to our Martin-Baker guy, his very last ejection nearly cost him his life, as it was itself a failed ejection sequence similar to what Jim had a few nights before. In that filmed training flight, it was noted that the base of the scattered clouds was around six thousand feet above ground, or slightly more. In the filmed, and carefully planned test, the guy already had about 30 previous ejections.

The Martin-Baker man was an expert at this type of an ejection emergency. It was daylight, and it was planned—but something had gone wrong, and he entered the top of the scattered clouds still in the seat. When he came out of the bottom of the clouds, he was still in the ejection seat and still over five thousand feet or more above the ground. This 30-plus ejection seat expert had fully two or more minutes of time, in daylight, to do the otherwise routine manual separation process.

The twist and roll technique simply did not work. Trying to separate from the seat using a twist-and-roll procedure, breaking away from a heavy seat falling with you is not feasible. We had been lied to: as if that made a difference.

Ultimately, the Martin-Baker test guy did get a manual separation, but it was so near the ground that the chute had made only a single wide swing, and the man fell to the ground from the initial outward swing, swinging laterally at that point, and had broken both legs on the impact.

Apart from the design failure of the seat that caused the drogue chute not to deploy, it is always pure bullshit that you could make a manual separation. If the test guy, with nearly 30 ejections, or more, could not do it but for just a couple seconds to spare, then the chance for any of us is—*zero*.

One realizes, sadistic to a point, but blindly flying into a mountain or exploding in flight has a lot to be said for a way to go—*instant*, or nearly so. No time to contemplate what is surely your end-of-life as Jim had to do.

3-2 / GEORGE IS LOST ON MY IR MISSION
(2-Fatal/MIA)

November 1970 - CW2 George Rogalla (20)
SP4 John King (20)
OV-1C #67-18897

George was, along with CW2 Russ Rowe, one of my two best friends of the time. Both these young men had been so for over a year since we first met in flight school at Ft. Stuart, Georgia, in early 1969 and then we went on to finishing flight school at Ft. Rucker, Alabama and onto the Mohawk schools together. George and Russ were two months ahead of me in the Army flight school. There were only about eight new WOCs a month in the Army's fixed-wing flight school, a small number, and because we all shared the same barracks, all the WOCs from six months before and after our particular classes were close friends. George, and Russ Rowe, already now dead from the friendly fire on our officer hooches from Fire Support Base Barbara a few months earlier, on July 19, 1970, had both arrived at the 131st just a few weeks ahead of me.

George's background was a lot like mine. He had learned to fly while in high school, as I had, and wanted to be an Army pilot and to do so before the war was over! He was just 18-years old when he enlisted in the Army and is selected to attend the Army's *Warrant Officer Pilot Program*. My friend all through flight school and then all three of us wanted to go to the deadliest of the Mohawk five units, the 131st Aviation Company in Phu Bai.

George was just twenty years old, a month before he is legal to vote or drink (!) when he disappeared on an IR flight. He was about five months younger than I was and as such he clearly held the record as the *youngest pilot to ever, from any of our Armed Services, to command a combat aircraft into or over North Vietnam*, and probably goes for Laos too!

X-The IR Mission We Swapped One Afternoon

George and I were both back at Phu Bai for a few days, staying out of Udorn and working on IR targets in Steel Tiger. The area was ugly not only for the intense anti-aircraft fire in that area, but the mountains were rough and many. Trying to fly IR strip targets along the trails and stream beds in near total darkness, often while under the clouds, was more than we should have been doing, especially with the –C- Model with only Doppler for assisted navigation.

Usually, on these types of mountain valley strip targets, we would stay a bit higher, get a mile or so of lead-in while still at altitude, like way up at 1,000 feet (!), and then drop down to our optimum IR flight altitude, which is only around 600-700 feet above the terrain and *well below the mountain ridges* on both sides and ends of the IR run. Any wonder it was mostly the warrant officers flying these missions; at night, low in the mountains, often moonless and overcast so not even able to make out the silhouette of a ridgeline?

Flying this low at night, in the mountains, always had the risk of hitting mountains. If you read down in this chapter, you see how many of our IR aircraft we lost. Most of us flying IR missions on a continual basis had hit at least some trees from time-to-time, and a couple of the guys crashed through the trees, unseen until they hit them, so hard at 230 knots that they stripped off all the lower antennas from the Mohawk and kept flying! I hit an upper-level tree and got away with one antenna gone and just tree scrapings. The terror is that if you had seen the trees, you would not have hit them. The best defense was: 1) be a commissioned officer with some other assigned unit duties, so you never, ever, never had to fly an IR flight, or 2) set the radar altimeter at just 400 feet and if the light went ON–*then jettison the drop tanks, the wing stores, and immediately* be pulling up. And to eject at 200 feet on the radar altimeter. The reality is that this sequence of events would all happen within a second or two and by the time you figured the—

Oh, shit...

—Factor, you would have crashed. Others did just that—*not just George.*

Back on George's flight; we always had to stay lower on *these specific targets* because of the anti-aircraft fire we would get climbing out of a valley run. Usually, it is an issue of too much anti-aircraft fire, .30 and .51 cal machine gun fire only, if we were low and an easy target, but not in these valleys. If we flew at a higher altitude so as to align the IR run, we would likely be shot down, as was the fate of some of the 131st guys in this chapter. If we pulled up too much on the end of the run, which in this target area is too dangerous, we are going to get shot down by the flak.

I had run the near identical target area be four or more times during the past weeks. *I did not like it.* No one did. The mountains were rough, the valleys narrow and steep, and the few and weak terrain references we might be able to see even on the small IR screens of the OV-1C model made trying to determine exactly where you were tough. Add to that is that we had the Doppler system versus the later Litton INS, and thus many navigation references were difficult at best.

It was mid-afternoon that fateful day and I was assigned this target area, again. On that particular day George had been targeted to be working IR targets further to the south, and spilling over from the *A Shau Valley*, an area we had just recently taken over from the 245th SAC at Marble Mountain.

I am ordered to take my IR aircraft and head back to Udorn and run that night's IR mission in the PDJ and then stay in Udorn until further advised. Like twisting my arm is going to be necessary for going back to Udorn, to stay in my room at the

Paradise Hotel, with one of the girls, a hotel, swimming pool, and real food? George was moved from the easier targets to the south and would take these particular ones I was to have flown that night.

Mostly what was going on in this time was that the ill-fated and disastrous *Operation Lam Son 719* incursion to cut *the Trail* in Laos is only months away and the NVA, knowing that this is coming, is building up large stocks of weapons and armor in the areas we were targeting night-after-night. Thus, the anti-aircraft and flak gun numbers had increased a lot!

I took off for Udorn and that night I flew that IR mission that no one wanted, or had the stomach to fly, made my fly-by of the pool at the Paradise Hotel and got picked up and over to the hotel within an hour of landing. The adrenaline, as usual, is heavy in my veins.

I am down at the hotel pool drinking for maybe half an hour when one of our maintenance guys came rushing from the base (only the officers got to live at the Paradise Hotel) with news that George—

> *That George had not come back from his IR flight this night and is down probably somewhere in his target area—near Tchepone.*

Damn! Ignoring my current drinking status, as it was, I went back to our ramp and had my aircraft prepped to leave immediately. I am flying back to Phu Bai to see what is happening as George had been working in my former target areas.

At that point, we did not know with any certainty where George is lost. Once an IR aircraft dropped down into a target area, we had no radar tracking to see where one had been. For coordination he would have checked in with *Moonbeam*, the Air Force's EC-130 C&C aircraft, but not on the individual IR strip runs, so now we did not know where in several hours he might have been lost.

I went over and over the IR targets and knew the area and the most likely sequence he would have run the targets. It is too late for any of us to go out there that night, with the morning light coming soon, and it would have surely been extremely dangerous to do so. Before grabbing a couple of hours of sleep I redrew the targets George had, as I would have flown them, and in the order I suspected he might have. We then used my IR target run diagrams and planning as our search pattern, to start as if it is his mission and go target-to-target. This is a horrible, deadly idea, but it was the only one we had that night.

Without any sleep and as the dawn is creeping up on us, a dangerous time as now the gunners could see you. We, and I think also the Air Force, started to fly camera missions over all the areas we suspected George had run targets. We had my aircraft and at least two others that had volunteered to go into the target area and make camera runs of the areas. This is incredibly dangerous. Looking down into this chapter you find, I think four, or more, of our Mohawks that were lost just while looking for other unit aircraft that were already down. Loitering around low enough to look for a crashed Mohawk is dangerous due to the anti-aircraft fire, while getting higher for camera runs put us into the flak—and that was getting very heavy leading up to Lam Son 719.

There are several good Air Force pilot books that covered a period around this time too of downed Air Force FAC, fighter and rescue aircraft all near Tchepone that had started with just a single pilot shot down, alive and hanging in a tree just above the bad guys. When it was over, some three days later, there were *at least five aircraft down*, several dead guys, just a couple rescued and several men shot down that were subsequently talked to on the ground and known to have been alive that were never found and never heard from again, even after the war. It was just that dangerous an area, day or night—and George is down there somewhere.

I think it is towards the end of the second day, or into the third day, after we had flown at least a dozen photo recon flights, and had taken what must have been thousands of frames of photos from individual runs, either as snapshots or mostly strip running film, that we found the aircraft wreckage in a single frame of a photo run. Our Spud Intel shop, under the control and command of my then hooch roommate, Captain Al Musil, is working 24-hours endlessly with all this film. Every person they could find is going over and over the film laid out on the light tables—and with even more guys going over the same film again just to be sure. Looking for anything that might be part of a Mohawk.

On about the third day of running VR camera missions in the target areas, dodging gunfire, a small piece of George's aircraft is found on a single frame of film. The irony is that what is discovered in a single photograph is just the image of the 131st Eagle Hawk that is painted onto the left vertical tail. There it was, one of them, clearly just that one piece visible in a photo—and it is in really, really bad guy land. A Mohawk, in wreckage parts, in a darkened jungle, is like looking for more than a needle in a haystack; it is looking for a color-matched needle in the whole field.

On the *Vietnam Wall* website is a first-person account from a Marine that said he was put on the ground and found the bodies and helped carry them up to the top of the ridge for recovery. So details differ and what we knew of anything at the time was probably filtered for our benefit.

What appears to have happened to George and John is how fate played out for too many of the guys in the 131st. The piece of the tail that led to the remains (more I were recovered just in the past years from one of the Hawaiian-based graves registration teams) is the result of hitting a ridgeline apparently just as George was coming up off of a run at the end of a valley.

The worst irony of the crash is that George was climbing this mountain route, ending an IR run, in complete darkness, no night vision goggles like we have today, and he needed only maybe one second, *two at the most*. He hit at the very top of a ridgeline, right there, right at the top and the wreckage flung over the top to where the tailpiece is found. This is why trying to find remains at all was nearly impossible; there is not a crash site, but just wreckage spread like an explosion flinging pieces down off the other side of the ridge. It is amazing that this brave recovery team found anything at all that day.

Had he been ten feet lower he would have crashed at the top of the ridge in an exploding pile. As it was, he just needed, what, *three more feet—just three more feet to clear*. A mere second in time more, two at the most.

George Rogalla's was the first name I put the little paper rubbing strips to on the *Vietnam Wall*, and I was in tears and nearly collapsing as I did so.

3-3 / IDENTICAL TWIN BROTHERS; ONE LIVED, ONE DIED -
(2-FATAL)

26 November 1971 Captain James Spann (24)
SP4 Lawrence Smith (19)
OV-1B #59-2634

It is November 1971, and the Northeast Monsoons were in full swing at the northern end of South Vietnam. The monsoons covered from where we were, about from Hue, northward through North Vietnam. The monsoon season ran day and night from about October to March. The Southeast storms, warmer, but very wet, were mostly south of us. So for months on end, each takeoff, and every returning post-mission approach is going to be on instruments with a Phu Bai GCA precision radar *talk you down* approach. We would climb out, usually, but not always, getting on top of the monsoon clouds and head northward with radar vectors to get into position for SLAR flights up and down the coast of North Vietnam along what was Route Pack-1.

It could not have been a worse time or place or circumstances to try to fly.

Jim, just 24-years old, and married, had arrived in Vietnam with his identical twin brother, Darryl, also a Mohawk pilot and, what should never have happened—they were both assigned to fly with the 131st. They had come to the 131st in about June 1971 while I was between tours, so I had no initial contact with either of them.

I did not know these two young men, identical twins they were; fresh out of Mohawk flight school and right into Vietnam. So identical were they that the only noticeable difference was that instead of just their last name on the sewn-on name tag on the jungle styled flight suits and fatigues each of them had a different first initial. After I had returned to the 131st, my only encounter I recall was a brief hello and chat at the Spud Club one night. I had come back to the 131st and went almost right away back over to Udorn. And here were these two, new to me, young captains—identical twins.

This kind of event is something we did not need considering our horrific losses due to crashes. Even at Phu Bai the night fighters, the IR guys, lived and worked totally at night, with seldom a day off. As such we had very little interaction with the other pilots in the unit other than occasionally passing by them. We ate at different times, showered at different times, and sometimes were seen eating breakfast (of too often hot dogs and powdered milk and eggs) with a beer or a bottle of Jack Daniels on the mess hall table. We worked (flew) on an opposite wake and sleep cycle.

As I recall that morning, the conditions could not have been worse. It is pouring rain, windy, with very low ceilings, requiring a full IFR takeoff and a climb out immediately into the blackness. Usually, in this stressful situation, we would get the engine and electronic system run-ups completed while off to the side of the takeoff area; take a deep breath, slowly taxi into position, roll forward a bit to be sure the nosewheel steering is aligned, and be ready for a powered up takeoff instead of a rolling run. You could see only a short distance down the runway, the windshield wipers are operating at a frantic pace even as you sat there, getting your nerve up, calming down, and mentally going into the fight or flight mode—but fight, or in this case, taking off in this horrible weather, is the only option.

Jim slowly taxied into position, carefully and correctly, and let the aircraft roll forward a few yards to be sure the nose wheel is aligned with what he could see of the few runway stripes. As Jim would have called—

"Seats hot."

—And both crewmembers would reach above their heads and press down the upper ejection seat firing switch, unlatching the pin holding the top ejection rope and then reached down and moved the lock level off of the safety position allowing for the lower ejection seat firing handle to be released and usable.

With only limited visibility in the rain, a slowly accelerating running takeoff is probably not used. For this situation, the power is first set to midrange so the turbines would fast spool forward at an even rate. This gives a jerking start on the runway. The runway, the inclement weather—one wanted as little time on the runway as possible, to get the aircraft into the air, a stabilized seven degrees or so of nose up attitude, and climb out on autopilot if need be.

The TO then would have put his left hand onto the external stores jettison T-handle located just below the power quadrant. The TO would hold the handle on takeoff so that if there is an engine failure right after takeoff—*our highest ranked way to die in a Mohawk*—the pilot would have only commanded—

"STORES!"

—And the drop tanks, rocket pods, machine gun pods, radar jammers, flare lights and whatever else slung under the wings that we could not fly with on one engine would be gone, *sometimes*. See my account of a lost engine and a hung full drop tank I had in the *A Shau Valley* for what happens with a drop tank decides to hang on.

At this time, Jim is talking to Phu Bai tower, the Army controllers who cannot see him, and is given, only for seconds, the runway sidelights to help with alignment. The runway lights were usually left off to avoid giving the local enemy gunners the airfield targeting they needed for the frequent mortar attacks.

While still sitting on the departure end of the runway, and just before brake release, Jim is switched over to make contact with the departure radar controller to be sure he is on the right ATC frequency for the climb out. Usually, we would change to departure control after a takeoff and while leaving the airport traffic area, but in inclement weather, the switch over is made while still sitting on the runway. After liftoff is not the time to be turning to the right and looking down at the radio panel and switching frequencies. Having to turn your head and look down to the right offered up more deadly confusing fluid movements in the inner ear and is long a problem with flying the Mohawk. One had to turn and look down to the rear of the center radio panels, sometimes all the way back to the back wall, just to tune the radios. Fortunately, we worked our UHF radios off of a set of 24 preprogrammed frequencies before we even started a flight. Thus, one could—

"Switch to Red Crown—Button 12."

—On command.

Everything is now set. The departure controller is talking to him. He powered up, engines and props stable and running high, released the toe brakes and rapidly moved the throttles full forward against the panel. The aircraft would have lurched a bit, the fluids in his ear canals moving, maybe lying to him now. This procedure would give him a minimum ground run as the faint white runway lines were all but disappearing into the rain and darkness. There were now runway sidelights and his single nose gear landing light to stay on the centerline of the black, rain-soaked runway

The Mohawk's main landing light, located outboard and under the left wing, would have been left off and kept in the up and stowed position, left there as the glare of the light in the driving rain would cause too many distractions to one's left side peripheral vision. The nosewheel light is mounted on the nose gear assembly and is turned on and off with a toggle switch on the pilot's overhead eyebrow panel. The nose light switch is just one of several near identical switches grouped together. Immediately after the takeoff Jim would have to reach up to the switch, with his gloved right hand, to toggle off the light as the nose gear is retracting.

Brakes now released, more pouring rain and the Mohawk leaps forward and is immediately swallowed up by the wet darkness. Jim's SLAR aircraft is now rapidly accelerated into the pouring night rain as more of the runway disappeared behind him. Everything is okay.

Takeoff speed is reached quickly, and he rotated into a climb, slamming the landing gear handle forward, and already, just seconds into the flight, he is on instruments and swallowed up by the low clouds and driving rain.

They had only seconds now left to live . . .

Following procedures then in place, moving rapidly now, scared at this point even for the most experienced of us, departing at night, low ceiling, rain, wind, right up into the cloud base. The gear retracted on command and keeping his eyes glued on the illuminated FD-105 flight director, ensuring that the nose is above the artificial horizon and wings level, in a climb configuration, now maybe just three seconds into flight.

Jim would have glanced, only briefly, up toward the pilot's eyebrow panel of gauges and switches, and in the darkness, somewhat scared as we all would be in that departure situation, with his right hand he probably moved from the landing gear lever and then up to toggle off the nose gear light just as the gear is still retracting with the light still on. If you forgot to turn the light off it would shine up through the cockpit floor area—a major distraction if on a night takeoff and climb.

In the morning darkness, the rain, the fear, the swiftness of this combat flight, his gloved hand may have betrayed him and with eyes glued on the flight director he moved the toggle switch to turn off the nose gear light.

*Pilot's Eyebrow Panel Had a Confusion of Like-Shaped Switches -
A bad configuration for using at night*

There is a difference of thought on just what then caused the crash. At the time, it is thought that Jim had accidentally toggled off the electrical inverter when he meant to turn off the nose landing light, two near identical toggle switches on the pilot's eyebrow panel that are right near to each other—*a clear cockpit design error.*

The other account and no one would know for sure, is that he had rotated, pulled the gear up, and turned on the autopilot for a stabilized climb—and the autopilot had caused the crash, not the inverter issue.

Within two switch widths of the nose gear light's toggle switch was a *near identical toggle switch*, one that would switch off the electrical inverter—the source of the instrument power bus and cockpit lights.

If it is the assumed inverter switch problem, then it is a *fatal error* and unrecoverable in the weather—***no matter who is flying.***

Now only mere seconds into this flight, everything would have gone dark: the cockpit lights out, and all the instruments suddenly switched off. He had likely toggled off the inverter power—and not the nose light.

Maybe, if there were not the weather, he might have been able to visually, in seconds, *perhaps*, in the darkness, have found an outside light or horizon reference to keep the aircraft upright and climbing—or maybe not.

In now total darkness in the cockpit with no instruments and no outside visibility, they were dead.

Jim would have desperately tried to control it, but he had no chance. Not even the best of us could have recovered from this event while on instruments. Within seconds, a fireball just past the end of the runway, outside of the perimeter near a small village, was all that remained. Full of fuel, the Mohawk exploded on impact. With no outside references neither of the two guys could know, in those few seconds, what happened and a successful ejection is not going to happen.

Jim died while still in the wreckage, in his ejection seat, maybe staying with the aircraft as he saw the village racing toward him. John had ejected just before impact but is well outside of the safe ejection envelope and is still in his seat, and alive, when they found him. However, he died a few minutes later.

As the day dawned, still heavy in rain and low visibility a search of the smoldering wreckage could be started. More troubling right then was that his brother is there.

I was not there that night, but I heard that the awkwardness was very difficult for everyone. The remaining brother, Darryl, insisted he wanted to stay in the unit, to return with his brother's remains and to then come back and fly. What do you say to someone in this situation? There are no rules or standards to cover this situation. We are living in a few small, wooden hooches held up on sticks, not really working together as we flew mostly solo missions, and here we have a young man, his twin now gone, and the remaining young man is there, right there, not over at some hotel, or BOQ or someplace, but right there, and we did not even know very much about him.

Darryl stayed, I understand, while what human remains could be collected from this explosive crash are recovered, and then he left. He did not come back.

For us, death like this is uneasy, to say the least. In most cases, and we had many deaths right at Phu Bai, not all of it being out on a mission and not coming back—but mostly we joked about it. Sick? No. Someone crashes or is shot down and tomorrow, or maybe in an hour, *you are going to be right there in the same situation*, perhaps under fire, maybe an engine exploding or failing on liftoff. If you did not make light of this you would lose your mind—or worse, *lose your nerve*.

It was this horribly deadly crash that caused a timely redesign and change to the pilot's eyebrow panel so that the near identical switches, the inverter, and landing light, were not in the same location, along with changing the physical size of one of the switches. Wearing Nomex flight gloves, at night, under stress, anything dealing with these switch locations was a problem.

3/ These Ended Really Bad 177

3-4 / DEADLY FSB BARBARA FRIENDLY FIRE HIT US
(1-FATAL - MANY INJURED)

November 1970 - WO1 Russ Rowe is killed by *Friendly Fire*

Phu Bai being hit by US artillery was worse than any NVA or VC attacks.

Three of us very young WOs had gone to the Army's primary flight school and then later the Mohawk school just a month or so apart. As there were only eight fixed wing WOCs a month, versus some 700 helicopter WOCs, and then only about four Mohawk warrant officers a month, so you understand we were all close to anyone from a few months before to a few months after our class time.

The three of us were Russ Rowe, George Rogalla and me. Some months later George and I traded missions late in the day, and he went on an IR mission, in really bad guy land, hit a mountain, and is lost. I would become the sole survivor, and frankly, I think always suffered a bit with what is *survivor's guilt* as it may be.

On this fateful night, we had an *ad hoc* officer's party in the CO's hooch with most of the unit pilots and a few of the nurses from the 85th Evac Hospital. It would end badly.

The eight or so small wooden officer's hooches were lined up behind the flight line across from the Spud Club, the officer's club that was merely two small wooden hooches itself. A little dirt and mud single vehicle wide road ran along the front of the hooches. At the far end of this row of hooches were the officer's shower and latrine shack. I was two hooches up from the latrine and two hooches down from the CO's. In between my hooch and the CO's was one that Russ lived in with three other pilots.

Can't believe I lived here, in these shacks, for years!

The Spud Club is to the far end on the left side of the road. The last hooch on the right is the officer's shower (once set with a grenade) and my hooch was two up from the shower. The artillery from FSB Barbara was air bursting along a line from about where the center power pole is standing.

About midnight the party had run its course and is slowly breaking up. The CO's hooch was crowded for a couple of hours. As I was already an IR pilot regular, I seldom saw who else the new guys were in the unit as they were all on opposite shifts of flying. Anyway, a couple of jeeps had headed back to the 85th Evac with the nurses. I left the CO's hooch and walked down about forty feet to mine, kicked off my boots, put my pistol in one of them, and fell face down on my bunk—still fully dressed in my black party suit.

Suddenly, there were **HUGE EXPLOSIONS,** maybe less than one minute after I got into my hooch. My small personal fan had been sitting on a plank just above my head, and it came flying across me, the spinning blades now tinkering against the shrapnel damages, which is only part of the new airing design of my hooch. I am lucky—*but at least six others were not.*

The explosions had been *massive*. This is certainly not any 82 mm mortars or even a large 122 mm rocket hit; this is something else, something massive. There are several of them almost at the same time that air burst almost right over the officer's hooches.

Instantly I rolled off my bunk and onto the floor, and not hearing more explosions, I pulled on my boots, taking my pistol from one of them, and shoving it into my holster as I got up, put the gun belt on and half-crawled as I went out the hooch door.

Maybe just 10-15 seconds had passed by now, no more . . .

There is smoke and an explosive smell heavy in the air while debris is still drifting down. It was surreal to be sure. Not like anything that we had experienced before.

A hundred yards or so—down past the officer hooches and to the right of the dirt road by the hooches—our Escape & Evasion (E&E) equipment hooch had a small fire, the result of thousands of bits of shrapnel from the air bursting artillery fire having blown through the hooch and lit on fire some of the signal flares that were in the crew member's survival vests.

We had been hit by several airbursts from the firing of the *large* artillery guns from American Army Fire Support Base (FSB) Barbara, off to the west of Phu Bai. A wrong set of coordinates had been put into a combat firing support mission, and these massive artillery rounds come right to our officer's hooches that night. At the time they were firing either the large 175 mm or the 8-inch artillery, really massive shells in relationship to the usual 82 mm mortars or the 122 mm rockets the NVA would fire at us.

The scene was horrible. I staggered, now noticeably sobered only these past few seconds, into the next hooch, between the CO's and mine. Three of the four guys present were wounded. The artillery airburst closer to the CO's hooch sending hundreds of pieces of burning shrapnel into this hooch and less into mine just one hooch over.

Several were on the floor, wounded and bloody and there were already blood pools around the beds and across the wooden floor.

A large piece of shrapnel had hit Russ in the back of the head while he was lying face down on his bed. We had both left the CO's hooch maybe just two minutes before. Two of the other wounded guys were on the floor as we were getting Russ off the bed and onto blankets on the floor. Russ is alive then, but not conscious, and he would never regain consciousness. A good part of his brain matter is on the bed and floor. For all practical purposes, he was killed immediately. To say the least, there is a lot of blood and carnage—not exactly what pilots were used to in our version of the war.

Next door, the CO's hooch has a lot of shrapnel damage but is not on fire like the E&E hooch is. The couch he had, as he had the only private hooch being the CO, just minutes before had four to six nurses and guys sitting or standing around it—and it is now heavily shredded. Had the artillery come in just two minutes before the death toll would have been much higher as surely some the nurses in the hooch would also have become combat casualties.

As it was, some of the pilots took shrapnel wounds from the attack. I think several are then sent back to the states. I did not even know these guys due to our mixed flight scheduling and that I had spent some time in Udorn and new pilots would come and go and if they flew SLAR or other day missions, we would likely never cross paths except for briefly, and only sometimes, maybe in the Spud Club.

We loaded Russ onto a makeshift stretcher on the back of a jeep and several of the guys, and another jeep of wounded left to go to the end of the airfield where the 85th Evac is. By now, not even sure the nurses that had been with us were even back to their compound yet.

A few hours later five of us took a helicopter and flew the 90-miles or so to the hospital at DaNang. Russ is still alive, legally I guess, but only barely. They had airlifted him from the 85th Evan Hospital during the night to try to save him.

I remember to this day that he is covered in black and blue bruises, a sheet covering him, and breathing tubes in his mouth. He had a toe tag. That bothered me for a long time, but I think everyone had a tag, so one did not have to look for a wrist strap.

He is not conscious. What do you do? What can you say? Nothing really. We said our goodbyes that morning and were taken back to the helicopter and flown back to

Phu Bai. By the time we landed, about an hour later, we were told that Russ had died just after we left.

I think, now in retrospect, that they had kept him alive *only* to allow us to go there and say goodbye—for him, for us, for his family. Later in my life, with my own boys as young men and myself more than a bit anti-war, even as I worked for the CIA then, that this is a touching moment to be remembered. I fear that so many young men had died and disappeared or were killed in mass, and no one was there for them. Dead in an instant, and who would be the last one to see or speak to one of my sons, to one of someone else's son or daughter, father or husband?

George is lost next, and then I am left alone . . .

3-5 / OUR LAST FATAL TAKEOFF CRASH -
(1-FATAL)

12 August 1972 - SP5 Daniel Richards (23)
OV-1D #69-17025

The irony of this fatal crash was that I would not even know who it was for many years.

On this fateful morning, I was medevac'd to the Air Force hospital at Clark AFB in the Philippines. I was waiting to be helicoptered over from the MMAAF field hospital to DaNang AFB, a few miles away, and from there put onto an Air Force C-9 (DC-9) and flown to the Philippines yet that night.

About two hours before my helicopter lift to DaNang there was an explosion near the hospital and crash alert sirens started wailing. See *My Last Flight and I Am in Trouble*.

It was one of our Mohawks going out on an RP-1 SLAR mission, and he had lost an engine on takeoff, rolled, crashed and exploded just off to the side near the end of the runway. There were too many accidents of this type, not just with us, and not just during the Vietnam War.

What we all knew was with an engine failure, you had only seconds, two or three at the most, to act and keep the aircraft upright and flying on the remaining engine. The immediate action is to jettison the external stores (drop tanks, radar or IR jammers), along with maximum power and if the aircraft is rolling, as it would on one engine, to reduce power on the good motor, stabilize the flight, or if necessary, to immediately close both throttles so the rolling action stops—***and eject.***

Got that? That is according to the checklist and training, but that seldom has happened. The most immediate action is to jettison the stores, which is okay, but if the pilot lets go of the throttles to eject, the Mohawk is rolling over, and you will go out sideways or inverted—and this was usually fatal.

In my following years, we found even high-time, highly-trained and old IPs that have lost a Mohawk from the failure to *do these steps immediately*. It is just not wired into our brains to act that quickly. We can do it on a pilot training flight or checkride because we know that is what we are to do, but in real life—almost no way will the pilot go that route.

In an unanticipated engine failure, usually on takeoff, the first impulse is a few seconds of shock, confusion—and those 2-3 seconds are just enough to ensure a crash is only a few more seconds away. If by chance the pilot does immediately jettison the stores, and then closes the throttles to keep the Mohawk from rolling so they can eject—well that is likely to cause a serious injury or death because you are ejecting too low, outside of the ejection envelope, and you come out through the canopy, even if right side is up. However, the main chute is deploying horizontally with you attached to it, and then one is hitting the ground at maybe ninety knots or so. Probably fatal there too as we had found out.

An engine failure on takeoff is dangerous, even for the most prepared, the most skilled, and the most experienced pilot.

In this case, the pilot survived, badly broken up, but still alive. The TO was not so fortunate—and he died.

Just before I am taken out to the helicopter to lift over to the C-9 at DaNang, word came that it was one of our aircraft, but we did not know who was flying or the TO's name. So I left Vietnam and went into the many weeks of the medevac system of those days, and a few months later got out of the Army for the first time without having known whom the crewmembers were. I would not know for many years, into the 1980's when I was temporally assigned again to Ft. Hood, Texas, where the remainder of the 131st had moved to just a few months later.

I did have a chance to go through some of the records when I was assigned there. Now the Internet has opened up access to more of the files, but the chaos that prevailed in the closing days of the war left many files and people in the dust, so to speak.

3-6 / MOHAWK HITS SHIP IN DANANG HARBOR
(2-FATAL)

This is an especially ugly one for everyone. I will leave out the names, for good reason. The right-seat passenger was a young man from flight operations and not a regular crewmember.

A Mohawk was sent out on a routine, daytime, local area maintenance test flight and it ended with the aircraft clipping the antennas on top of a South Vietnamese ship that was in DaNang harbor and then the Mohawk immediately flipped into the water and disintegrated. The *rest of the story* is just horrible.

A new pilot was brought into the unit, as a captain as I recall. I was on my second tour, and while walking to operations I meet this new captain—*and he looked somewhat familiar to me.*

As it was, this now captain had been a Warrant Office Candidate (WOC) with us at Hunter AAF early in our fixed-wing flight school in the spring of 1969. We had some strict rules at the time, as always, and this guy broke one of the main ones—the flying or attempting to fly formation on another training aircraft. We were flying the Army's version of a single-engine training T-41 (Cessna 172 with some modifications). In those days, for a rules breach, or academic shortcoming, the individual just *disappeared*. We might come back from the mess hall, or classroom or flight line and where a fellow WOC had been was now a vacant, neat, and completely setup room as if no one had ever been there. That is what happened to him some years before.

If you are put out of flight school, you lost your WOC standing and the E-5 pay that went with it, and you were reverted to an enlisted grade, generally as an E-3 Private First-Class based on your time in the flight program and sent off to someplace. We never knew. We never heard from anyone, *ever*. Some WOCs had been higher ranked enlisted guys, up to E-6 I think we had, and if removed, then they could go back to their last status.

Well, here he is, *and wearing Captain bars*, a Mohawk patch, and assigned as a new pilot. In talking, I discovered that after being kicked out of the early flight school he is assigned to training as an enlisted armor soldier—driving a tank or something in training. He had the good sense, smarts, and skills to apply immediately to then go to the Army's Officer Candidate School (OCS) and because he was not discharged from flight school for anything atrocious in his actions, he got the assignment and was off to the 90-day OCS course.

He came out of OCS a few months later, while we were still WOCs in flight school, but now as a newly minted Second Lieutenant. He had managed himself a new post-OCS assignment to go back to the fixed-wing flight school and in his orders, as it was with the commissioned officers then, assigned that after graduation from basic flight school to go then on to the Mohawk qualification school—regardless of his flight or academic skills or achievements. This was a long ongoing problem in Army aviation because only the top two to four of the new warrant officers got Mohawk school while the commissioned guys were going there no matter what their relative skill level was. Many of us felt this was later a significant factor in the number of accidents we had with the Mohawks, as perhaps too many guys were in over their heads in a very sophisticated aircraft on tough missions, and that was not their fault at all.

So here he was, nearly three years later, not a 131st guy. He had gone to flight school and then to the Mohawk school and was probably an okay pilot and thus by this time he was now making his first tour. He had moved up to being a captain, which only took a total of two years then, one year for promotion to First Lieutenant and just one more year to Captain.

I was back in Udorn when this happened, but the details I got was that he had not yet flown a combat mission and had been that day assigned to fly a local area maintenance flight. He had been checked out on the local flight area so he could do the flight. He had asked around flight operations if anyone wanted to go on a flight and a young man, not a maintenance tech, requested to go with him.

Less than an hour after takeoff flight operations got a call asking if a Mohawk was missing?

Apparently he had made a diving run on a South Vietnamese ship in DaNang harbor, to buzz it only, as perhaps all of us have at one time or the other also done. While diving close in for a low pass on the ship, pushing about 230 knots, or more, had clipped the antennas on the top of the ship and immediately the Mohawk flipped into the water at such speed that it mostly just disintegrated right then and there.

I have always wondered what the official records for this lost Mohawk showed? Not like it was anyone's fault other than the pilot, who had already been kicked out of flight school for illegal and unsafe screwing around—and no one there would have known of that or would have even cared.

3-7 / JACK AND AL ARE SHOT DOWN NEAR TCHEPONE -
(2-FATAL/MIA)

31 May 1971 - CW2 Jack Brunson (22)
Captain Clinton "Al" Musil (31)
OV-1A #59-2615

CW2 Jack Brunson was one of only a few of us warrant officers in the unit on my first tour. A neat guy just a year older than I was. I had known Jack before going to Vietnam as he was in a class only a few months behind us and with only eight new warrant officers a month in flight school, we knew most of the guys pretty well.

Captain Al Musil was a Military Intelligence (MI) branch captain and was our non-pilot 131st senior intelligence officer and as such, Al was running our Spud intelligence group. Al was also my roommate in our four-man hooches, so I knew him *very well*. Because he was our Intel briefing officer we worked together with him daily and the pilots knew him better perhaps than the other officers that were doing unit assignments. Al was someone we saw and talked with nearly every day and who personally gave most of the IR and VR mission briefings, one-on-one with us.

It was just shortly after I had left from my first tour that Jack and Al were flying an armed OV-1A model gunship with another aircraft in a flight of two. As was the norm then on any armed VR flights, there were two planes in flight when attacking *the Trail*. The guys were running gun and camera recon near the most dangerous area in Laos, *Tchepone*, in Savannakhet province in the northern end of Steel Tiger North and just about 90 miles to the west from Phu Bai.

According to the guys in the other aircraft that day, Jack had made multiple passes on a target area, taken some light fire, but when the other plane came around from a turn, all they saw was a burning area on a hillside. It was Jack's and Al's Mohawk.

There had not been even a call or warning in those few seconds it took for this to happen. No chutes are seen, and Jack and Al went onto the official MIA list. Some decades later the status was changed to KIA.

From somewhere or someone before my time, there was this song we would sing with our drinking and telling war stories, but it was so true that here it is. It is meant to be respectful to not only Jack and Al, but all the guys we lost—and that was a lot you see in this chapter—when working anywhere near Tchepone.

3-8 / Don't Go To Tchepone

Jack and Al were just more names on the long list of guys lost at or near Tchepone. We had a special Spud song just about—

Don't go to Tchepone . . . ,

> *I was hanging around Ops, just wasting my time . . . ,*
> *Off the schedule . . . not earning a dime . . . ,*
> *When a major steps up and he says . . .*
>> **"I suppose . . . you fly a Mohawk in those black flying clothes?"**
>> **"Well, yes sir I do . . . and a good one says I . . .**
>> **Do you happen to have me a mission to fly?"**
> *He says*
>> **"Yes I do, it's a really easy one . . .**
>> **No sweat my boy it's an old time milk run . . ."**
> *Well, I gets all excited . . . and asks where it's at?*
> *He gives me a wink and tip of his hat . . .*
>> **"Its two eight zero for ninety from home . . .**
>> **It's a small quiet little hamlet that's known as Tchepone . . .**
>> **Oh sure, you will like Tchepone!"**
> *I grabs up my helmet . . . and straps on my gun . . .*
> *Out through the door on the dash, I do run . . .*
> *We fires up our Mohawks . . . and takes to the air . . .*
> *Two flying Mohawks locked in tight and we haven't a care . . .*
> *In twenty-five minutes, we are over the town . . .*
> *From eight point five grand, we're looking around . . .*
> *I push in the breakers . . . and dial in the mills . . .*
> *Racks up my wings and goes in for the kill . . .*
> *I feel a bit sorry for the folks down below . . .*

The destruction that's coming . . . they surely can't know . . .
But the thought passes quickly; I know war is hell . . .
Downward we scream to that town called Tchepone . . .
Unsuspecting, peaceful, Tchepone . . .
My panel's all hot . . . and the pipper's just right . . .
I pickles a couple . . . I lays them in tight . . .
I pickles those beauties from two point five grand . . .
Then started my pull-up . . . when the shit hit the fan . . .
There's an air burst in front . . . and two off my right . . .
There's eight or ten others . . . I sucks it up tight . . .
There's small arms, there's tracer's, there's heavy ack-ack . . .
It's scattered to broken . . . in all kinds of flak . . .
I jinks to the left . . . and pulls up for the blue . . .
My wingman cries

 "Lead, they're shooting at YOU!"

 "No shit!" I cried as I points it towards home . . .

Still comes that fire from the town called Tchepone . . .

 "Dirty, deadly Tchepone . . ."

I gets her back home . . six holes in my bird . . .
With that major that sent me . . . I'd sure like a word . . .
But he's nowhere around, though I look near and far . . .
They sent him to Saigon . . . to help win the war . . .
Well, I've been over this land for many a day . . .
I've seen all the shit . . . they're throwing my way . . .
But I'll bet my flight pay the Hawk jock's not born . . .
That can keep all his cool flying over Tchepone . . .

 "No, don't go to Tchepone . . .
 Dirty, deadly, Tchepone!"

3-9 / OUR COMMANDER DIES ON TRAINING CRASH AT PHU BAI - (1-FATAL)

24 February 1970 - Lt. Col. Frank Newman (42) /
Captain McClenathen (Badly Injured)
OV-1A #60-3739

Comment: This recounts as best I can because it occurred just a couple of weeks before I arrived in Phu Bai on my first tour. The story of the fatal training crash that took the life of our commanding officer, LTC Frank Newman, and severely injured right to near death, a new pilot that the CO was training, Captain McClenathen.

Warrant officers Russ Rowe and George Rogalla, both of them my class friends, and both whom would perish within months had arrived at the 131st with another newly assigned officer from their Mohawk class, Captain McClenathen. Captain McClenathen survived this accident, though he is horribly injured and near death for some time. We knew him also as he had spent nearly a year progressing through the fixed-winged flight school with the few warrant officer candidates (WOCs). It was a bit of an irony that the 131st got these three new guys all at once, and the only survivor was himself nearly killed.

LTC Newman was also the unit standardization instructor pilot (SIP), a position I would take over on my second tour. As such the IPs and the SIP had to give the new pilots several local training flights before they got started on training on unit SLAR, IR and VR missions. For now, it was that most pilots got three to four flights with an IP going over aircraft emergencies, engine failures, the local area procedures, any ATC issues, the enemy situation right around Phu Bai, and orientation generally to flights in I Corps. Usually, these local flights were done within three to five days of arriving at Phu Bai.

The training needs may have been pressed a bit with three new pilots arriving all at about the same time. Furthermore, looking deeper into this chapter, *These Ended Really Bad*, you get the feeling of how many crashes and shootdowns the 131st was suffering.

On top of all other things, takeoff accidents, engine failures, and multiple deaths in this aircraft, and especially in the 131st, were getting out of hand, right down to the fatal takeoff crash at Marble Mountain within just hours ahead of my medevac to the Philippines in 1972.

X-The Engine Failure Issues with the Mohawk

The primary factor in takeoff crashes, as related to too many sudden engine failures, was that the large Lycoming engines swinging a big propeller generated more running torque than the short wing of the Mohawk could control. The OV-1A and OV-1C models both had short wing spans with not enough aileron control. Lose an engine on takeoff and in just seconds one could be rolling inverted into a burning hole in the ground.

The first significant change that Grumman made was to add inboard hydraulic ailerons, which are large moveable flap surfaces between where the fuselage started and out to the flaps, about three feet across. The inboard ailerons have rapid sudden up and down movement of about 25-26 degrees and are workable only when the flaps were lowered, either for a landing or takeoff position or full down flaps. As such, as you put the flaps down you had the advantage of those big articulating inboard ailerons to give you more instant control.

With even more crashes the Mohawk remained the Army's *Widow Maker*. As the OV-1B model (SLAR only) and the Super-C (IR) and all the OV-1D models came into production, they had about three feet of extra wingspan on each side and more aileron control on the outboard side.

> *Still the Mohawk wanted to go over on its back within milliseconds of an engine failure on takeoff.*

An *autofeather* system was installed to help control the aircraft during an engine failure on takeoff. The autofeather sensed a low turbine power setting—along with having the engine power lever, through micro switches, in the full takeoff power position. Three things had to happen: 1) the system is armed with a switch just below the throttles and an AUTOFEATHER light is showing, 2) the throttles are both fully forward on the power pedestal, and thus a micro switch is armed, and 3) the sensed engine torque is too low. If these conditions were met, such as with an engine failure on your takeoff, then the supposed affected engine would suddenly autofeather the propeller on that side—almost INSTANTLY I will add, and thus give you a fighting chance to fly the aircraft out.

Assuming you *have* performed **Step 1** on the Emergency Checklist—to have jettisoned the wing stores, the fuel tanks, the machine guns, the rocket pods or other things that are hung on any of the six underwing hard points, three on a side. To make this happen, on a takeoff, the right-seater, the TO or the other pilot, or the IP as the case may be, would put his left hand on the stores jettison T-handle that is right below the throttles. The last item on takeoff, for the right-seater, is that his hand *is visible on the T-handle* and would await the call of the pilot, not acting on his own: the call of the pilot to—

"*Jettison stores! Or just "STORES!"*

Probably preceded as the case may be, by . . .

"*Ah, shit . . !*"

With both throttles held full forward, the wings cleared instantly, the pilot not having to try to figure out what engine had failed, and he has a chance—*only a chance*—to fly the Mohawk out of this situation. In this book, and overall in the history of the Mohawk, I would guess that at least half the takeoff crashes, even if the autofeather worked and the stores were jettisoned—still crashed. But with the fuel tanks, or rocket pods or other things still on the wings, the likely chance of flying out is terrible.

In an early OV-1A model, the dual stick aircraft used for guns and training, as the guys were flying, that chance is about zero, in my estimate of over 20 years of flying the Mohawk in two different armies, the US Army, and the Argentina Army. That is why, while there are emergency checklist items that one follows in a reasoned order, the **Engine Failure On Takeoff** almost has to be done as an immediate action set and the jettison of the stores has to be done immediately. *Period*. There is, was, zero room for one's excellent airmanship skills to save you in an OV-1A model with only one engine burning and turning.

With the wing stores gone, an engine failed, or in autofeather, and with good luck, and quick rudder control, the Mohawk may continue to fly—not likely, sadly, but maybe. Sometimes—*but sometimes not.*

X-What Is Thought That Happened That Fateful Day

This was a training flight, making things even more dangerous, not less. They had been doing local training and were at the time practicing landings and some emergencies. They were doing this with an OV-1A model, with both drop tanks, *and* with empty rocket pods slung out there for even more troubling frontal drag.

And, they were supposedly doing touch-and-go landings.

> *I never, ever, do touch-and-go landings in any aircraft, even on a long runway.*

A *touch-and-go* is a training maneuver wherein you briefly touchdown on the runway, and before stopping or even slowing down, you reset the trims and flaps, and the throttles go forward—and you are taking off again. This obviously saves a lot of time in stopping and taxiing back for another takeoff, but it has huge risks also, as this deadly event showed.

I have been a flight instructor since I was just eighteen; with an FAA flight instructor license since then for airplanes and multiengine airplanes, an Army IP and SIP pilot for about 20+-years, also an Argentina Army IP and SIP pilot, a civil jet training pilot, and an FAA pilot inspector, FAA training pilot for inspectors and an FAA type rating examiner—**and I never, ever, do touch-and-go landings** in anything other than a small, single-engine airplane. *But never in any multiengine aircraft. Never.*

The problem, the danger is, that while it is not illegal, and in fact most places want you to do touch-and-go landings to lessen the training time needed as you do not have to stop and then taxi back, get in line, and make another takeoff: you just touch down, reconfigure the aircraft while it is rolling on the runway and go again.

But, to do this, after your touchdown, you (the IP) has to *immediately* be reconfiguring all three of the control trims, the elevator, rudder and aileron trims, reset the other cockpit indicators, and recheck the items on the BEFORE TAKEOFF and the TAKEOFF checklists—all the while you are trying to control the aircraft and being sure you do not take off before you have it reconfigured.

> *There are simply too many things to go wrong, and the aircraft is already leaping back into the air.*

On this flight, I was told a few weeks later, they had touched down, and the IP called for a touch-and-go and while it is usually the IP, the training pilot in the right seat to reconfigure, it is believed that the autofeather was *armed* again. It is turned off after takeoff and during the climb out.

In this rush on the runway, as any IP knows, with the *Autofeather* armed, as it should *not have been* in a training situation, and with the IP's attention probably diverted to the trim reconfigurations, the pilot put the throttles to full power, as would be expected, and the engines were not yet spooled up *above the autofeather set level*—and, sure enough, one of the engines autofeather just as the aircraft was lifting off.

Ah, shit . . .

I cannot imagine any way an IP could have reacted quick enough to avoid this, other than: 1) not doing any touch-and-go landings, and 2) to be sure, *absolutely sure,* that the pilot DID NOT rearm the Autofeather. But it is suspected that the autofeather *was rearmed,* the engines are not spooled up enough, the throttles were forward and just at liftoff—with too many things going on in the cockpit—one engine autofeathered. Even though there was nothing wrong with it: it just had not, in those seconds, let the turbines spool up above the autofeather low torque setting—so the system sensed an engine failure, as it would with both throttles full forward, and autofeathered the engine that was maybe only a single second from being up to speed. Disaster followed as surely as day follows night.

Well, they *might* have been able to fly this out **IF** they had jettisoned the stores. While a routine, non-rushed takeoff would have the right-seater with his hand on the jettison T-handle, it probably was not. The drop tanks and rocket pods stayed where they were.

There is no way, none at all that this aircraft was not going to crash within just a few seconds. My decades of training pilots I suspect in the milliseconds of the autofeather acting that the IP, and the pilot, both waited, just a brief hesitation to see what happened? Only a second or two, at most, that is all the time they would have had. Did the IP create this engine failure as a training event, or did the IP think the engine had actually failed, right then? Who knows? It happened too fast.

What the IP did that at least saved the pilot's life, but not his, was that as the Mohawk was impacting at the end of the runway, probably with the landing gear already into its retraction cycled by the time the pilot got the engine failure/autofeather indication, that the IP slammed both the throttles closed and thus stopped what is always an assured roll-over, the torque of a single engine at full power and the opposite engine dead and the propeller feathered.

On a short-winged OV-1A, the aircraft would have been heading onto its back side in a second, and no amount of rudder or stick control could stop that—unless the pilot slammed both throttles *closed*, which would have the effect of preventing the unequal engine torque and kept the aircraft's wings somewhere near level. In doing so, to have bought that critical second or two to then have ejected at something other than upside down.

Then in this instant, just at impact, not really in the air, they both ejected, but were well outside of the ejection seat's safe ejection envelope.

The pilots both ejected through the Plexiglas canopy, which is the standard process. There was no seat separation for either pilot as they were propelled horizontally, still strapped into their ejection seats, doing about 90 knots and headed for a personal crash. Generally, this is not survivable either.

LTC Newman apparently came down onto a concrete pillar, still in his seat and was decapitated. The pilot, he too still in his seat, went into and through a building to the side of the runway and out of the backside, surely dead, his broken body still in the ejection seat.

With this exploding Mohawk right on the airfield, it was not immediately acted on that anyone got to the two ejection seats. LTC Newman was dead, to be sure. When they finally got to the pilot, something like up to fifteen minutes later (no rush as he is surely dead too), they found him alive! Not by much, but the structure of the ejection seat, as you can see in the photos later in this book, go above the heads of the seat occupants; That is what saved him as the ejection seat went tumbling through this building—*the seat still saved him.*

My understanding is that nearly every bone that could be broken was, and he was sent home pretty much in a complete body cast. What was amazing, is that about three years later, when I was getting out of the hospital myself, there is an Army article about this man, the pilot, and it recounted much of this story and that now, some three years later, he was back on flight status as a pilot in a U-21 King Air. **Good for him!**

3-10 / EASTER BEAR IS LOST ON MEDEVAC IN LAOS
(MULTIPLE FATAL AND MIAS)

Event Note: It was during Lam Son 719 in spring 1971. There was a US military Stars & Stripes news article about him and his crew, and other Army helicopter crews by then too, that had to shoot many RVN (South Vietnamese) soldiers right off the chopper skids.

The RVNs had overrun the medevac helicopters while the Dustoffs were trying to evac wounded from bases inside of Laos that were *right then being overrun* by the NVA forces. This was a dreadful situation in a whole war of dangerous situations. A few days later, and probably dozens of more missions by then, Easter Bear was brought down—and on the run. This is just part of the story.

Dustoff ships took such heavy losses in the war.

I don't remember his actual name, and when I went looking at the online records, I was stunned by just how many had died in only a few weeks in the spring of 1971, just in the Lam Son 719 campaign. It was at this time, during the opening days of the campaign, that I took an SA-2 SAM missile while on an IR mission in southern North Vietnam, just northeast of Khe Sanh at the end of the *A Shau Valley* (the *Valley of Death*).

At Phu Bai, an always-unsecured airfield with a number of internal compounds, like ours, we had some units combined into one of the other internal compounds. The 131st was at the far south end of the airfield and to the west of the landing threshold. Sharing our officer's club, the Spud Club as it was, and the mess hall was the medical Dustoff unit with several UH-1 medical helicopters. The 85th Evac

Hospital sat at the far north end of the runway, where we, or at least some us, were in some troubles from time-to-time.

One of the advantages of having the Dustoff aircraft with us was that when the commander at the hospital was trying to keep the nurses in check, or something like that, we would have the medevac pilots take a Dustoff Huey from just a hundred yards past our Spud Club and then hover taxi down to one of the medical hot pads at the hospital, pick up a few of the nurses, and hover taxi back to our end of the runway. With the nurses back at our club we could party, and when done, have one of the Dustoff helicopters take them back, thus bypassing the check gates designed to keep the nurses IN and all the airfield's young pilots OUT. Must have been the sexual pheromones at play as the nurses were the only American women north of DaNang.

So it was as might be expected that we were drinking friends with some of the Dustoff pilots in the Spud Club. One, in particular, I knew as Easter Bear, a young, maybe like me, 21- or 22-year old warrant officer command pilot. Nice kid, but we were all *old kids* by then.

Some background is needed to show how this terrible situation developed. Lam Son 719 was an ill-fated and disastrous attempt in the spring of 1971 to insert about 20,000 RVN troops to make a cut across the Ho Chi Minh Trail inside of Laos at a point to the west of Khe Sanh and going as far to the west in Laos as Tchepone. *Dirty, deadly,* Tchepone. The RVN forces were backed mostly by American air support, helicopters and our firebases and artillery.

The NVA knew months in advance that we were coming in strength and instead of running or hiding, they planned to hold and aggressively attack—something new in that time of the war. Their attacks were incredibly useful and within six weeks the numbers of soldiers, aircraft and crews we were losing were staggering—*and everyone was on the run out of Laos.*

Supposedly, over 10,000 RVN soldiers were dead or wounded. That was more than half of all of them. The estimates for losses to the NVA were around 15,000 dead, but who could know?

For the Americans, we lost *176* crew members killed, *1,952* wounded and *42* more MIA. Easter Bear would be one of the 42 MIAs and never found or heard from again, as too with his crewmembers shot down with him that day.

Of the staggering *800+* US Army helicopters we lost to battle damages in just a couple weeks, *just in that area,* an incredible *108* of them were *completely* destroyed.

Of just the Dustoff crews from Phu Bai, *6,* including Easter Bear, were either killed in action or MIA and another *9* of their group wounded in action. They were a small unit, and those losses made our Mohawk unit losses seem pale in comparison.

In the days immediately before the action started from Phu Bai, we had hundreds of helicopters moving through the Phu Bai airfield from aviation units that were from way down in the delta, in II, III, and IV Corps. These fleets of mixed helicopter types would land, maybe 20-40 of the aircraft within a few minutes, in the grassy areas between the runway and taxiways, and nearly as soon as they touched down, the rotors still winding down, fuel trucks were moving from one to the other.

There was also a half dozen jeeps pulling small trailers with generators and paint equipment and moving quickly from aircraft-to-aircraft spray-painting off of each helicopter their unit designations and emblems. When done refueling they were quickly spray painted over lifting off again moving north toward Quang Tri and then west, just below the DMZ, to Khe Sanh and onward into Laos.

When the disaster got fully spooled up over the next weeks the dead started arriving back at Phu Bai, but not as expected. Usually, a Dustoff helicopter would bring in the wounded and sometimes the dead, though other helicopters were often tasked to bring in bodies to Phu Bai and take supplies back.

Then we started to see what *thousands* of dead RVNs, and hundreds of dead Americans, looked like on arrival. The large twin-rotor CH-47 Chinooks were coming to the ramp with sling loaded Army deuce and a half trucks piled in with just bodies, dozens in each vehicle set down on the ramp, day-after-horrible-day. Hundreds of bodies, not in body bags, at a time, were coming in and being unloaded there on our side of the airfield. Where they went from there, we had no idea? **The carnage was staggering!** Whole trucks full of bodies slung under a helicopter and carried back to Phu Bai. *Unreal*!

The hundreds of American helicopters were running nearly nonstop missions and maybe even more so with the Dustoff aircraft. The gunfire was like nothing ever seen in the war to that date or after. I took my SAM during this time, and at least a dozen other small aircraft were shot down with these big missiles, including an Army U-21 crew from Phu Bai with guys we went to flight school with and worked with at Phu Bai. The tape recording of their last call, with the missile coming right at them, was chilling. The NVA also used these SAMs on helicopters and others, as never, ever, been used before, as their intent was to push the helicopters and small aircraft down into the ground fire range. Helicopters that had never been shot at above 1,500 feet were now being taken down with heavy weapons while flying above 2,500. The missile campaign worked.

Our helicopters moved towards Tchepone, into the most anti-aircraft intensive areas ever. And for the first time, these units faced not only a host of heavy .51 cal machine guns, but there were dozens of flak weapons, literally everywhere, taking down helicopters—or more directly, forcing them down and closer to the otherwise deadly ground fire from the .30 cals.

For the first time, instead of our forces chasing the NVA around, it was reversed, and the NVA were the hunters in force.

Until this time, when we used the nearly round-the-clock waves of B-52 bombers creating what were known as *Arc Light* strikes were all planned and set in place many hours in advance. When I would be in Spud Operations, plotting my many nightly IR missions in Laos, I had to plan to fly around the bombing strikes. Generally, we knew exactly when and where these massive attacks were going to happen. That would change as things quickly worsened for all of us.

Within days of the start of the assault, there were waves of B-52 bombers used for the massive *Arc Light* strikes were being sent loaded to Laos *with no known targeting*! **None.** They were getting last minute instructions, often to try to drop now waves of bombs very, very close to the RVN fire bases we had just set up that were now overrun in mass by the NVA ground wave attacks. But now, for us, we were running IR or armed VR missions, and only getting a notification of the bombing on the UHF 243 MHz Guard frequency—and only about the time the bombs had left the wings of the bombers several miles above us.

I had two cases where I was running low, under fire, and a row of explosions arose from my lower left side and across to my right front. I had flown right through a wave of bombs, twice in a week. There was no way for our TOs to take the called-out bombing locations quickly, usually referencing a TACAN site, and then check the map before there were already hundreds and hundreds of mass bomb explosions. Often by then, the massive B-52 *Arc Light* bombing waves were targeting three sides of a firebase that was being overrun so that there was a possible escape route out from just one side. **These were ugly times.** And those were the same ugly and dangerous targets we were running on in the daylight VR and the night IR missions

It was in these situations that Easter Bear first came to shooting the RVNs off his helicopter's skids. He and others by then were routinely being swamped by RVN soldiers trying to escape the fire bases—for good reasons of course and they were either jumping into the Dustoff or other helicopters or wrapping themselves around the chopper's skids to get out. Not that anyone could blame these Vietnamese kids whom were sent out there to fight and were now trapped on fire bases being overrun much like the endless waves of soldiers we had seen in the Korean war.

Of course, the helicopters could not fly with that kind of load, and it was to either get rid of the guys hanging off the skids, or the helicopter would crash within a matter of seconds. I cannot imagine the horror that the RVN soldiers, just kids like us also, were going through as waves and waves of NVA soldiers were overrunning other camps. This is why there is so much censorship of the media, to avoid panic in our troops. For good reason, I might add.

Anyway, a Stars & Stripes story hit the news with a reporter that had been with Easter Bear and his crew, including the pilots, had pulled their pistols and were leaning back and shooting the RVN soldiers, *the friendlies,* right off the helicopter skids.

By that time the regular single aircraft rescues were no longer able to survive and nearly every attempt to extract, and this was *over 200 a day* by then, had to have covering helicopter gunships (Cobras) or Air Force or Navy close fighter/bomber attack support for nearly every mission.

Just a few days later Easter Bear's Dustoff was one of the over **800** aircraft shot down and one of the **106** destroyed, and he and his crew were suddenly on the ground, and *on the run.* For several days, there was intermittent contact with him, or other members of his crew, as they were fleeing through the jungle on foot. Then there was nothing. Easter Bear and his guys, all just kids, of course, became some of the staggering **42 MIA** helicopter crewmembers just from those couple of weeks. Taken prisoner? Not likely in those days and that was why our Laos mission survival vests had all the ammunition we could sew onto them—to fight to the end because no one, no one, came back out of Laos. Not even at the end of the war.

Or, they could have become casualties of the Arc Light strikes, or the snakes, or the Bengal tigers, or the spiders, or the bombs, or the mines.

While the 131st suffered huge combat and other losses of people and aircraft, this did not compare with the accounts of the gunfire, the crashes, and the shootdowns that so many of the Army helicopter units went through. Wave after wave of Army Huey's, with kid pilots, taking many hits, on the mission, and keep going to pick up others that were themselves shot down, and then back and taking another helicopter right back out for rescues.

3-11 / OUR IR OR VR MISSION AIRCRAFT LOST IN LAOS -
(2-FATAL/MIA)

Event Note: No details just the names and date from online records.

16 October 1969 Captain Lawrence Booth (34)
SP4 Dennis Rattin (27)
OV-1C #??

3-12 / NEW AND OLD UNIT COMMANDERS DIED IN FLY-BY CRASH (2-FATAL)

It was our practice, and the Air Force too apparently, to make a low-level, sometimes with acrobatics, runway *fly-by* performed by a departing pilot usually just days before they would start the movement to Saigon, the jumping off point for returns to the states. This zooming fly-by is clearly an old tradition I am sure. Helicopters would do it too, but keeping the greasy side down—although we have some helicopter folks crashing due to fly-bys and them a quick pull up and *return to target maneuver* that is sometimes deadly also.

For us, this usually involved a lead up to a later afternoon, or early evening, drinking event wherein you would make your Mohawk *fly-by* with a fast, very low-level run just a few feet above the runway, pull up slightly and then do a low-level rapid aileron roll, pitch up and come back and land. The unit guys would be all sitting up on the aircraft revetments, beers in hand, probably waiting for a crash anyway. When you landed and taxied in, they would have a poster with your name and things, and then the guys would lift you up and carry you down to the remains of the O-Club, the shack with the barrels two levels high around it.

So here you would come, low-level, right above the runway, high speed, pull up a bit and do an aileron roll and come back around. The procedure needed a light aircraft for maneuverability, so one had to be sure to arrange to have an OV-1A or Super-C with no external fuel and only minimum main fuselage fuel to go up, make the fly-by and come back.

In reality, these aerobatic fly-bys were usually only done by the IR and VR pilots and not the SLAR guys who spent their missions always flying with the greasy side down and banked turns usually no more than 30-degrees from level flight. Aerobatic maneuvers for dodging heavy flak, .51 cals walking up your butt and missiles was generally not in the mission flight profile of a SLAR-only pilot.

For obvious reasons, these fly-bys were usually flown solo as no one wanted to be sitting in the right seat with the intent of having the runway striping showing through the upper canopy Plexiglas. Because of that issue, there would never be a chance to practice precisely what are the sensations, the visual sighting, and the predictable fear factor to overcome from doing this maneuver.

Because you never took a Mohawk out alone, even for a maintenance test flight, so just when would one practice this event? Maybe get a Mohawk and check with Spud Operations to see who wanted to go out for a couple of hours of very low-level aileron roll practice was not going to get any takers at all. Never. So there was no practice.

We did perform aileron rolls all the time on our missions, a barrel roll once in a while, or loops on some of the VR missions, if you were not too heavy. Even an

Immelmann out of a gun run to keep from a vertical stall, or occasionally rolling a SLAR ship rolled over on its back so as to check through the top canopy on flak coming your way—and doing that roll fast enough and with enough G-force, so the SLAR equipment did not leak fluids. However, flying low-level, near the trees, was not part of their regular work.

By the time I was leaving at the end of my first tour I had seen enough of these *fly-bys* to know this was dangerous; too many things to go wrong and low-level work was not the best plan. Some of the guys were very lucky as they were departing during the monsoon season and it would rain endlessly for weeks. Others, sometimes the SLAR guys, would do a *fly-over*, not a *fly-by* and a routine aileron roll at 1,000 feet. Playing it safe.

The IR and VR guys lived on the edge anyway, flying either daylight gun attacks or nights of low-level mountains, endless flak and heavy machinegun fire with the associated and continuous bar talk stories of just why they had gotten back alive from the mission. So for them, for us as it was, it would have seemed somewhat anti-climactic—dare I even suggest a bit fearing if *we* did not do a low-level *fly-by*. Such a lack of showing could inevitably cause our flying stories of harrowing encounters and assorted near death events into somewhat of a state of *suspect*. So we did it. We would do the low-level *fly-by*.

I had not carefully planned for my first tour fly-by, and my aircraft had full fuselage *and* wing fuel. I took the plane anyway, against my better judgment, and then flew around for some time burning off what fuel I could: All the while getting up my nerve to do a low-level roll with a heavy Mohawk. Finally, I came in, hot, out of a dive, props forward, power ready to go to max on the jerk and roll—and still too heavy. Maybe forty guys are sitting on the top of the flight line revetments, mostly with a beer in hand and waving as I made my pass, pitched up slightly, rolled to the left, pushing the stick forward as the sky and perimeter minefields exchanged places—and rolled.

As recounted later, many of the revetment sitters figured right then and there they got what they were waiting for, **a crash**, as my sluggish Mohawk rolled slow, *very slow*, and I had dipped below the tree level sighting out to the end of the runway instead of the climbing pitch I needed and all that while I was still inverted—only to come popping back up to a disappointed bunch of guys.

Well, between my tours, the Air Force OV-10 Bronco unit at Quang Tri had made a fly-by with the departing CO and the newly assigned CO.

They hit the runway inverted and exploded.

As we had just that year lost *our* old CO, and new pilot horribly injured and medevac'd out from an exploding crash at Phi Bai on a training flight, we knew exactly how bad that situation would be for everyone.

We did not do any further departing aerobatic fly-by*s*—*ever*. I think no one was ever disappointed with that decision.

3-13 / IR AIRCRAFT EJECTION ON TAKEOFF - (1-FATAL)

24 September 1968 - SP4 Dennis Giles (24)
OV-1C #64-14264

You cannot survive an off-field crash landing in a Mohawk—or as we all believed. The aircraft would break up, or explode, or you would be smashed and trapped in the cockpit. But, that was not true.

It was fall of 1968, and the aircraft had taken off on an IR mission. I thought this was a daytime SLAR flight, but my online sources show an OV-1C model, so had to be an IR aircraft so must have been at night.

One of the engines failed on takeoff, a very, very common happening you see just in my records of Mohawk crashes. Anyway, supposedly the pilot dragged the Mohawk back around to try to land but kept the drop tanks in place. The engine failure on takeoff procedure is to drop the external stores immediately, drop tanks and whatever else was hanging out there as the aircraft simply did not have the power or control. This aircraft was a straight OV-1C model, not a Super-C, and thus had shorter wings and less control ability.

He gets the Mohawk around the traffic pattern and pointed to the runway but cannot keep it flying. For whatever reason the pilot decided to put it down into a rice patty short of the airfield instead of ejecting—and with the drop tanks still in place. If he had jettisoned them, he could still be flying.

The fear of any ejection was very real. They are dangerous and so often fatal even under controlled situations, so the issue of no ejecting clearly was at play here. The pilot stayed in his seat while the Mohawk went belly landing in a rice patty and he survived. The TO, knowing that you cannot survive an off-airport crash, had ejected at the last moment.

Unfortunately, he was too low for a seat separation and was thrown forcefully into a rice patty, still strapped into the ejection seat and died there.

3-14 / IR/VR Aircraft Lost in Laos - (2-Fatal/MIAs)

> 19 February 1967 - Major Johnie Wright Jr. (38)
> SP4 Harold Wilson (20)
> OV-1C #61-2682

No details, which was so common on single-aircraft IR missions. You just disappeared, and usually, the aircraft is never found. Whether they were shot down, or shot up and ejected and did not survive or flew into a mountain is not known.

3-15 / VR Gunship Lost in Laos - (1-Fatal/MIA)

> 20 December 1966 - Captain Larry Lucas (26)
> Captain Kulmayer (Injured)
> OV-1A #63-13123

There are no details I can find but this being an OV-1A model was flying an armed VR mission in southern Laos. Because only one died I am assuming that they ejected, rather than crashed or there would have been two fatals and that another crewmember, most likely an officer pilot, had ejected and was rescued—*that being very rare also.*

3-16 / VR Gunship Lost in Laos - (2-Fatal/MIA)

> 19 November 1966 - Major James Whited (42)
> Captain James Johnstone (28)
> OV-1A #63-13115

20th ASTA Avn Det - Predecessor to the 131st Aviation Company.

Beginning a routine recon in an area of high ridges and valleys their wingman, another OV-1A model Mohawk flying armed, was observed to climb, as if to fly over the top of a hill, keeping close to the trees. It then crashed.

3-17 / Our Mohawk Shot Down By Soviet SA-2 SAM Missile - (2-Fatal/MIA)

> 28 September 1966 - Captain Jimmy Brasher (25) (Spud 19)
> SP4 Robert Pittman (20)
> OV-1B #64-14266

They were flying a SLAR mission on RP-2 just off the coast of North Vietnam. It was assumed that one or more of the SAM missiles launched that night hit the plane and that it crashed into the Gulf of Tonkin approximately 40 miles east of Phuc Loi. No trace of the aircraft or crew was found.

However, in my research for this book, I come across the same incident with the same guys only the location is in the far northwest of North Vietnam and to the north of the PDJ and more along the Chinese border. In that case, these guys were probably flying out of Udorn in the CIA's secret war and were running SLAR about a hundred miles further to the north of the PDJ than where I had over a hundred night missions. In that case, they may have been brought down by an SA-2 SAM, but more likely they were jumped by Soviet MiGs the North Vietnamese were flying, and as such was the same fate as some other 20th ASTA/131st guys we know we lost to MiGs. I suggest this because the SAMs were mostly kept in and around Hanoi and Haiphong harbor or down the coast towards Vinh, where the other account of this loss indicated.

If so, the Army would have manufactured the account of a SAM downing the Mohawk on an RP-2 mission off the coast rather than give information about our years of CIA operations up against the Chinese border.

During Lam Son 719 in the spring of 1971 I took a SAM missile in southern North Vietnam while flying an IR night mission. I was the only other 131st pilot to engage a SAM successfully and supposedly one of only two US aircraft not equipped with an active ECM or radar jammer to evade a SAM. The other aircraft was an Air Force OV-10 that engaged a SAM and successfully escaped it about ten days after I did.

3-18 / STILL ANOTHER MOHAWK IR/VR AIRCRAFT LOST IN LAOS - (2-FATAL/MIA)

14 July 1966 - Lt. Col. Robert Nopp (43)
SSG Marshall Kipina (33)
OV-1C #61-2875

They were on a night, single-aircraft IR mission in southern Laos and simply never returned.

3-19 / TWO MOHAWK GUNSHIPS LOST IN LAOS ON SAME MISSION - (2-FATAL/MIA, 2-RESCUED)

6 April 1966 - Captain James Gates (43)
Captain John Lafayette (34)
OV-1A in Laos #63-13117

6 April 1966 - Captain Harry Duensing
SP4 Larry Johnson
OV-1A in Laos #63-1316

20th ASTA - A then MAC-V mission as a predecessor to becoming the 131st SAC.

In the spring of 1966, the 20th ASTA was under the direct operational control of MAC-V Headquarters in Saigon, and it was represented that although the other three men were assigned to the 20th ASTA, Captain Lafayette was assigned to the Operations Directorate (J-3), MAC-V Headquarters. Interesting.

The two aircraft, with Duensing as lead, proceeded west toward Laos, checking in with *Hillsboro*, the Air Force EC-130 airborne command post aircraft.

Hillsboro matched the Mohawks with two Forward Air Controllers who would help work the recon mission. Shortly before five p.m., Hillsboro received Mayday calls from *both Mohawks*: Captain Duensing was downed by anti-aircraft fire, and when Captain Gates took a position overhead he too was hit and downed.

Ah, shit . . .

Search and rescue efforts began at once, and by 5:30 PM the FACs had located both crash sites and established radio contact with all four crew members. They were about a kilometer apart on the lower slopes of a hill some 9 kilometers inside Laos. At approximately 6:15 PM Captain Lafayette radioed that enemy troops were closing in on him and Gates and they were in imminent danger of capture. Shortly after that radio contact was lost. While Gates and Lafayette could not be rescued, the two crewmen from 63-13116 were picked up by an Air Force SAR helicopter.

Gates and Lafayette were classed as Missing in Action and were continued in that status until the Secretary of the Army approved Presumptive Findings of Death for them, Lafayette on 15 Nov 1973 and Gates on 28 Oct 1977. Their remains have not been repatriated.

None of the 20th ASTA/131st crewmembers captured or missing in Laos were recovered after the war. **None of them.**

3-20 / MOHAWK GUNSHIP DOWN IN LAOS
(2-FATAL/MIA)

15 March 1966 - Major Glenn McElroy
Captain John Nash (29)
OV-1A #63-13124

Flak hit this aircraft, and it crashed while searching for another Mohawk crash site. This sad event then involved the loss of *four Mohawks* and *all the crewmembers* in March and April of 1966 with the searching aircraft being shot down in both cases and losing all the crewmembers in each instance.

3-21 / MOHAWK LOST ON IR FLIGHT IN LAOS
(2-FATAL/MIA)

9 January 1966 - Captain Thaddeus Williams Jr. (23)
SP4 James Schimberg (24)

OV-1C #61-2705

Aircraft was on an IR flight when communications were lost, and the aircraft disappeared due to unknown causes and no good location.

3-22 / CHINOOK CRASH NEAR PHU BAI - (MANY FATAL)

I had come off a SLAR mission to North Vietnam on a bright day, was handed off to Phu Bai approach control and started a radar vector for an extended downwind and long final. ATC was trying to sequence me into a series of inbounds so extending the downwind was not an issue. Underneath me, some flights of helicopters, including Chinooks, were maneuvering downwind and would eventually turn onto a right base leg and come for final approach aligning to the helicopter ramp area on the east side of the runway.

Nothing seemed out of the norm that day. The Phu Bai approach plates and military airport directory did have a warning that aircraft may be fired upon in the traffic pattern, but that warning was standard across our part of the country. There was always some guy out there with an AK-47 firing, and occasionally maybe a light machine gun (.30 cal), but it was rare. Mostly we would just see *sparklers* on approach at night. No big deal.

I was about three miles out on my final approach, in good weather, and Phu Bai approach control asks if I see any smoke or aircraft on the right downwind? Nope, nothing in sight. He then turns me off final to the right and says there is a Chinook *down* on the downwind and if I can see it. By then there is smoke billowing up, and

I make a wider right turn and maneuver so that I can come down with the burning Chinook on my left side, watching for other helicopter traffic that was converging on the scene.

What happened? This was a good weather day, midday as it was with no other indication of gunfire and no trouble call on the radio. The Chinook was maybe a half-mile off the east side of the runway, burning. Was he shot down? No calls and no indication of gunfire and apparently no witnesses, even as this was the airport traffic pattern.

There was something like over 30 dead in the wreckage, and I never heard what the cause was. I did some research for this book, and it was perhaps a mechanical failure of one of the transmissions and the Chinook suddenly went over inverted and exploded, killing everyone. Not for sure that was the accident. I do not think it was gunfire that day.

Like any given day, any given time, any given event, things happen—horrific things by any measure—and one just moves on hardly without a glance. Dwelling, in reality, is not a good thing to be doing for your mental state of mind.

3-23 / HEAD INTO THE PROPELLER AFTER EMERGENCY LANDING - (1-FATAL)

This terrible accident did not happen to us at Phu Bai, but one of my flight school classmates in another Mohawk unit had gone on a maintenance test flight as the pilot and with a senior maintenance guy (senior is like maybe 25 years old or so) went along to run some in-flight engine tests.

Whatever else was right or wrong was set aside as when they came back the landing gear would not lower hydraulically and lock down. They tried whatever other means they had, cycling the gear, rudder slamming or whatever, but the landing gear was not coming down.

The backup to the hydraulic gear lowering is a high-pressure air bottle that routes past the hydraulics to the lowering mechanism and pushes the gear down. It is a one-time blow down of the gear.

They pulled the gear blow down handle; the blow down worked fine, and they had three green landing gear lights showing a safe gear down and locked condition. They went ahead and landed without problems. The procedure at that point is to shut down the aircraft and have someone come out and retrieve the gear lock pins, located in the left side underbelly compartment, and safety pin all three gears.

With both engines shut down, a man takes the gear pins with the long red flags and inserts them on the main and nose gear. A tow vehicle is there to pull the aircraft off the runway. Even taxiing an aircraft after a gear blow down is too risky and unless it was an urgent recovery of other aircraft, a few minutes on the runway, engines shut down, is all it took to set the pins, hook up the tow bar and take the aircraft away. That was apparently not what they did.

With the engines still running and the props swinging dangerously close to the cockpit, the maintenance guy got out through his right side cockpit hatch window, right in front of the moving right engine propeller. He then went around the nose of the aircraft, around the outside of the left wing and from behind the wing and engine and retrieved the gear lock pins himself from the belly holding bags. He then carefully, from behind, inserted the left main gear locking pin and then also secured the nose gear pin in place.

Then somehow, distracted as this event has happened other times with private and commercial aircraft, while safety-pinning the right main landing gear, distracted, maybe even mesmerized by the moving propeller and the noise: his head was taken off, and parts of him were instantly inside the cockpit in a surreal, bloody mess.

As the pilot, you do not easily get over these things like you would a crash or shoot down death. This death is right there, right then, right in your face.

In all fairness, we all routinely had right-seaters climbing in and out of the cockpit with the right engine running just feet from them and mixed with the flickering effect of a moving propeller this could have been any one of us.

Chapter 4

TIDBITS AND OTHER SCREW-UPS

4-1 / THE BENGAL TIGER IN THE 131ST COMPOUND

It was a night when one of the most bizarre and strange events of our part of the war happened. On that *first night*, one of our unit's internal guards had come running to the Orderly Room saying there was a tiger—a tiger down near the motor pool. I think his weapon was carefully taken from him, and of course, no tiger was found.

We had the tiger inside our little 131st only compound at Phu Bai

The base at Phu Bai was never *secured,* so we had three layers of minefields around the airfield and more concertina wire to stop intruders. Inside the airfield were about eight smaller unit compounds, like ours, secured again with their own minefields and wire. The internal compounds were patrolled at the unit level, around the hooches, mess hall and the motor pool area. Getting to our internal compound would take much doing by any enemy—but this was different.

> *The next day, sure enough, there were tiger tracks around the motor pool.*
>
> *Big tiger tracks!*

We did not have another encounter for several days and nights; Then about three nights later this big Bengal Tiger, perhaps over 400 pounds as they were known to be, had come from wherever it was hiding, then walked through the motor pool area that was only 40 yards to our unit mess hall and was there digging for food. This time, a lot of people came out and saw this huge tiger. The mess hall was surrounded on three sides by rows of NCO and enlisted soldier hooches, so this big cat was right in the midst of our compound and wandering around.

Sadly, within days, the cat was flushed out of the hiding area down and behind our motor pool and killed. A picture of this magnificent animal was in the Stars and Stripes military paper showing it hanging from the front end of a forklift. It was huge. So sad to see it gone. Surely it was a mystery how something this large had worked its way through the primary perimeter mine fields, to our area, and through our internal minefields.

4-2 / RATS IN THE COCKPIT ON TAKEOFF

This event could have ended dreadfully in flight. As it was, this was a large rat—*and we had many rats everywhere*—but this one that had somehow found its way into the cockpit of a SLAR aircraft that had been sitting in the maintenance hangar for many months awaiting parts. It was now time to put the plane together and back into service.

The aircraft had been a *Hangar Queen* for many months and was cannibalized for parts. It was holding down the floor and pushed against the back wall of the hangar. Maybe that had something to do with the events.

Engines were now put on to the aircraft; ground tests run, and a brief flight test was conducted. Everything seemed well, so the plane is scheduled for a sensor mission test flight and moved out of the hangar and prepped with SLAR film for a local flight.

The taxi out to the runway was okay. Lucky for them. An engine run-up is completed, and Phu Bai tower gave clearance to move into position on the runway and hold for a takeoff clearance. They just never quite got there. As the pilot moved the few yards from the power-up area to enter the runway the right-seater, the TO, started yelling in the mike, unfastening his harness and opening the right side hatch (with the right side engine running). His intention was to leave—*now!*

There was one of Phu Bai's finest, an enormous, hideous, **rat** that came out from under the right side SLAR console and up between the TO's knees and was staring the TO in the face, only maybe a foot away. Pretty ugly.

The pilot immediately shut down both engines. The guys both made a hasty exit, and the aircraft towed back to the hangar. Not sure when it ever did fly again, or who was ultimately tasked with doing a very intensive search through the cockpit and under the floors looking for the rat—or maybe that Mohawk did just continue to live back in the corner of the hanger.

4-3 / THE ISSUE OF FEAR

Fear is more dangerous than all the enemy guns, maintenance screw ups.

This is always the real enemy you had to face.

We were all volunteers to be sure. My *first fear* was that the war would be over before I got to go to Vietnam. I had been working as an 18-year old bush pilot in South America, Brazil mostly, in 1968 after I ferried a single-engine Cessna 205 from Washington State to Brasilia, the then very new wilderness capital of Brazil. I had worked alone in nine countries and spent time sleeping in my airplane at remote or abandoned places in the Amazon basin like Amapa, or Belem, Carolina and the Plateau of Bahia in Brazil. When I came back, I knew I had to be an Army pilot, in the fight, and in the action.

We all knew that fear is the biggest enemy of all. We tried to ignore it, *as men do anyway*, and to make light of it—*as we knew we had to*.

When someone died or went missing, we had a rather macabre sense of gallows humor almost immediately. *We had to*, for we might be next, and *the next* might be in the same place on the same mission against the same guns in what, a few days? Tomorrow? How about a few hours? Fear could eat you alive, or your fear could eat up someone else that may already have been on the edge. Or, your personal fear in the almost constant fight-or-flight responses of being in combat could cause the death of others.

Flying low-level IR in the PDJ or Steel Tiger was a good example of dealing with your hidden fear, as you were flying directly into the mouth of the beast. As you flew towards your target area, you could see the streaming rows of flak tracers weaving back and forth across the sky. Usually, multiple guns were firing at someone. This was *not* the intensity of the flak covering the skies around Hanoi or Haiphong, but it only took one of these to end your days.

So as you moved toward your target area, you had some time to contemplate, to get your nerve up, and to ensure that your state of mind was not becoming *your enemy*. A cigarette, or two, was helpful at the time.

However, once the anti-aircraft gunfire started then your personal fight-or-flight responses jumped in with a massive dose of adrenaline flowing through your veins. It was always the fight response you had to have, for, as a rule, you had to continue to press the attack. This is no different from getting the soldiers, or even the sports teams, to be yelling or throwing their hands in the air and more yelling. Adrenaline is the drug to your brain that ran the rest of you. It instantly made you sharp, alert, physically and mentally at your best game—and your best game was usually to fight, not flight.

It was a game then, a very deadly game, that you could out fly what they threw up at you. You could anticipate the next round of flak guns. You could deny them—*you could win*—whatever winning means. And you might as well have had a medical drip of adrenaline going directly into your arm.

When at last you came out of a dark and dangerous valley on your last target from a night of IR flying it was, like WOW! Wow! And you turned for home. You had won—*again*! You had not beaten *them*, but you had overcome your own fears. You had stayed on target. You had not cut-and-run with some excuse. You were home free and by the time you got back you were pumped up, drunk without a drop of alcohol in your system!

The issue was, for us, that you usually could not turn and fly away: you needed to press the mission. If you left, then someone else was going to have to go and refly your mission—which did not bode well with the other pilots. So you needed to, except in the most extreme situation, use the *fight* part of the fight-or-flight response and press ahead.

A terrible night flying IR in Steel Tiger or the PDJ would be one where *no one shot at you!* That was horrible. Typically, once the shooting had started you knew what you faced, pretty much how many guns and what types there were, and your skill level then. But to go over and over on targets when you *knew* there were guns and no one shot at you was troubling. You were on the edge—sometimes for hours, waiting, waiting to face this, and it never came up to fight you.

When you got home from one of these, you are emotionally beat. You had been denied your much needed, and well deserved adrenaline fix, and you were feeling like some junkie without his fix.

My best defense from fear was hours and hours of mission planning, target strip-by-target strip all made into little 5-1/2 x 8-inch sheets and put on my right kneeboard with the lead-ins, the terrain, the guns, the various *Oh shit* possibilities on each target and which way to go if in trouble. There was nothing like being prepared when you could be.

4-4 / SEABOARD WORLD DC-8 ACCIDENTALLY LANDS AT MARBLE MOUNTAIN ARMY AIRFIELD - AT NIGHT!

This is a great story! Our somewhat short 4,300-foot and narrow runway at Marble Mountain was considered a bit tight and short even for our Mohawks, and I do not recall ever seeing even an Air Force C-130 land there.

This had happened in the months before I arrived in Vietnam on my first tour. In 1969 a *Seaboard World* stretch DC-8 airliner, carrying a full load of R&R guys, made a night approach to DaNang and when they came out of the clouds, angled I think away from a straight-in to the very long, twin runways at DaNang AFB, the pilot's attention caught the runway lights at Marble Mountain—located a couple of miles to the east of the DaNang AFB. They were cleared to land, but over four miles to the west at DaNang AFB. It was about two a.m. when this happened.

The copilot was flying and mistook the lights of the Marble Mountain runway and made what has to be an incredible, *absolutely incredible*, landing and stopping on the short Army runway—one that even we in the Mohawk had to be very careful of. He came to a stop at the end of the airfield, just 21 feet from the end. Passengers said he used full maximum reverse thrust right to the very end to keep from overrunning the runway.

Usually, an aircraft like a Mohawk would be working from a 5,000 to 6,000-foot runway: We had less than 4,300 feet, and it was narrow besides.

What to do now? The passengers were bused over to DaNang AFB. Over the next hours, the aircraft was first completely unloaded, then defueled down to what would be the very minimum needed to get off the ground for a five-minute flight over to DaNang AFB.

On the next morning, an hour before noon, as the aircraft not be turned around, they used a large ground tug that was brought over from DaNang AFB and towed the DC-8 backward to the approach end of the runway. The wings hung wide over the sides of the narrow runway and could suck up gravel into the engines.

If you Google **DC-8 Lands at Marble Mountain** there are a couple of YouTube videos of this event and some discussion boards too.

Does the pilot get punished for being so careless and reckless to have landed at the wrong airport—*a really wrong airport*, or does he get the fantastic flying award of 1969 for that landing?

I should imagine that right there, on short final, committed to landing as they were—that something along the line of—

Ah, shit . . .

. . . *May* have been uttered. The copilot had made the landing.

4-5 / THIS IDIOT (ME) DIVES ON TIGER ISLAND OFF THE COAST OF NORTH VIETNAM

A classic example of utter stupidity—something I undoubtedly excelled at over time. When we flew SLAR on RP-1 off the coast of North Vietnam, our primary starting point was at *Tiger Island*, a mostly uninhabited small island just to the north of the DMZ and about 8-12 miles out from the coast. That was the starting point as we turned then to the northwest and started our first mission leg.

All I had ever seen of the island from overflying at 10,000 feet was an occasional fishing boat, or what looked like fishing boats.

On this particular flight, I had a first-time new to our unit SLAR TO in the right seat. It was daylight in good weather and visibility. After we had run our three turns on RP-1 and were about to head home, my new guy was asking about Tiger Island just below us. I had some answers, I thought, and being a bit of an idiot *show off* at the time; I decided to dive down and do a pass around the island before heading to the DMZ and back to Phu Bai. What could go wrong? With me flying—*everything actually*.

I started a left rolling and diving turn, keeping Tiger Island out of my window and down to the left. I rolled over about 120 degrees and was careful to keep a positive G-force so that the liquids in the old SLAR system film developer tray did not spill as I went in for the kill—*err*, the run around the island.

I had come down to maybe 3,000 feet just off the shore and sure enough, only fishing boats—until I got around one bend and then the basketball sized .51 cal tracers started coming past us in a steady stream. There was a North Vietnamese gunboat on patrol that I had not seen, and I was his new target.

What an idiot I had been (and, sadly, often continued to be for a few more years)! I rolled to the right diving toward the ocean to mask our profile and put my tail to the tracers and headed low and out to the open sea.

Nothing more was said of this, but I had no idea how I would have explained large bullet holes in a SLAR aircraft that was supposedly at 10,000 feet over the ocean?

4-6 / MY ASSIGNMENT AS THE 131ST STANDARDIZATION INSTRUCTOR PILOT

Event Note: In early to mid-1971 I was back in the states for only a few months between combat tours. I had gone through Ft. Hood and then almost directly to the Mohawk Instructor Pilot School at Ft. Rucker. I was back in the 131st with many of the same guys in less than six months.

The Mohawk units had, or at least we did, 2-3 instructor pilots (IPs). One of them was designated as the unit's Standardization Instructor Pilot (SIP), a position that had overall responsibility for training new pilots; not only as group pilots but also to provide the mission and AO training.

As a side note, when I retired in 1996 I was a Mohawk IP & SIP in both a US Army NG Mohawk unit *and* the Argentina Army Mohawk unit outside of Buenos Aires. I retired with both US Army and Argentina Army Master Aviator Wings. I had also been an Army Special Forces IP/SIP in the C-7 Caribou and C-23 Sherpa, a converted Shorts 330—*and the box it came in*.

Arriving back in Phu Bai in the fall of 1971 I was refreshed in the new OV-1D models and their systems and operationally put back into flying night IR missions, my specialty as it was. No one, and I mean, **NO ONE**, wanted to fly IR missions.

Within a few weeks, I was assigned as one of the three 131st IPs and started doing routine checkouts, annual flight checks, and some new pilot work. Not long after that, one night I was taken aside at the Spud Club and the CO told me I was now assigned as the 131st SIP, a position usually reserved for a commissioned major or at least a very senior captain. It was the CO's reasoning perhaps that gave some light. If you have already read some of this book, then you know that I excelled at screw-ups and close calls usually of my making, not so much as being a show off, but as someone that was always pushing the envelope, as it was.

That night the CO said he was making me the SIP because, as he put it, night-after-night I was in the club admitting to doing some the most stupid things either operationally or with the aircraft—and surviving it. We had had a string, a long and enduring string you see in this book, of accidents, many of them fatal, and other flying troubles with some of the pilots.

What the CO wanted, he said, was that I could come in, talk about my screw ups, without the embarrassment *that was so justly deserved*, and then go on. The CO felt that my willingness to be so open, so admitting, so frank—*plus skilled as I was for sure*—could be what was needed to draw out the other pilots with their problems—of which flying the aircraft was only part of the issues. Many of the flying troubles and accidents, I felt anyway, were from personal issues including self-doubt, *fear*, and often knowing they are in over their heads with this aircraft and the nature of the missions we were flying.

So it was that at 22-years old I was holding the most senior flight position, the 131st SIP, overseeing two other IPs and deciding on both our flight and operational mission training and qualifications and what pilots would be qualified, and trained, to fly certain missions. Clearly, all of them were okay for RP-1 SLAR missions, and usually fine for routine SLAR/IR combo boxes in Steel Tiger South and some to the north, nearer to Tchepone.

Fewer were ever allowed to go live in Udorn and fly SLAR or IR in the PDJ. Ultimately, the issue was both IR and VR in Laos, both of them incredibly dangerous and requiring not just exceptional skills, but also an absolute focus and concentration on the mission at hand, especially the IR tasks, down low in the mountains at night and under gunfire.

As time went by, and particularly in the end for me, I had morphed into some sort of a protector of the unqualified or the ones with wives and kids and I often found myself flying more and more of the most dangerous missions—*often more than one a day/night*—while some guys that should not be flying with us at all were flying only 2-3 flights a week, and those often were simple RP-1 SLAR missions.

4-7 / THIS JUST HAD TO HAPPEN - AIR FORCE GUYS LOST

It was just another night coming back up from the southern Steel Tiger box I had worked with my IR ship. I had overstayed my welcome working tank targets and while my high bird, the SLAR aircraft headed home I had dropped into Pleiku AFB to pick up some spare fuel. I was now angling back towards DaNang when I heard a fascinating exchange between a flight of four Air Force jets.

F-4 Phantom used in Vietnam. The USAF lost 445 F-4s in Vietnam, with 382 of them being direct combat losses.

Mindful, that this was in the night, with the aircraft's running lights out; this Air Force flight had apparently just reformed and was heading back to DaNang AFB. When they came up on the ATC controller's frequency with a *Flight Check*, or whatever the Air Force might call it, when a group of aircraft, two or more, come over onto another frequency and check to affirm that each aircraft is on the same frequency.

Usually, the check-in might go something like this, supposing it was a flight of four (unusual, but has happened) of our Mohawks using the call sign Spud. The flight leader would have, before changing frequencies, have made a call on their private channel to go to Button 4, or 12, or whatever preset the new frequency is. Then, a moment later before the lead aircraft has called ATC, he would have ensured the other aircraft are on the frequency—

"*Spud Check . . .*"

—Would come from the flight leader, usually the front aircraft initiating the call and expecting an *in-sequence* response such as—

"Spud 2..."

"Spud 3..." and

"Spud 4..."

Each of us, and probably the other Services too, had personalized Call Signs; mine usually being *Spud 22*. When running a group or formation flight you would have been assigned a flight sequence number at the dispatch planning time so, in some flight missions while my call sign used if I broke away, would be Spud 22, my mission call sign might be Spud 2. Alternatively, a flight may be given a call sign only for that flight, such as HoBo flight and then I might be *HoBo Leader* during the joint part of the flight and Hobo 22 when on my own. Using a non-related mission call sign might be helpful in confusing an enemy as to what type of aircraft the flight is.

Here, on this night, early in the post-midnight, time I hear this Air Force flight checking in—

"DaNang Approach...

HoBo flight...

A flight of four is checking in."

Then from the cockpit of the pilot who *thought he* was the flight leader—

"HoBo Check"

The lead aircraft making a call in the blind to be sure the others came over to DaNang approach control and are on his wing, even if in the darkness, and everyone is running with lights out; he cannot see them.

"HoBo 2..."

—The pilot whom apparently **thinks** he is in a formation with the leader, HoBo 1. He is likely really tucked in with Hobo 4 under his wing, and only Hobo 4, instead.

"HoBo 3..."

—The pilot that thinks he is sitting on the wing of Hobo 2.

There is silence for a bit. An awkward silence to be sure.

HoBo lead breaks the deafening silence—

"Hobo 4, **where are you?**"

Silence.

There are more seconds of *deafening silence* until this rather squeaky, meek, awkward, *Oh shit response . . .*

"I thought I was the flight leader, Sir."

Ah, shoot! This is way too funny.

About that time, I figure that Hobo leader has risked cranking his neck back and finding out there is ***no one on his wing***. No one. He is alone, and Hobo 2 is likely tucked onto the wing of Hobo 4, not on HoBo leader, who must think *he is leading the return flight home* (not unusual to switch and might explain the confusion).

4-8 / RECON THE DESTROYED CAMBODIAN BRIDGES

Typically, we only operated in Laos and North Vietnam until the near end of the war, but I did get a flight request to go south, to Saigon, Bien Hoa specifically, for a special MACV mission.

All of our missions were *secret,* but I must have been in someone's occasional good graces to have pulled this particular assignment. This required a *three-night stay in Air Force transient officer quarters*, with a *real bed* with a *real mattress* and eating *real food* that was not hot dogs for breakfast, lunch and dinner as was sometimes the fare at Phu Bai.

There were all four of the other Mohawk units closer to the mission area, specifically, the 73rd to do this mission, but I suppose that because it was outside of South Vietnam, that the 131st, the only unit *officially* flying outside of South Vietnam, was tasked by MACV HQ to go into Cambodia.

It was a milk run to be sure. Over a couple of days flying, only about three hours a day, I flew daylight VR flights with cameras along roads in Cambodia. I was tasked to take pictures of the bridges on that route. At that point, they were all but a couple already down or destroyed. I suspect the mission reasoning was that someone wanted to see if the tank flows from the southern end of Laos into Cambodia and then attacking into III and IV Corp was being stopped. We would do anything for a real night's sleep, on real beds and real food. Such were the times then. I milked this mission for as many days of sleep, food and drink, some shopping in a real PX, as I could muster.

Then it was back to cold, rain-soaked wooden huts, no mattress beds, nightly mortar attacks, hot dogs (or some mystery meat to be sure) at sometimes for all three meals.

4-9 / DRUG CONTROL OFFICER

Drugs were everywhere.

By early in my first tour I was already a drug addict—but my drug of choice was *adrenaline* while so many others were less fortunate.

The penalty for being the unit's youngest officer was that somehow I got tapped to be the *Drug Control Officer* on both tours. The primary function is watching guys pee into a bottle and making sure it was not something hidden they were using.

4/ Tidbits and Other Screw-Ups

This is also interesting in other ways. For example, whenever there were these random drug raids on the enlisted guy's hooches, usually by the NCOs, the loot from the raids would be taken to my hooch.

In the weeks following an NCO-led drug raid, my hooch would look to be the very envy of the most notorious drug dealers of our worst cities. I would have the standard rows and rows of bags of pot, to be sure, but the main haul was always heroin—and a lot of it and very pure stuff compared to what was in the States.

Oh, there was LSD around, usually sent by marking some part of a letter from home with liquid drops and then one would just eat that part of the letter—*a bit hard to detect for sure.*

The Vietnamese were getting the GIs hooked on heroin, strong heroin, by lacing marihuana cigarettes with traces of heroin and then throwing free smokes over the fences. It did not take long to get someone that would never, ever, think of using hard drugs to become a heroin addict and from there it was a short—very short—step to free basting and injecting heroin. *Just that quick—and that easy.*

There was a mechanic guy, a draftee to be sure, from New York that had been a long time heroin user and he became my source on the ins-and-outs of the drug world, such as where to find the stuff hidden in our guy's rooms. What he *really* wanted was for me to recommend him to be sent back to the states for excessive drug use, which I would not do: he was clearly too valuable to me for what he could do and help with. He was a nice young man, and after he did go back, I later got a neat letter from him. Still a drug user, but someone I had changed his opinion of the officer group.

The most notable incident for my drugs was after I had been working in Udorn for a few days and came back to be met literally at the aircraft—before I was even out of the cockpit—to go immediately to the CO's office.

In my then hooch, I had a young non-pilot first lieutenant intelligence officer as a roommate. This guy liked to burn incense; particularly when I was gone. There had been another NCO-led drug raid, and a lot of narcotics had been found and taken to—well, to the Drug Officer, *me*, at my hooch—only I was not there of course. So the NCOs left this vast new stash of drugs, including maybe thirty or so nickel or dime (as they were called for $5 or $10) caps of heroin and a few pounds probably of pot in dozens of bags. And of course, my roommate had been running his usual incense burning because I was gone for a few days. *This was then a perfect storm of trouble.*

It seemed that somewhere in that time span my CO was visited by a higher up from the battalion and they wanted to talk to me, as the flight unit SIP, about some flight standards issues—so they went to my hooch thinking they might find me there. **Major mistake.**

My CO is telling me the story—*and he was not happy*. He had this colonel in tow and walked into my hooch, apparently reeking of this odor of burning incense like an Asian heroin den of *Edger Allan Poe* days and besides the smell hanging heavy in the musty air of our small hooch, was that all over my tables and window shelf was a drug dealer's dream of a stash of tremendous value. *Huge*.

On my side of the small room were these rows and rows of small plastic *caps* of heroin, hashish, and lots of marijuana in all sizes of bags. As the NCOs would make small raids they would just come by my hooch and toss it all onto my table and leave.

Well, I was good at collecting this stuff, mostly because my NY City mechanic, a pretty heavy heroin user himself was coaching me on where druggies were likely to stash their goods and who was buying the drugs. But I had no plan or guidance on how to dispose of all this. It just piled up in my hooch and with my roommate being one of these incense-burning guys, popular in those days and harmless, the overall scene looked like something out of a 70's roadie drug movie.

4-10 / Sending The New Pilots and TOs Back Home

This was the summer of 1972 and was just a few weeks before I was medevac'd out of Marble Mountain. The 245th SAC, our sister unit that had been at Marble Mountain and then moved over to DaNang, had been shut down and sent home the year before. The 245th flew missions in I Corps so when they shipped home is when we took over our first in-country missions in late 1971.

By this time, mid-1972, the end was near—*and we all knew it*. With the 245th gone we had an excess of people. As it was, then several assignment officers from the Pentagon showed up for a few days of briefings and to interview mostly just the line pilots and TOs—the mission critical people—to decide about a reduction-in-force and who would go home early. This did not work out as we had hoped. They did the interviews and then left before they sent back the cuts they were ordering. That sequence was probably for their own personal protection as the recommendations were not what some had expected, nor felt fair.

I had volunteered to stay over on my first tour, but that was denied to the officers, and I had returned to Vietnam just months later after my few months of Mohawk IP training, so I had no reason to complain about being there—it had been my choice to come back so soon.

As one might have expected, all the new guys were being sent home *immediately*. A few had been there only a month or so and maybe had not even flown any combat missions. Those were the ones that got the ticket home. If you were on your second, or third tour (I think we did have one third-tour guy), and I was on my second, then you were staying. The logic was right, for them, the missions were so very dangerous that to send home the experienced guys, and hold back those that already had a few hundred combat missions, was the only real outcome to be expected.

In our view, there should have been at least a cash bonus payment like there was for extending, which I think at the time was something like $10,000—a fortune then—to stay for another six-month tour. They should have done something like that for the ones that involuntarily stayed so the new guys could go home.

4-11 / DUMPING THE 131ST COMPOUND DOGS INTO THE OCEAN

Tears to my eyes just to look at this.

Not sure if this came before, or after, the grenade fragging of the 131st officer's shower, but we had a deadly kill day for many dogs that had been living in our compound and that had often slept with the enlisted guys. Various diseases were rampant, while fleas and other nasty things were passed to the guys that often slept with the dogs. Plus, there were other issues with the dogs too. With the rats in and around the hooches, the other health problem was moving plague from rat to dog to the guys that were taking care of them.

The command had tried to clean up the compound a number of times and then started to put restrictions on the stray dogs, most of which were very mangy looking and not exactly like the one you would want to share your bed with anyway.

The cleanups just did not do the job, and warnings went nowhere. One day the officers were briefed just before the NCOs started a roundup of the dogs, just in case there was going to be any violence, and apparently there was some of that.

With hundreds of thousands of people dying, horribly, still the images of helpless dogs.

The senior NCOs started a new dog sweep about mid-morning as most of the guys were out of their hooches and working, but of course, word spread very quickly, and the confrontations started.

Previous attempts to just remove the dogs had not worked and this time, the dogs were loaded into a truck on the flight line and driven away only to be put onto a helicopter and taken out over the ocean and dumped. This apparently did not sit well with the enlisted guys, not at all.

Chapter 5

THE 131ST MISSIONS AND AREAS OF OPERATIONS

There were five Mohawk units sent to Vietnam—one for each of the Corps: I Corps at the DMZ in the North down to IV Corps in the far south. The last unit, the 20th ASTA/131st Aviation Company, later changed to the 131st Military Intelligence Company, was flying the only armed Mohawks (rockets and machine guns).

Our area of operations was *entirely* outside of South Vietnam; covering North Vietnam, all of the central and southern Laos, and northern Laos in the CIA's Secret War along (or into) the Chinese border. This was our mission status right until the end of the war when the 131st took over some I Corps missions, and the 245th Surveillance Airplane Company was removed from DaNang in late 1971.

"Someday the World Will Know What a Bunch of Army Pilots in Black Flight Suits Really Did"

- Spud Club Wall with Names

*"Spud IR - We Will Go Anywhere-**Once!**"*

- On the Wall at our CIA Operations Offices at the Udorn RTAFB

5-1 / THE 131ST WAS COMPLETELY UNIQUE

When the 131st SAC converted from just a detachment (20th ASTA), then with about 16 aircraft, many of them being the armed OV-1As, they had lost—in a single year to combat and crashes—a staggering 28 Mohawks and dozens of crewmembers were dead, MIA, or injured spread across Laos and North Vietnam.

Here is a cut from the annual official report records, for just one of the years

Link to Official Unit History from 1966

http://www.OV-1.com/131st_AVN/131st-history66-a.html

"Flight hours for the first seven months of the company's history totaled some 5,638 hours of combat time. The Night Hawks have compiled an extremely noteworthy record. Many individual awards have been presented and several others are pending approval by higher headquarters. These include 33 awards for valor, 20 awards for meritorious achievement, 320 awards for sustained aerial operations against the enemy, and 23 purple hearts.

Although the Night Hawks have an outstanding record of achievement, they have paid dearly for their accomplishments in both personnel and aircraft losses.

In Less Than Seven Months

Combat operations have claimed 13 crewmembers killed or missing in action. In addition, 10 crewmembers have been wounded in action.

Aircraft losses have included 6 OV-1A', 20 OV-1B's, and 2 OV-1C's.

Also, aircraft have received over sixty ground fire hits during the year.

The 131st Aviation Company (AS) has compiled an enviable record of performance. Intelligence furnished by this unit has proven invaluable in the conduct of combat operations. With a continuation of the unit's past record, it can be assured of an important position in the history of the United States Army in Vietnam."

In just these seven months the 131st lost 28 aircraft and 13 KIA/MIA and 11 more guys missing or wounded. That was a Mohawk a week and one crewmember dead or MIA or wounded every week.

* * The number of OV-1B aircraft lost by the 20th ASTA (20) seems too high based on my research of the loss of tail-numbered Mohawks. * *

5-2 / About The Missions - We Flew Alone, Mostly

Unlike many aviation units, when one flew a mission, other than an armed attack flight with an OV-1A, it was usually as a single aircraft. Nightly we flew three SLAR/IR combo combat missions in hunter/killer teams with Air Force AC-130 *Spectre* gunships in the south of Laos, and AC-119 *Stinger* gunships in extreme northern Laos, near the Chinese border in the CIA's Secret War in Northern Laos.

While we might have worked as a team on those missions, each IR mission aircraft was actually flying alone, often many miles apart with the SLAR ship, which was usually flying at around 10,000 feet above the ground while the IR ship, doing point spotting of targets called down from the SLAR ship, would be dodging, *or not*, trees and mountains and facing the endless anti-aircraft fire and flak.

We flew eight daily individual SLAR missions just a few miles off the southern coast of North Vietnam in what was known as Route Pack-1 (RP-1), which I later found was sometimes called Route Package-1. Before my arrival in early 1970, we had flown RP-2 up to points northeast of Vinh and just south of the North Vietnam harbor city of Haiphong. The Soviet SA-2 SAM missiles and MiG issues had caused us to move our 24/7 SLAR missions down to just RP-1.

In Laos, other than the SLAR/IR combos in the extreme north, usually to the north of the Laotian Plain of Jars (PDJ), we often flew solo IR missions in the southern part of North Vietnam: usually close to the DMZ, and all over Laos, and flew daytime VR (photo recon) missions in the armed OV-1As, *everywhere* else.

The solo IR missions into southern North Vietnam, all over the Ho Chi Minh Trail in the south of Laos, and nightly in the CIA secret war in extreme northern Laos, were flown against targets, spot or strip runs, determined by higher intelligence entities. The IR film was then taken back to be read out for examination of points of interests, versus the SLAR/IR hunter/killer teams that worked targets we were attacking right on the very mission—in real time.

As a result of this mixture of secret missions and countries, this is likely why we did not have good company records, as the unit was not operating as *unit*, or even a *squad*, or a *flight* as it might be, but as one guy's solo combat mission (or two sometimes) and what they did on that mission.

Because we made many screw-ups, as things may be, our recounting of what we did or met with on a flight of our own was seldom part of any record. Combat awards were an issue as no one was there to see you do something ~~stupid~~, err . . some act of incredible skill and bravery while on a single aircraft combat mission.

One of our night, solo IR combat mission reports from a mission in Steel Tiger North in Laos, near what was known to us as *dirty, deadly,* Tchepone, might have read:

COMBAT MISSION REPORT

131st Avn Co, Phu Bai, I Corps

IR Flight 223 - Steel Tiger North, Laos

~~"There I was, at five-hundred feet, flat on my back, with two MiGs on my ass, a pocket full of nickels and not a coke machine in sight . . ."~~

Err . . .

"There I was, with ~~a~~ two MiGs on my ass, one of which I managed to kill by dragging him into the side of a mountain in the darkness.

The other MiG was destroyed by NVA ground gunners when I cleverly maneuvered him into following me to the heavy and intense fire from at least ~~four~~ six assorted 23 mm, 37 mm & 57 mm flak guns located to the southeast of Tchepone - most of which were filling the sky with hundreds of rounds of exploding flak at any given time.

It is possible that one of the MiGs was lost from the half-dozen or so .51 caliber heavy machine guns working me over, with one of them likely being a track mounted Soviet ZPU-4 quad-.51.

The ECM worked fine, and I was able to engage and dodge two more Soviet SA-2 SAM missiles while coming back home.

I managed to get back home with just six holes in my bird . . .

With that major that sent me . . I'd sure like a word . . ."

Or, a report of this general nature.

I believe our last known *armed VR mission fatal* combat loss was pilot CW2 Jack Brunson, whom I went to WOC flight school with, and with him was our Intel officer, and my Phu Bai hooch mate, Captain Al Musil. Another of our gunships flying with them was not shot down, but we did have dual shoot-downs in this book.

5-3 / THE FATALS WERE TOO MANY

When you start reading through Chapter 3, ***These Ended Really Badly***, you get to taste the flavor of how circumstances had pushed so many brave guys to have ended up dead or missing. So often these fatal events were by flight accidents that we had in this tough aircraft to fly—especially if anything was not working right, like say an *all-too-often* sudden failed engine on takeoff.

If you are a pilot of any sort, you may, at times, find yourself consumed by the anxiety of seeing some of these fatal accidents and the crashes being played out in slow-motion, knowing what the end is going to be, but not for sure how it is getting there.

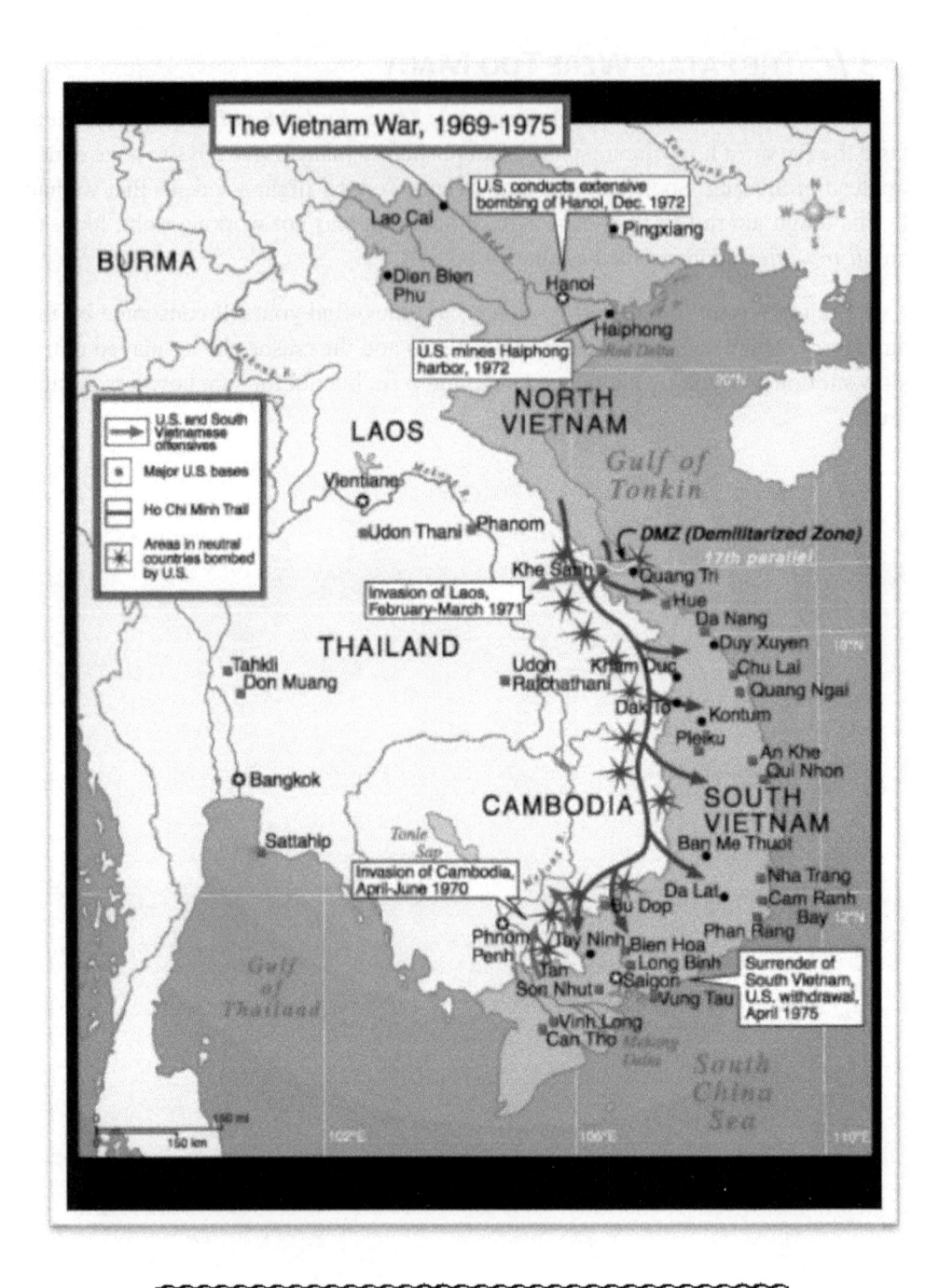

5-4 / NUMBER OF UNIT MISSIONS FLOWN

I could only find the last numbers for 1970, and they showed a high of about 935 missions in one month and a low of just under 600, so averaging maybe 750 missions, which includes all flying in combat and maintenance test flights and admin flights that we might have used one of the Mohawks for. So around 25 flights a day was a decent average.

Right out of the box, eight (24/7) of these missions were off the southern coast of North Vietnam on the RP-1 SLAR flights, then two more were SLAR/IR combo missions on hunter/killer teams with the Air Force AC-130 *Spectre* gunships in Steel Tiger North and South, and another SLAR/IR combo in the PDJ in northern Laos for the CIA missions with Air Force AC-119 *Stinger* gunships. So, about 11, more-or-less, fixed SLAR missions in each 24-hour period.

With just 14 to 18 unit aircraft, and maybe a quarter of them not flyable at any given time, this meant that a plane probably had to fly at least twice a day and with aircraft down a lot we got into the situation of swapping engines between day flights on a SLAR or VR bird to do a night IR flight and then do a single or dual engine change again. Insane! Might want to read the little encounter in this book about the ejection on short final at Phu Bai after a failed night maintenance flight gone badly.

If a SLAR aircraft was down or had problems while flying in RP-1, then another one was immediately launched so we could ensure round-the-clock coverage of the lower part of North Vietnam. If a problem were in Laos on a SLAR/IR combo flight, it would be too late to get another SLAR aircraft out there because the IR ship would not have the fuel to continue. So, if there were any problems on the SLAR aircraft in Laos or the PDJ area, then the mission was down for the night. The IR aircraft would then come home too unless he was also targeted with other specific task runs that were other than just checking out the SLAR *Movers*.

For IR flights, we always had two aircraft with the SLAR/IR hunter/killer missions in Steel Tiger North and South and another one, or sometimes two, in the PDJ. The PDJ missions would have been mostly *untargeted* flights supporting the SLAR targets that were then flown over by the IR aircraft, looked at on the screens in real time, and evaluated for any target information was then called up to the AC-130 *Spectre* (Steel Tiger) or AC-119 *Stinger* gunships (PDJ). Those were the fixed IR flights every night that the monsoons did not stop us. These, while always challenging and dangerous, were over and over in the same area and one could learn the terrain and the anti-aircraft situations.

We usually had 2-3 more IR missions each night that was *specifically targeted,* and these ranged from southern North Vietnam over to the west, past Mu Gia Pass in the Annamite Mountains on the North Vietnam / Laos border far to the west of Dong Ho. I have a Spud Party suit patch of *Ski Mu Gia Pass* that was sort of funny and colorful.

Before my time, the 20th ASTA/131st was running VR and IR missions deeper into the southern parts of North Vietnam, and I think up to the area around Vinh. Our IR and VR missions, in my years, only worked the southern North Vietnam areas during Lam Son 719 and then during the massive tank invasion, or just ahead of it, in 1972 and usually not more than 20-30 km north of the DMZ.

We flew solo IR missions from the area near Mu Gia Pass, on the North Vietnam and Laos border, and then down through *anywhere* in Laos and often right through where the SLAR/IR combo flight were working. Those missions were combinations of spot targets, something the folks above wanted to look at on IR film, to road, stream and trail recon flights that were read-out back at our Spud Intel section. Lastly, we flew many box pattern flights. Some nights we would put a second IR aircraft into the PDJ just for precisely targeted areas in addition to the IR ship working the real-time SLAR/IR hunter/killer times with the *Stinger* and *Spooky* gunships.

We would also fly a couple of VR flights each day doing camera, or armed recon runs in Steel Tiger. These flights were two aircraft if running missions in Steel Tiger North, anywhere near Tchepone, and often single ships if farther to the south. We lost the most aircraft on VR flights, unfortunately, and then the IR flights. The only SLAR aircraft I think were lost was one down by a SAM on RP-2, and Captain Shereck's shoot down, crash and the failed ejection at Phu Bai. When flying an *armed VR mission,* we always had two aircraft, but an unarmed VR-only mission could be run with just one aircraft in most areas.

5-5 / How Our IR, SLAR, and VR Missions Were Flown

X-Side-Looking-Airborne-Radar (SLAR)

We flew three SLAR missions; RP-1 (Route Pack 1) up and down the coast of North Vietnam, two nightly boxes in Steel Tiger North and Steel Tiger South in southern Laos paired with an IR aircraft and the same pairing in the Barrel Roll, the Plain of Jars in the CIA's Secret War in Northern Laos.

RP-2/RP-3 Missions

Before I arrived, we had stopped flying the RP-2 missions going farther to the north, past Vinh. Those missions had fuel enough for only a single mission pass while the RP-1 missions were three loops on each SLAR mission.

We had lost a SLAR aircraft to what was believed to be one of the SA-2 SAM missiles while running a mission on RP-2 in 1966. I have read that the RP-2/3 missions later were performed by US Navy P2V Neptune aircraft flying from someplace in South Vietnam.

RP-1 Missions

We flew about eight of these missions a day to ensure a 24/7 continuous coverage of the truck and tank traffic coming down into the southern part of North Vietnam. RP-1 SLAR missions were flown about 12-15 miles off the coast at 10,000 feet MSL so that you could look down at an angle to the beach area, but far enough out to avoid anti-aircraft fire.

RP-1 SLAR was the standard no-brainer mission mostly for the commissioned officers of the 131st whom otherwise had some important unit duties, like maintenance, motor pool, admin, mess hall, etc., and yet had to fly an occasional *combat* flight. No special skills were needed and no time was involved in mission planning; one could just show up for a short Intel and threat briefing, get the new *Safe Letter*, and be off.

To be sure, this was really an entire TO mission to run, and the success of each flight was almost entirely in their hands. We would fly from Phu Bai out to Tiger Island, a small island just off the end of the northeast end of the DMZ, and from there we ran the RP-1 route three times, to a point just below Vinh in North Vietnam.

The TOs use the SLAR image to keep us about 8-15 miles off the coast and give us maximum coverage as deep into North Vietnam as possible. This distance was outside of any of the flak guns, but well within the range of the SA-2 SAM sites.

Looking at a map of this part of North Vietnam one can see that the SLAR aircraft had to be making course corrections every few minutes. Thus, the mission was almost entirely the TO's. While the pilot may get the plane out to Tiger Island using our Doppler, TACAN, or INS, or when none of that was working (!) using a radar vector to get to the start point. From there the TO used the autopilot to make the course corrections needed to maintain this distance from the coast. The pilot may be sleeping at times (?!) as long as the ECM was not screaming something in the helmets, but the TO was running all of this.

There were reported cases of the pilot having fallen asleep sometime in the climb, even in the weather, out of Phu Bai only to have the TO take the aircraft control from the autopilot on the climb out, fly the course, do all the communications, run the entire RP-1 SLAR mission, and bring the Mohawk back to Phu Bai on autopilot only—and do all of the coordination with ATC and Deep Sea and Red Crown. I know of this because that happened to me once, falling asleep on the climb and when being shaken awake, ready to continue to the mission I had found we were being vectored around, at night, in the weather, for a recovery GCA to Phu Bai. I am sure it happened to others too. This shows that the term TO, **_T_**echnical **_O_**bserver, was so far off base. The SLAR missions were entirely the TO mission. The mission time on RP-1 was just short of four hours' total.

The SLAR targets, the *Movers* on the roads in the southern part of North Vietnam, were plotted on the film and counted back at base by our Intel group and then sent as updated reports multiple times a day to MACV headquarters. No in-flight target fixing was done as it was on the SLAR/IR combos in Laos.

Steel Tiger in Southern Laos

Generally, the SLAR ship would head into Steel Tiger (north or south) each night about 30-minutes ahead of the IR ship, thus giving time for the SLAR TO to find and plot out a series of targets, the *Movers* as they were, before the IR ship arrived. There were occasions discussed herein where the IR ship had their own objectives for the night and might have gone out ahead of the SLAR ship to start working these targets. So each mission had a particular variance for the IR guys, but not so much for the SLAR crew.

We had dual SLAR search boxes that were about 45-60 miles on a side over known areas where we were watching ground traffic of tanks and trucks on *the Trail*. The *Movers* were manually plotted in real time by the SLAR ship TO and then the coordinates were called down to the IR aircraft, checked out and also called over to *Moonbeam*, the Air Force EC-130 C&C. The SLAR pilot had little to do other than fly the box and watch for the flak while the TO was always working to plot targets.

Captain Jim Shereck was flying the only SLAR aircraft I can recall that was hit on a mission, and that was by a .51 cal. This took his plane down and killed him back at Phu Bai because of a failed ejection seat less than an hour later. Jim and I had flown *that mission together*, with him running the SLAR ship and I was the IR aircraft.

Sometimes the AC-130 *Spectre* gunship would themselves directly check out the *Movers* from the SLAR ship and attack if they wanted to, though most all attacks, or bombing too of course, whether in Steel Tiger or up along the Chinese border, had to be checked through the Air Force C&C ship to be sure some friendlies were not being attacked.

Other times the IR aircraft would be down on the road traffic checking the *Movers* before *Spectre* got over to them.

The C&C aircraft are usually coordinating the attacks as they had the Intel on whether the targets were near hidden friendlies, were friendlies, or other situations, not the least of which was the latest, up to the hour, reports on known or suspected anti-aircraft fire.

Once an attack was okayed, and all this was in just a couple of minutes, then the IR aircraft would move away from the targets, maybe do a bit of trolling for gunfire, and let *Spectre* attack. Unlike the AC-47 *Spooky* gunships in the PDJ, with triple mini-guns firing tracers, the *Spectre*, and the AC-119 *Stinger* gunships did not use tracers on any of the various types of weapons, so they would only say they were about to "*sparkle now*" and we could look up and see these intense sparkles from the barrels of the guns and then down on the target is all these hundreds of small explosions!

If the trucks or tanks stopped moving then the IR aircraft would go back in and look to find and count them using their engine and exhaust IR temperature signature to locate them, even when under the jungle cover.

If *fast-movers* were in the area with bombs we would, the IR aircraft, usually offer up the anti-aircraft fire and flak situation by *trolling*, with our lights on as needed, just to draw out as many of the guns as we could. We did not control, nor ever talk directly with the *fast-movers*, that would be an Air Force FAC function, but we would be right there.

The other IR Mohawk in Steel Tiger was usually not working with our SLAR aircraft as we had our own targets to run IR film on, not real time targeting working with a SLAR ship, and the film was read out back at Phu Bai with specific Intel requirements of why we were running any particular target or strip. On these missions, the really scary ones, the TO had to keep you alive—*every second.* He had to know *exactly where we were*, watch the rapidly scrolling IR screen(s) and continuously update the Doppler or INS for our position, *or die trying*. That was why a *targeted* IR mission took hours and hours of planning so the pilot and TO would always be on the same sheet of music.

You run these IR missions in the mountains, under a variety of enemy anti-aircraft fire, and the adrenaline was a toxic drug running in your veins *for hours and hours* after you got back home.

X-IR Sensor Missions

These were the killer missions. Flying IR took a lot of dedicated, *mission-area specific training*, not just for IR itself, but also for the work areas themselves, to get to know the terrain and weapons in this field. The same few warrant officers were usually working the same mission areas, Steel Tiger North and South, the Barrel Roll, etc., over and over. There were, in all fairness, some very fine commissioned officers flying IR missions, but only as a dedicated IR pilot, not as a spot assignment for a night. You could fly most any SLAR mission, but I suspect no IR TO would get in a Mohawk with some pilot that was doing this mission just to get his minimum flight time.

When doing these missions, you are flying low-level (600-700 feet AGL was optimum for IR coverage), at night, in the mountains, and often under anti-aircraft fire. From Chapter 3 here, you see we lost many of the aircraft to these missions, and usually, they were fatal and MIA. From mere moments or just seconds, of inattention, several of us *had* hit trees, at night doing 220 knots, and not even knowing what was coming. The issue of the emergency *jettison* of the drop tanks when trying to blind climb out of a mountain valley and to clear a ridge that you could not even see, and that was not supposed to be there had happened. One of the

IR warrants came back one night with all the lower antennas stripped off his Mohawk and was lucky to be alive.

What the IR could do is find the SLAR's identified *Movers,* targets that had pulled over and stopped, and thus, were no longer trackable *Movers*. Usually, the vehicles, tanks or trucks, had then been attacked by either an AC-130 *Spectre* gunship in Steel Tiger or an AC-119 *Stinger* gunship in the PDJ. The IR could find the heat signature of a vehicle, even it had shut down the engines, for an hour or more and continuously if they had simply stopped under the jungle and thinking they were safe from our prying eyes.

X-The SLAR/IR Combo Flights

These missions took little mission-specific preplanning on the part of the pilots, as it was the same basic task done over and over each night in Laos. From high above the jungle, at about 10,000 feet, running a 40-60 miles' box pattern in Steel Tiger North and South. And do basically the same in the PDJ, the SLAR aircraft found *Movers* and the SLAR TO would pass the coordinates down to the IR aircraft and over to Moonbeam or Alley Cat. The IR aircraft would then make low-level runs seeing if we could determine what the target was—tanks, trucks or other, or sometimes nothing.

We usually did not make direct calls to the gunships, that being the forte of Alley Cat or Moonbeam.

In making the target runs it was also part of the task to figure out the anti-aircraft fire so you could pass that to the *fast-movers* that would be making the attack or even to the *Spectre*, the AC-130 gunship in your box. If there was no, or only limited anti-aircraft fire, then turning on the aircraft position lights (going Christmas Tree as it was known) and trolling for gunfire, crazy as it may seem, was sometimes used.

We usually did not fly the Steel Tiger SLAR missions in the daytime, as valuable as the movement information might have been, because, in these areas, with the flak and heavy machine guns that could reach up to the SLAR altitude, the aircraft would have quickly been taken down. Ditto on the Air Force gunships, just too dangerous, though I know some were flown in daylight if flak was not a significant issue. Most of the truck and tank traffic was found and attacked at night as the NVA did not like to be driving in daylight and risk being attacked.

I do not recall any time that we had acted in an FAC function for the Air Force and Navy *fast-movers* doing bomb runs. At most, when they were doing their runs, we might have used the IR aircraft only to draw out any anti-aircraft fire.

> *And I volunteered for two nearly back-to-back combat years for what reason?*

X-Single-Aircraft IR Missions in Laos

Often, in each of the Steel Tiger boxes and sometimes in the Barrel Roll (PDJ), there was also a lone IR aircraft running individual spot and strip targets. To stay alive at this, one would generally get the target lists by mid-afternoon from our Spud Intel guys, and then you would start to plot each and every pass in great detail. That involved *hours of detail work* and studying the maps, the known or suspected weapons, the anticipated weather and, yes, the moon cycle, which was often so important when down in the mountains.

For each of my targets, I would draw a single sheet for carrying on my right knee pad (we had knee pads strapped to both thighs on every flight) and on each, I had altitudes, run in headings, known or suspected anti-aircraft weapons nearby, the terrain information and more. Then I would assemble the sheets into a determined order to fly them, as the targets may sometimes be 15-40 miles apart. This process often took three or more hours of just target work. You did this detail work with your IR TO. The TO then was usually using a larger map so he could match some of the IR screen images to the map images, to be sure we were following and filming the right road, trail, or stream beds. This was why the IR missions were *mostly* flown by the few warrant officers—we had to have full-time, dedicated every night pilots. Not so with any SLAR flight, thus, most of the commissioned officers flew SLAR and not the IR.

You could not expect one of the commissioned guys, who had other unit duties, to spend hours of mission planning and flying and still do their unit functions at the same time. The skill and target area knowledge was so critical that one needed to be flying these missions over and over and over, not just occasionally as one might be doing as a SLAR pilot.

Sometimes the tasks included IR boxes that you ran that could be 10 x 12 miles on a side. You flew these with the old Doppler or the new (OV-1D) INS navigation system so as to track along a line, then get to the end of a run, which might be ten runs in a box, and have a well-practiced turning maneuver so you rolled out usually two kilometers over, ran that, and repeated the turning at the other end. While these were easy to fly, and usually above the surrounding terrain, it was also an invitation to take anti-aircraft fire as you were straight tracking and going back and forth. You had to decide if the anti-aircraft fire was a reason to get off target. **And the phase of the moon was always an issue.** With a new moon, you were probably okay from the gunfire, but a full moon and you were the witches on the broom going right in front of the glowing moon. Way, way too dangerous.

Generally, these were not *real-time* targets. The IR film was read-out back at our Spud Intel section, as they determined what intel was being looked for.

X-Moonlight

Your friend and foe at the same time.

You wanted a new moon so the gunners could not see you, which was great. A new moon also meant you could not see the terrain. On a night with a full moon, the stress level was very high. I could see the mountains, get a visual position fix, and run my IR strips, but every second I was just waiting for the sure anti-aircraft fire.

On the night I made the radar targeting run on a 57 mm gun in the Barrel Roll/PDJ, (Chapter 2) we used *Candlestick*, the C-123 flare aircraft, to coordinate laying a line of large flares timed to be below the view of the ridgelines. This was done so we could fly a new moon run on this target area and still be able to climb to the right, upward towards the mountains with the flare's backlighting in the next valley over.

There were times, too many times, especially when flying with the OV-1C model IR aircraft with the two *little IR screens*, that we would miss the road, trail, or stream and for seconds not know if we missed it to the right or the left. For a few seconds, was it that we were now too close left or right to the mountains, which would cause an *immediate* full power climb? It only took 2-3 seconds—*very, very, very long seconds*—to lose your position. Some dedicated pilots IR pilots would set the radar altimeter to 400 feet and a blink of the RA (radar altimeter) light—meaning we were only *seconds* from impacting something—meant the drop tanks were jettisoned in a power climb.

Sometimes you ran two IR flights in a single night. At other times, near the end of my second tour before being medevac'd to Clark AFB, I ran *four IR missions* during one night. The night (early a.m. actually) I took an SA-2 SAM in North Vietnam during Lam Son 719, I was on the third IR flight of that night. These usually resulted in up to 10-12 hours of cockpit time and often not getting out of the aircraft on a turn, just having someone change the IR film while the fuel truck was plugged in—then push back, reach up and press the engine start buttons, and be off again.

X-Visual Recon - Guns, Rockets & Cameras

I think the original Mohawk detachments all had armed OV-1A model Mohawks that carried pod-mounted .50 cal machine guns and 2.75-inch folding-fine aerial rockets (FFAR). We had both the 7-hole and 19-hole pods. Before my time at the 131st, our Mohawks carried a variety of bombs and other ordnance on VR flights.

The VR missions were usually flown with two aircraft and often flown with two pilots in the dual-stick OV-1A models.

A non-armed VR mission could be flown in any Mohawk as every model, even the new OV-1D models, had the three cameras—two sweeping pan cameras, one in the nose shooting wingtip-to-wingtip and another identical one in the belly pointing down and sweeping wingtip-to-wingtip.

Another large lenses camera was in the belly, and that could have anything from a 3- to 18-inch lenses. The 18-inch lenses could only point down, but the other lenses, usually a 12-inch, could be electronically pointed outward to two side aiming angles. The pilot had a flexible arm on his side of the cockpit with a 2-inch round aiming lenses he used to run the target over the lenses circles and either have a running camera or individually be pressing a camera button on the control stick.

X-Maintenance Test Flights

I put this in because we flew many maintenance test flights either for aircraft issues, usually an engine swap or for testing the IR or SLAR. In the *It Was All Too Real* chapter herein is the event of a maintenance test flight that ended in an ejection at Phu Bai.

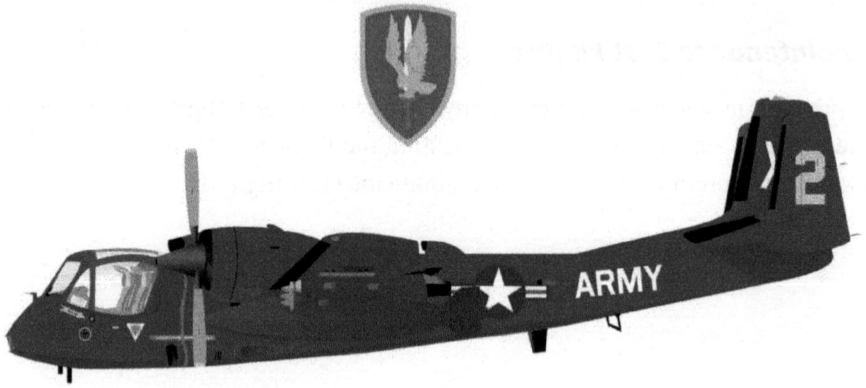
2
ARMY

Chapter 6

WEAPONS WE FACED

Southeast Asia was full of the left-over weapons of both World Wars and awash in a variety of weapons for individuals and light combat, most of which came from China, but also a lot of old Russian arms

The newer weapons in what had initially been a limited ground war turned out to be the Soviet SA-2, the big Surface-to-Air Missiles and then, in 1972, the game changer, the shoulder-fired, heat-seeking SA-7. With the SA-7s also came the track mounted, radar fired, 57 mm anti-aircraft flak-type weapons, which effectively closed the airspace where we had operated for years.

6-1 / ANTI-AIRCRAFT GUNS, FLAK, AND MORE

Because we flew only in North Vietnam and Laos, at least until near the end of the war, it was only the 131st that had to deal with the heavy machine guns, the flak, and the SAM missiles. Not that the other Mohawk units did not also face deadly anti-aircraft guns, mostly .30 cal machine guns—and for sure a .30 cal can kill you just as sure as a 42-foot SAM will.

Here is how we mostly, or at least how I was shown and worked, to deal with the guns in Laos.

X-.30 Cal Medium Machine Guns

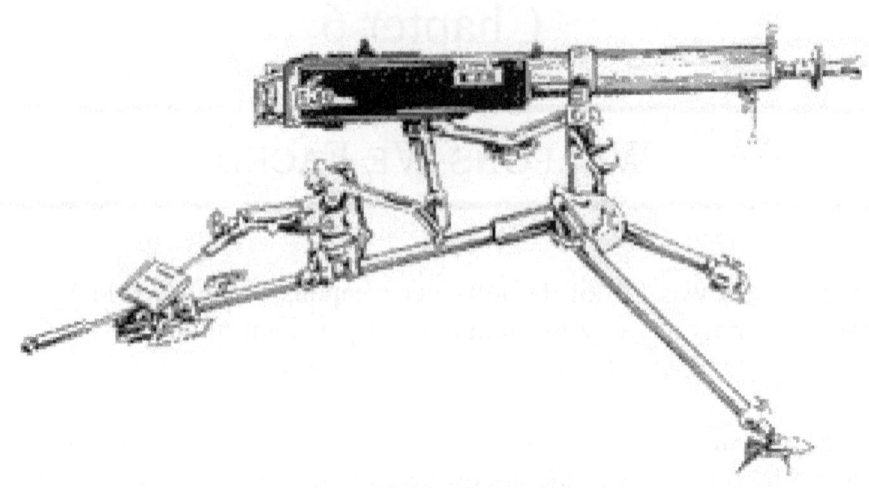

Not necessarily this old model of gun.

These were a standard weapon all over Southeast Asia, on every trail, hillside, road or down a riverbed we flew over. The NVA and VC versions had bullet sizes that were close to our .30 cal, but slightly larger so they could use our ammo, but we could not use theirs. Ditto on the .50/.51 cal heavy machine guns.

The velocity was slow enough that a gunner had to lead an aircraft and anticipate their speed. In Chapter 1 you can read about one of the Mohawk guys that took three direct hits to his chest and neck, in the cockpit, from a .30 cal, and brought the aircraft back home.

X-12.7 mm / .51 Cal Heavy Machine Guns

This is the single barrel, but imagine what the Russian/NVA quad-gun could do to you . .

These heavy machine guns were surely more deadly than the flak weapons. The bullets were not only very large, but the real issue was the velocity of bullets. These guns could start firing on you and then literally walk the tracers right onto you. They did not have to lead the aircraft like the slower moving flak rounds did, and while they had a best effective altitude of about 5,000 feet, they could reach above 15,000 feet.

At night, the tracers from this weapon were visible from a long way off and offered a good warning to stay clear. In the daytime, this gunfire was less easy to see coming at you, plus the gunners could see you. During the night you were harder to be seen; but once they saw you, they would start firing. The flaming basketball sized tracers racing at you in the darkness meant you had immediate attention to this, but in daylight, the tracers were less visible to your peripheral vision and thus taking fire from these guns was much more deadly and linked to more of our shoot downs.

And of course, they would move them sometimes several times an hour to hide from attacking aircraft.

14.5 mm AA heavy machinegun ZPU-4

No way, no way to get close to one of these .. and survive.

The Intel guys had kept track of two of the quad-.51 cal guns, the ZPU-4s, one each in Steel Tiger North, near Tchepone, and another that would come up firing in the PDJ in northern Laos. If they were in firing order no one, ***absolutely no one***, wanted to be anywhere near them.

X-23 & 37 mm Flak Guns

Most of the flak taken was from 23 & 37 mm guns. They would fire a clip of 7-9 rounds, with each round being a tracer. The velocity was relatively slow, and the appearance was as if they were drifting up at you in an arching stream of red tracers.

If you looked at the tracer streams coming up and if the relative position of the tracers did not change then you were merging with them and needed to take immediate action. However, if during a brief second or two you perceived even a slight shift in the relative position of the tracer stream, then you could forget them and focus on the others.

Usually, these guns worked in groups of four to maybe a dozen guns in a localized area. It was not unusual to be pulling streams from four or more guns at a time. Frankly, this was *nothing* compared to what the Air Force and Navy pilots faced in the Hanoi and Haiphong area where there were *hundreds and hundreds* of these guns.

Because they were not very accurate, and the rounds showing the tracers were somewhat slow, the best way to use them was to try mostly to fill the sky up with flak and hope that an aircraft is hit, or the air burst was close enough to damage, and maybe take down an aircraft.

Try a few hundreds of these all over the sky, day and night.

At night then, if you could see the streams coming up you could make the near instant 1-2 second visual judgment on whether to maneuver out of the danger or to change course or not. The slow speed did mean that they had to lead you to get a chance for a hit or an airburst near you. Hitting the aircraft would almost surely bring you down, but a sky full of hundreds of exploding airbursts could also knock you down with the shrapnel.

We did have one of our armed VR flights, and I wish I could find the pictures, of one of our Mohawks on a VR mission that took a hit in the tail, lost the right-side horizontal stabilizer and vertical tail, and still made it back to DaNang AFB. However, like my hung drop tank misadventure, in that case, the aircraft was out of control for some seconds while the tail was still hanging on. Looking for a long runway to come down on with this control-damaged aircraft, the guys recovered their plane back to DaNang AFB. That was one of the few incidents I recall that someone took a direct flak hit and made it back. Another of the aircraft took a direct hit to the aft fuselage section, forward of the tail, and blasted a hole through that section, and the aircraft made it home. Another reason we usually referred to the Mohawk as having been built by *Grumman Iron Works*.

However, in the daylight, where we lost so many aircraft, the gunners could see you, lead you as needed, and because the tracers were not so easy to see in the daylight, it was not as instantly obvious that you were under fire as it was in the darkness.

The most anti-aircraft fire I had taken, and the basis of the Silver Star nomination from the US Embassy in Vientiane, was for working against about a dozen of these guns while offsetting the NVA and Pathet Lao attacks on the CIA base and airfield at Long Tieng, (Lima Site-20a), some miles to the southwest of the PDJ. See Chapter 2 for some details.

X-57 mm Radar Fired Flak Guns

A Soviet AZP S-60 57 mm flak gun is aimed by a radar system.

I put the issues of the radar aimed and fired 57 mm guns as a separate item because it possessed a different threat to our operations than did the 23 & 37 mm guns.

During the 1972 Easter Offensive these weapons and the deadlier track-mounted ones came in force across the DMZ and ended our flying in that area.

First, these guns fired a very *large* bursting round so if they hit you; you were toast, and if they were even close the bursting shrapnel is many times more dangerous than the smaller guns.

We initially encountered only a few of these weapons in Laos—but when they did fire, there are no tracers, no warning—you are just flying along, and suddenly there are these huge airbursts near you. Because of this, you could not dodge anything, as you had no idea from where the flak is coming. Do you dodge left, or to the right? There was nothing you could do. Here are these *huge airbursts* near you and the only defense is to turn a bit immediately because you had nothing to see to decide how to dodge.

You could, and would be, in the weather in a SLAR aircraft, invisible to the standard .51s and 23 & 37 mm guns, and there are suddenly these explosions near you! **In the clouds!** Big ones!

Like the quad-51's, we tried to keep track of these weapons; we had located only a few of the 57 mm guns in Laos and when found they became the highest priority to attack and destroy. We had at least one, and maybe just one, in the PDJ, and several nearer Tchepone in Steel Tiger North. I do not know of any of our Mohawk aircraft that were hit by any 57 mm flak—but it did get your attention when the airbursts would come out of nowhere.

While we had the APR 24/25 ECM running on the radar scans, I do recall that we were able to use the ECM radar paints to help us on these guns to the extent the ECM would be pointing in the direction of the 57 mm radar.

X-Soviet SA-2 SAM Missile

At the end of the war, I was the only known recent 131st pilot that took a SAM and made it home. That was during Operation Lam Son 719, and the whole story is in the first chapter of this book. In late 1966 we had lost a SLAR aircraft on RP-2 that is suspected to have been a SAM, but could have been a MiG.

Having said this, in my online research, I found at least one case of another 20th ASTA Mohawk that had taken one of these huge missiles and survived, so maybe I was not the only lucky one.

6/ Weapons We Faced

This weapon is incredibly dangerous and highly effective. The same missiles had taken down our CIA U-2 spy planes over Russia (Frances Gary Powers) in 1960 and another U-2 over Cuba in 1962.

For example, in just 11 days of our attacks on North Vietnam in late 1972 these SA-2s destroyed **14 B-52 bombers** and damaged another 6, *in just a few days*. Saying nothing about so very many of the other Air Force and Navy aircraft brought down all over North Vietnam. In one night in December 1972, a staggering **8** B-52s were downed by the SAMs on a single deadly bombing raid over Hanoi.

The SAM sites were not deployed into Laos but during Lam Son 719, they were firing these SAMs from the tri-border region into Laos from the same location that sent a missile after me in February 1971.

With the Easter Offensive of 1972 setting the stage for our ending defeat, the SAMs were brought back down to the DMZ area with more deadly results.

X-Soviet SA-7 Grail Heat-Seeking Shoulder Fired Missile

SA-7 - A game changer for sure, starting in 1972

These were a game changer for all of us. The SA-7 was brought into the war with the Easter Offensive in 1972 and immediately changed the battlefield. Within the first 24 hours of the invasion, there were reportedly 23 aircraft downed in northern I Corp, in our AO. This weapon felled many of these.

6/ Weapons We Faced 249

The SA-7 took down helicopters, jets, and even an otherwise untouchable AC-130 *Spectre* gunship, just with its small warhead going up the engine exhaust. While a pilot might be able to eject from a crippled aircraft or bailout, the helicopter guy's faced immediate crashes.

Within weeks, many of the I Corp helicopters were equipped with exhaust deflectors, or dubious value while the Mohawks later had electronic IR deflectors mounted on the back of the right wing drop tank.

X-AK-47 - The Deadliest Weapon in the World

The deadliest killing weapon in the world is the AK-47

Putting aside the issues of missiles, bombers, flak, machine guns and even nuclear weapons—the most lethal weapon in the world has been any one of many versions of the AK-47, known as the Russian *Kalashnikov*. Unlike our then M14/16s, these are a field weapon that one can pick up out of the mud and start firing.

Apart from the thousands of rounds of flak surely thrown at me, and how many hours of combined streaming of machinegun fire, and a SAM missile to boot, the only hit I ever took on my aircraft, and one that very nearly brought me down or to an ejection, *was a single round from an AK-47* on takeoff from Pleiku that went into my aft electronics bay. That is the opening story in this book.

It goes to show, that apart from the dangers of the big stuff, sophisticated weapons, radar guns or missiles, mortars or more, it is often the single personal weapon of an individual soldier that killed then, and now, so many people.

This is actually showing the quad-51 cal, but in Cuba, not Vietnam.

Chapter 7

ABOUT THE MOHAWK

Built by *Grumman Iron Works* in Bethpage, NY

7-1 / MOHAWK - THE ARMY'S WIDOW MAKER

In the years leading up to the Vietnam War, the OV-1 Mohawk is being developed for the Navy for use as a rugged aircraft to operate from an aircraft carrier as a light attack bomber and close support gunship.

Early short-winged OV-1A with Speed Boards Popped Out

We routinely flew formations too close—
and lost some aircraft doing just that.

7/ About the Mohawk

OV-1A with .50 cal machine guns and seven-hole rocket pods.

OV-1A with both 7- and 19-hole rocket pods.

All of them armed. A hunting we will go . . a hunting we will go . .

We did not have air-to-air refueling in our Vietnam aircraft.

OV-1D with an IR configuration and with dual radar jammers for North Vietnam flights.

131st OV-1D (large SLAR tube) with a flasher pod under the right wing.

OV-1A with a small, single rocket mounted on the left side.

OV-1D with Dual Controls

7/ About the Mohawk   257

Late model OV-1D with SLAR

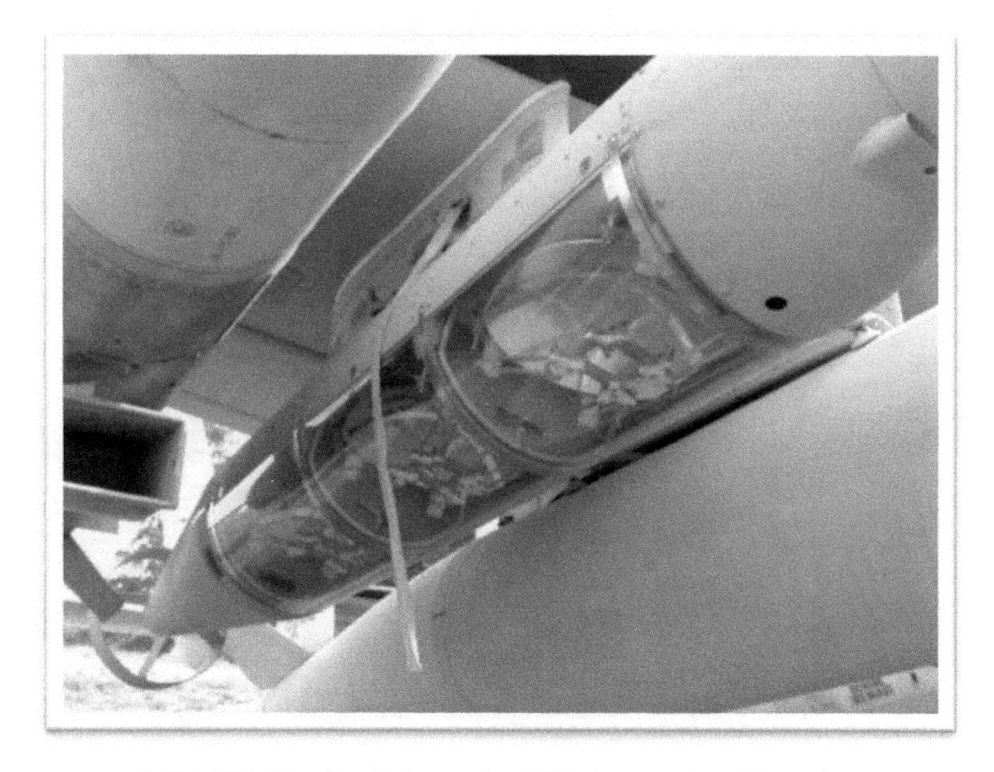

A 131st OV-1D with a flasher pod and IR defuser outboard from that.

On the left of this photo is a large IR missile *Defuser* nearly the size of a drop tank and is there for defense from the shoulder-fired, heat-seeking SA-7. With drop tanks, radar jammers on one side, and IR Defuser, this is a **very heavy Mohawk**

Early OV-1A with armament packages of rockets, guns, and bombs.

Our .50 cal machine guns and droppable flare pods

7/ About the Mohawk 259

OV-1D cockpit with SLAR. 131st aircraft with ECM on the glare shield for North Vietnam flights.

Early vertical tape instruments and still running Doppler navigation before the Litton INS.

OV-1A view from the gun camera on the other Mohawk on an attack

The Mohawk is a single-pilot, single-flight control (most of the time other than checkrides and some armed gun attacks when we had two pilots) aircraft.

This armored, and sometimes armed, aircraft is designed to carry a wide variety of weapons, ranging from .50 caliber pod-mounted heavy machine guns, up to six 7- or 19-hole pods of 2.75" folding fin rockets, or an assortment of bombs—all to be used for the close air support missions for which the Mohawk was originally designed. In a conventional configuration, the Mohawk carried two 150 gallon drop tanks and then either the rocket pods or machine guns or sometimes other under wing equipment, like radar jammers, IR missile deflectors or photo flash pods that looked like big torpedoes hanging under our wing.

The 5" Zuni rockets, once used to down a MiG-17 that had jumped a flight of two of our attack Mohawks, were gone before I get to the 131st.

The guns and rockets were fired from the control sticks of the OV-1A and aligned using a heads-up gun sight on the pilot's glareshield panel. A more usual configuration would be the drop tanks and two 7-hole rocket pods under each wing with one of the four pods firing White Phosphorus (Willy Pete) warheads, so you had a visible burning mark on the ground as you came back around for another target run.

I never saw any of our aircraft go out with the 19-hole pods, but I did see one plane that had six of these large pods (empty as they were) mounted under the wings and with no drop tanks. I suspect this was only for a photo as I could not image the Mohawk staggering into the air with 114 rockets under the wings—to say nothing of the issue that a single burst of all six would probably stop the Mohawk in mid-flight.

We sat on our Martin-Baker J5 ejection seats in an armor-plated cockpit, behind a thick and supposedly bulletproof (?) windshield.

While the Mohawk is incredibly dangerous to fly—*even when people were not trying to kill you*—it is also fun! The control stick moved forward and aft, but is only about six inches high, and you rolled only by twisting your wrist and could go from a full rolling to either side back to the other way, all the way around, just by moving your wrist.

The Mohawk is fully aerobatic for anything other than outside maneuvers. Flying VR missions we did full rolls all the time, often while dodging flak, and loops (full loops when not too heavy), and aileron rolls gave way to barrel rolls and Immelmanns. The back side of a Cuban-8 was often used on a gun or camera run as you pulled heavy G's and could not stop at the top of the loop or you would stall, so you usually came down inverted on the back side, half rolled and completed one-half of a Cuban-8 maneuver.

As the Mohawk was being developed in the early 1960's, it was moved over to become an Army development program. There were initially three models: the OV-1A is the armed gunship with dual controls; the OV-1B is dedicated to a SLAR (Side-Looking-Airborne-Radar) system, and the OV-1C, and later the Super-C, were devoted just to IR (Infrared) systems.

By late 1971, while I was training to be a Mohawk instructor pilot between tours, the Army fielded the advanced OV-1D model Mohawk. This is a single airframe that could be deployed for either IR or SLAR missions by swapping out the systems in the cockpit and the aircraft's electronics bay. The changeover sometimes took a few hours to do, so this is not routine by any means, but we could make any aircraft to be used on IR, VR or SLAR missions. The OV-1Ds replaced all of our other 131st unit aircraft by about mid-1972.

None of the OV-1D models carried any armament, but we did have, besides great new, big, and working SLAR and IR systems, things like large underwing radar jammers, outboard of the left wing drop tank, and a huge electronic flashing pod for night camera runs versus our old ejecting of flares.

When the 1972 Easter Offensive brought in the game-changing Soviet SA-7 shoulder-fired, heat-seeking missiles, we had a large IR Defuser hung under the right wing that was designed to confuse the missile's infrared sensing. Fat chance!

Later the ejection seats were upgraded with a rocket assist allowing for a better chance to survive a runway-level ejection. The Litton INS replaced the old Doppler in the OV-1D also.

A 131st OV-1D with radar jamming pods under both wings.

The OV-1A and OV-1C model aircraft were designed and built with dangerously short wings, giving them terrible flight characteristics, especially in a single-engine configuration. The OV-1B, Super-C and all the OV-1D models had longer wings and thus much better lateral flight control. This short-winged aircraft had terrible single-engine flight characteristics and resulted in many of the fatal takeoff crashes, though later the OV-1D had fatal takeoff crashes also.

All the aircraft series had three visual cameras units, though they were not always installed on any given aircraft: a nose pan camera that swung from wingtip-to-wingtip for very low—*very low*—pan camera shots on a flyover, such as making a run on a SAM site in North Vietnam at 100 feet or less altitude. There is another identical pan camera in the bay looking downward and swinging wingtip-to-wingtip and is used mostly to orientate images from the third camera, a vertical, rotatable camera that had from 3" to 18" long camera lens.

With anything other than the 18" lens, the pilot could select to rotate the camera to several angle positions to either side and through opened doors may either do snap-by-snap shots or turn the cameras on and make an aerial camera run for strip target work. With this equipment, even an OV-1B model SLAR aircraft, or an OV-1C model, could be used for dangerous daylight VR (Visual Recon) flights.

7-2 / MARTIN-BAKER EJECTION SEATS

The Mohawk is the only Army aircraft with an ejection seat and, unfortunately, the technology of the day was not fully up to speed. Any ejection is high risk, and many died from ejecting while out of the ejection flight envelope—which is that you needed to be right side up and several hundred feet in the air. Some survived that had ejected at a lower altitude or on a descent path, but it was rare.

Just about as deadly as the flak shooting at you . . .

If you were outside the ejection envelope could not get main chute deployment. If you were too low, you only fell to the ground. However, the deadliest and most common fatal ejections were on takeoffs with an engine failure and propeller torque rolling the Mohawk onto its back—onto the runway.

X-Attaching Yourself to the Ejection Seat

You wore your harness, your personal one because it took a long time to make the right adjustments to the straps, over your survival vest. When you got into the aircraft, which itself is a chore and sometimes needed help because you were climbing through a window onto the seat, you worked your legs down past the control stick. Your first attachments were the detachable leg garters positioned around your calves. You could have unclipped them and put the straps on before climbing into the Mohawk.

The leg garters attached to straps from the lower part of the ejection seat and went down to breakaway (hopefully breakaway pins or you were screwed) pins in the cockpit floor. This caused your legs to be pulled tightly against the ejection seat as it went up the rail, the pins broke, and you could separate—hopefully?

There are harness attachments on both sides of your hips locking you down to the main part of the ejection seat. The main parachute harness attachments were above each shoulder and went directly to the personal parachute. The other attachment points would separate, hopefully again, when the seat came out.

After takeoff, you reached down between your legs and attached a cord that led to the under seat pack; which is either a raft for over water flights or a much larger, about forty pounds or so, of an overland survival kit. The seat pack would be left hanging several feet under you after seat separation. You detached the cord when inbound on final approach to be sure it would not cause a drag during an ejection sequence.

On your left shoulder is the clipping of the supplemental oxygen hose that your helmet mask would attach to. Each seat had about 10-15 minutes of oxygen in the case of a high altitude ejection; you would be getting these few minutes of oxygen as you descended, still latched into your seat until you are below 15,000 feet when a barostatic sensor would release you from the seat. Not sure what the plan ever is when we flew over the Rocky Mountains; and had mountain peaks at that altitude to hit upon while still locked into the ejection seat.

With all this hassle and the vests and harnesses and guns, you can understand why having a maintenance stand pushed to the side of the Mohawk to help get you up to the cockpit is best; then a crew chief to help with the various connections is important. You can climb the side of the cockpit using several foot insert steps, but it is difficult, and then you still had the extended step to pull up with your toes after you climbed in.

X-The Ejection Sequence

There are two ways to fire the seat: an upper looped pull rope above your helmet, or a lower looped cord between your legs. The preferred method is to lean back and pull the lower cord so your body is in a more upright position and you may then suffer less injury to your back. If you pulled the upper loop rope handle, this also pulled a mask down over your face. All of this is happening of course in about two seconds.

7/ About the Mohawk

The upper ejection cord had a flip down switch you reached up and pressed down before takeoff while the lower firing cable is armed by moving a flip lever to the right side. You armed the ejection seats only when on the runway with a takeoff clearance for fear of accidentally causing a ground ejection in the case you had to abandon an aircraft before takeoff. At the clearance for takeoff you pulled into position and both crewmembers call—

"Seats Hot!"

—as the final words before brake release.

Once either the upper or lower cords were pulled this first fired a lower seat explosive charge and started the ejection seat up a rail— going through the Plexiglas canopy. There is no *command ejection* system that would cause both seats to go out. You have to make your own seat eject, and if injured or unconscious then this is the end of times.

The seat is *unpadded* and *hard*! We did not (then) have an under seat rocket boost to help on the ejection, so the only way to get this seat out of the aircraft is a series of three pancake explosive charges built into the vertical rail. With the ejection based on explosives, the seat could not be padded as the sudden explosive compression would, or could, damage or break your back. It goes without saying that hemorrhoids were very common after some months of flight operations.

The seat is exploded up the ejection rail and through the overhead canopy. This sequence is only a mere second or so from start to finish; the series of pancake-shaped explosive charges fired in sequence and propelled the seat up and out. Only after Vietnam did we get ejection seats with an under seat rocket assist, so there are less sudden injury-producing G-forces—and allowing for an ejection at a lower altitude or even on the runway when moving forward.

Air Force ejection seats, and maybe also the Navy ones, mostly had *zero-zero seats* that could make a successful ejection from sitting on the ground and maybe too then high enough to survive a seat separation and personal chute deployment.

We needed a minimum of 90 knots on the runway to do an ejection, and even then you would find yourself deployed sideways, just above the runway, and about to be *hurt really bad* on impact, or killed as several were in this scenario.

After your seat moved past the top of the rail a firing pin discharged and that pulled out a stabilizing chute, which then pulled out another seat chute that would keep you in the seat until a barostatic device determined that you were under 15,000 feet before the seat would separate and the crewmember would be in his personal parachute.

7-3 / AIRCRAFT ELECTRONICS

X-ECM - Electronic Counter Measures Systems

Only the 131st flew with ECM gear. We had an APR-24/25 (whatever that means) ECM system with a control head and displayed in the pilot's cockpit window to the left side. There were sensors built into the aircraft at various locations. The ECM has a three-inch round display screen that showed different types of radar *paints* from all sorts of radars and the direction and strength represented by the length of the strobe outward from the center of the screen through a series of concentric circles, each representing some level of relative strength.

At any given time, you had radar paints from Air Force and Navy aircraft, from ATC controller radars, and our own air defense radar systems. Above the round screen is a row of lighted blocks showing what radar signals were being sensed, such as air-to-air, or ATC, SAMs or others.

The critical stuff is that it had SAM missile lights for two types of SAM radar that were being used. If you were just *painted,* you got something like an **E SAM LO** light. When the SAM site stopped on you, just you, the system went to **E SAM HI**, with more screeching in the headsets and the screen showing strobes as the direction and relative power or distance, maybe—*but only maybe.*

If they were about to fire a SAM at you—*after kissing your ass goodbye or ejecting*—you got a flashing amber **ACTIVITY** light and more and louder screeching in the headsets. The **ACTIVITY** light is supposed to mean a missile launch is imminent, and they had stepped up the power to the missile to exercise the flight control fins. When the missile launched, in theory, you got a red **LAUNCH** light. *Then you can kiss your butt goodbye.*

As discussed already in this book we lost a SLAR aircraft off the coast of North Vietnam on an RP-2 SLAR mission to a suspected SA-2 SAM missile. Just before the end of my first tour, during our work in Lam Son 719, I was the only other Mohawk to take a SAM missile and survive without any active ECM jamming gear. The details are in this book. *I should have ejected.* It being not survivable, that luck is the only thing that saved us that night. The sequence of alert lights was not how my missile came to me as it linked to two different SAM sites that both had locks on me with their missiles and one fired without me getting a warning **ACTIVITY** light at all.

On the OV-1D models, again only the 131st had the ECM systems, we had to get an active radar jamming system that hung from a wing pod and had a panel of lights indicating information about what type of radar is tagging us and if the ECM is responding. I would probably have taken my chances with an ejection, rather than see if this worked for if it did then why does the Air Force fly all the dedicated versions of the various Wild Weasel aircraft with all that gear, and we had only a pod under the wing. We had little or no confidence in the ECM system and on my second tour when the SAM lights started flickering it was time to move on along.

X-Navigation Gear

The non-OV-1D model aircraft had a Doppler navigation system that was of very dubious value and often very dangerous. Doppler is meant for high altitude navigation with little or no variance in the terrain, such as for over the ocean or plains, but trying to use Doppler while flying low in the mountains and valleys was nearly worthless, or even worse.

The OV-1D models had a Litton ASN-86 INS *inertial navigation system*, of dubious value at times also as it took as much as 40-minutes on the ramp, powered up, to get an INS initial position alignment. If the INS could not get in-flight updates from a TACAN station, then it too would get lost, and while flying low on IR missions, we usually did not have TACAN connections until we climbed back out of a valley. The INS would update okay on a SLAR mission if they could get a TACAN signal, but this did not work when you were down low. Each INS had an accuracy history log that we recorded at the end of flight, so we knew to keep the very best ones only in the IR aircraft. Even then one did not want to use INS to fly blindly down a valley when you cannot see even an outline against the stars or a ridgeline somewhere. Not that we *did not do* that, just that we did not like it.

The Mohawks have two ADFs, a single TACAN, and a single VOR. As it was, there were times when we launched RP-1 SLAR missions in the monsoons with no working navigation gear at all, just radar vectors. *Insane!*

X-Transponders

The dual transponders had the usual Mode 3 ATC codes you would program while in the cockpit, and a Mode 4 IFF (Identification Friend or Foe) and I have no idea how that worked. On a mission to North Vietnam, we also had programmed in a mission-unique Mode 2 secret codes. The Mode 2 secret codes were set by hand, in the left aft electronics bay, *only after power is on the aircraft* or the engines are running. Someone would be standing there, an engine is started, and he would put in the four-digit codes. If aircraft power is lost, the Mode 4 code disappears. The code is changed for every flight, every launch, and tied to what *Red Crown* or *Deep Sea* could see of us in North Vietnam without having to make direct contact with us.

X-Communications Gear

We had a single FM radio used mostly for communications with our Spud Operations on a line-of-sight basis, so that was usually only during arrivals and departures. Most helicopters had dual FMs as the ground troops they supported used

FM radios. We had a single UHF radio with about 24-programmed frequencies so that you could simply say—

"Go to Button 14 . . ."

Those would be a preprogrammed frequency, usually for control towers, sometimes the EC-130 C&C aircraft, or for Red Crown and Deep Sea. These also had a permanent emergency guard switch at 243.0 MHz, so you were always hearing not only the routine calls on the UHF radio but also the emergency calls, which at times were keeping the calls nearly constant and very confusing.

We had a single VHF radio also with presets and emergency always on at 121.5 MHz also.

There is a single HF radio that is almost never used for anything, but could be for global communications.

A gaggle of extraordinary pilots . .

This represented our combined, warrant officer and commissioned officer Mohawk class at Ft. Rucker, Alabama in spring 1971 before heading to Ft. Huachuca, AZ for the months of sensor flying school.

Chapter 8

TECHNICAL STUFF

This chapter is meant to give you a feeling of some of the technical background material that is unique to the aircraft operations in general.

8-1 / GETTING LOCAL TRAINING

There was about a week or so of aircraft-specific local flight training with one of the 131st flight instructors. On my second tour, I was first, one of the three unit instructor pilots and later moved up and took over the position as the Standardization Instructor Pilot (SIP). As such I had oversight of the other IPs and all the training—both aircraft-specific and combat mission training. Mission training did not require a certified aircraft IP, just someone with good mission skills to fly some missions with the new pilots.

Everyone would start off flying our bread-and-butter mission of the 24/7 SLAR missions on Route Pack 1 (RP-1) off the coast of North Vietnam. That would amount to eight flights a day. Only later would one move over to flying SLAR in Laos in Steel Tiger North and South and even later to the CIA's Secret War in North Laos where one got to live in the Paradise Hotel in downtown Udorn, Thailand. The Steel Tiger South SLAR missions were done for some weeks first, as the ones in Steel Tiger North involved dangerous flight operations near Tchepone.

The reality was that the training times had to be used to determine who would fly what. The safest and easiest missions were clearly RP-1. These were hard to screw up—though I did a few times—but I had to work at it.

The 131st at one time had been heavy with up to a dozen majors, and an LTC or two as CO or XO, and occasionally a captain or lieutenant as pilots. We lost many them in the process, too. Most of these guys were older and more experienced.

By the time, I went to flight school in 1968 the Warrant Officer Candidates for fixed-wing aircraft had, in our group, an FAA Commercial Pilot's license and averaged over 500 hours of flight time *before* entering the Army flight program.

X-Flight Training

A new company pilot received three or four local area flights that were routine and were working up over a few days to doing emergencies and then starting onto the RP-1 trips. The new mission trips were done first with a couple of flights with a training pilot doing the TO functions and then the best of the TOs assigned for the first few flights.

Our commander, Lt. Col. Frank Newman, was killed in a training crash at Phu Bai just weeks before I arrived when one of the engines seemed to have autofeathered on a touch and go landing, a maneuver I almost never, ever, did just because of this. They both ejected at the end of the runway, but neither one got seat separation, and the CO died.

X-Weapons Training

That was limited as we had to go off the airfield and over to Camp Eagle for weapons work, so that was usually passed up until our annual rifle and pistol qualifications. Along with my Colt .38 Special, and a personal M16, I also had a personal M3 grease gun, a .45 caliber machine gun that I got from who-knows-where that I fired a few times on the range. With a short barrel and only one moving part, a spring actuated firing bolt; I might as well have thrown the gun at someone than trying actually to hit them.

I had one of these, too.

I kept this particular gun by my bed, along with my pistol that was either under my pillow or in my boot, also right at my bedside.

Our personal M16 was under lock-and-key in our armory hut, so having something besides your pistol was helpful. This was just another *delusion of safety* and *security*.

8-2 / SURVIVAL VESTS & GEAR

Because of the Martin-Baker ejection seats, we wore survival vests that were different from the other Army pilots and were special only to the Mohawk to accommodate the ejection seat crewmember harness and its attachment points. The vest is worn over the flight suit, and under the ejection seat harness assembly, so it took a few minutes to get this on.

You had two vests, one for over water flying so that would be on SLAR missions on RP-1, and the other for overland survival in Laos and North Vietnam. Our Escape & Evasion (E&E) hooch/shop had a wide assortment of gear you could select from to customize your vests to your own likes. The E&E NCO would also sew on the holsters, pouches, more ammo strips or whatever you wanted onto your personal vests.

For the most part, the survival vests had a pistol holster, supplementing your own personal piston you carried on your belt, and for either a Browning Model 1911 .45 cal automatic pistol or a .38 cal revolver. Most of the Mohawk pilots carried the .38's; while I observed that most of the helicopter guys took the Browning .45 automatic, a better pistol for sure if you got into a real fight. Might it be related to the ejection issues with a much heavier .45 cal?

You usually had extra ammo strips sewn onto the vest. Because we flew mostly in Laos, and we never got anyone back alive, we had as many pieces of ammo sewn on as there were open spaces on the vest, and then right on down the sides, under the arms, etc. The idea was to shoot your way out, but keep one for yourself as no one, *no one*, came back from Laos. **No one.**

You carried identical twin survival radios and extra batteries for each of them. A large blade survival knife is on your chest, and a smaller one, a flip out knife with a curved parachute cutting blade is up on your shoulder so you could get it out, held on with a string and cut the parachute cords if you were hung up in a tree. Most of us wore another knife strapped to our ankle or on our pilot's pistol belt.

So you understand, we went into combat with two pistols, three knives, two radios, four batteries and all the ammo you could carry—*and the heck with the fishing gear.*

You usually took a few pencil flares and an electronic flashing beacon with a restricted aiming cover so it could only be seen from above on a rescue and not mistaken as gunfire, which I understand it sometimes was by a rescue crew—sometimes to bad outcomes.

There is also an assortment of fishing nets and food and medical pouches with first aid and narcotic pain injectors, which are nice to have.

The vests used for North Vietnam SLAR missions carried as much shark repellent as could be attached. Sharks were a very deadly issue. Some crew members from the Services, who had ejected or downed into the South China Sea, were killed and eaten.

Your personal flotation is *water wings*, automatic or manual inflation flotation, which is under your armpits. On the overwater vests, the water wings are sewn onto the vest. While flying over Laos, we usually had the water wings as a smaller strap on harness under the vest so we could shed them as need be. You would have inflated just one of the water wings before going into the water, then surfaced and inflated the other wing.

Then you waited for the sharks . . .

While you always carried your personal pistol with you, before each mission you checked out another pistol from the E&E NCO and loaded it at the shop door before you went out. As you started working towards your mission of the day, or night, you might customize the vest with some other stuff and then take it, and the ejection harness, out to the aircraft and hang it on your side drop tank while you went working on the mission planning.

Under the ejection seats, and going out with it, is either a small raft for overwater flights or the overland kit with much more survival gear. The small raft you could inflate before going into the water and try to climb into it after you surfaced in your water wings.

The bad news here is that when we had all tried at survival school to do this in a swimming pool, no one could actually get into the raft when wearing the harness and vests. This surely being a *fly-in-the-ointment* for survival issues. The overland seat packs had more food, water, a tent, and more medical stuff: the idea being that a sea rescue probably only hours away while surviving in the jungle might be much longer.

8-3 / SURVIVAL - BLOOD CHITS, SAFE LETTERS, AND RESCUES

X-*Blood Chits*

Your personal Blood Chit is stuffed into your flight suit.

All the crewmembers carried a personal, serial-numbered, *Blood Chit* that we stuck down inside our flight suits. The *Blood Chit* is a waterproof, tear-proof, silken large napkin-sized item that has the American flag and financial offers in several languages of rewards for helping you survive or getting you back to safety. The program payouts are a secret as to who used it and who has been rewarded. This secrecy is because of evidence regarding deadly reprisals to individuals, families, and even whole villages if discovered they had helped an American to safety.

Flying in northern Laos, in the CIA's war, most of us also wore solid gold *Baht Chains*; usually, several of them, around our necks to use to barter for helping us survive. Frankly, I think the other side would only kill you, and take the gold, and not have to mess with you. We also routinely wore solid gold *Four Seasons* bracelets for the same reason.

X-Safe Letters

Just before a mission departure your personalized Intel briefing, besides the anti-aircraft fire situation, you would receive a quick briefing on any recently downed airmen and a showing up on the wall of the current *Safe Letter*. Safe Letters, once used, are retired, and a new one is started. The Safe Letter is something you are supposed to try to make visible on the ground so that aircraft or our always running aerial photographs would see it. It had to be something that could look like a letter, such as –S-, -H-, etc., and could be created in an open area out of whatever is at hand, such as branches, or stomping on the grass or anything large and in contrast with the background. It thus would not be visible to someone, the bad guys, whom might be walking right over it while looking for you.

When someone is rescued using the *Safe Letter,* then the next one is used so that a new rescue is not attempted on someone already found or known to be dead or captured. It also meant that a Safe Letter could show up months, even years after our guys were shot down and are either on the loose or had escaped. No one ever (or few) escaped that were downed in Laos, and no one ever returned—thus, the extra pistol ammo sewn onto your vests.

X-Search and Rescue (SARS)

Most rescues in our area of operations were performed by the Air Force *Aerospace Rescue and Recovery Service.* There are some great books online and in the stores by some of these brave rescue teams—many of who were lost trying to save others. More than 40 of the HH-53 rescue helicopters were lost just in combat operations, with a lot of lost crewmembers to boot.

What you were supposed to do if downed is to hide and use your radio and go on the run only if you have too. In Laos nearly all our attacks were on the Ho Chi Minh Trail so in theory if you only moved away from *the Trail*, you should be okay and preferably moving to the west from *the Trail* towards Thailand would be best.

Not to discard the issue of snakes, spiders, more snakes, Bengal tigers and other natural dangers to your life, and the lack of food and medical needs to boot. Being shot down and not captured is only a part of the problem.

If in hiding and a recovery by ground forces is used, the process was a team of South Vietnamese soldiers, dressed as NVA, are inserted. They are to come looking for you. To tell them apart from the NVA the plan was that they would be two things: 1) they would be visibly more heavily armed than most NVA or VC, and 2) they would be walking through the area in silence. No chatter, no talking. These were the two primary clues that these guys were friendlies and even then—wait to be found. Do not get up and run to the rescue teams.

In our flight suits, we routinely had one or two of the four plastic water bottles in our flight suit's thigh and calf pockets filled with something like Scotch so that you had something to drink after landing to calm your nerves perhaps, or use for medical purposes.

X-CS Gas Was Often Used on Rescues

Four A-1 Skyraiders, carrying CS gas, HH-53 Jolly Green and the KC-130 Fueling Tanker

If during a rescue the issue of the bad guys being nearby then the Air Force would often use the A-1 Skyraiders, call sign *Sandy*, carrying a form of *CS gas* to blanket the immediate area or even for some hours I have seen them setting most of an entire hill covered in CS gas.

The gas would incapacitate you completely in the manner of throwing up and bowel movements and maybe worse, but it also did the same to the bad guys. Then the Air Force rescue guys would come down on a jungle penetrator and with their own gas masks and either get you out of the trees or go looking for you if they saw your chute nearby or otherwise get you out.

8/ Technical Stuff 277

The Air Force's A-1 Skyraiders were critical to most rescues using CS gas and guns for very close support for downed airmen and the rescue guys.

A-1E Skyraider escorting a HH-3C as it goes to pick up a downed pilot
1966 Vietnam, USAF photo

Chapter 9

AS IT WAS - HUE/PHU BAI

Phu Bai, while landing to the east

9-1 / THE VIETNAM ARRIVAL EXPERIENCE

Just like in the movie Platoon, people mostly came in one's and two's as replacements and as such they individually had little connection to others. Fortunately, maybe, the Mohawk community is so small that you probably knew all the guys within 2-3 months before and after your flight school class. Generally, that was less than a dozen guys, versus the helicopter classes that had about 700 pilots a month. As replacement pilots arrived, you likely did know someone either from Army flight school or past unit assignments.

It took maybe 3-5 days for Army replacements to migrate up from Bien Hoa, near Saigon, after a 22-hour flight from Travis AFB in California or McCord AFB in Washington with fueling stops in Anchorage and Japan.

During the few days at Bien Hoa, we slept in bunk beds covered with individual mosquito nets and were moved around in buses with armor and screening on the windows. One had arrived!

I am issued the new Vietnam-era Army jungle fatigues and a minimum of personal gear, as our unit would supply the rest. New name tags are sewn on, and new jungle boots were given to us. We did not need to worry about polished boots here. For flying, we had full leather flight boots as the issued jungle boots were partially constructed with nylon that would melt to your foot in an aircraft fire.

There were some orientation classes dealing with medical issues, hygiene, the taking of the daily or weekly malaria pills, and the very critical importance of carrying your own toilet paper with you wherever you went even in your flight suit as you would seldom, if ever other than at an Air Force location, find toilet paper in a latrine. Nice things, *important things*, to know and do.

Our money was taken from us and replaced with the Army Military Payment Certificates (MPCs), as actual US currency, greenbacks, are not allowed by US soldiers inside Vietnam. Later I would find that the 131st did not comply with these rules because we routinely worked on any given day back and forth to Thailand and we needed real US currency. When you went on R&R, they would exchange back your MPC for real money and reverse that when you return.

No weapons, of course, were issued. We would get all that from our own unit's armory, but we did certainly all feel a bit barren as we looked around and everyone is carrying at least one weapon and often two counting a pistol for the officers and NCOs.

From Bien Hoa, if assigned to the Mohawk units, the 131st at Hue/Phu Bai or the 245th SAC at Marble Mountain Army Airfield, you rode on an Air Force C-130 Hercules north to I Corps while making some stops along the way to drop off other new guys.

One had arrived! In a real war! If we only knew then what . . .

At the assignment station in Bien Hoa, I had started to express my preference for where I wanted to go, me being a fresh-faced, 20-year old warrant officer one, a WO1—*a mere kid pilot dressed up like a real soldier.* The NCO working the paperwork in a crowded building had immediately shut me down, clearly thinking I am looking for a cushy assignment in the south, where they had real beds and food in the mess halls. However, as he is rebuffing me to shut up, I blurted out something about going to the 131st at Hue in I Corps. *Dead silence followed.*

Did I want to go to I Corps? Was I nuts? From that moment the NCO started treating me like I was a colonel—this guy *wants* to go north so don't say or do anything but let him move there as soon as possible. I suspect that there was a quota to be met and anyone that intentionally pissed off some assignment NCO, or someone they just did not like—is sure to be headed to I Corps.

After the Air Force C-130 ride north I spent a few nights in the buried bunkers at Marble Mountain where our Army headquarters battalion was based. They controlled the pilot assignments to both the 131st Aviation Company and our sister company, one of the other four Mohawk units in Vietnam, the 245th SAC, based there at Marble Mountain. The 245th operated Mohawks only inside of I Corps. Unarmed Mohawks I might add.

After about three days in this bunker, apparently because they had no transient quarters or at lease none then, and being just a WO1, I am pretty low on any assignment priority. After a few days, I am given my Orders and to get on a helicopter that is going to Phu Bai. Incredible! I was there! Over the jungle and beaches in I Corps and going to the 131st—*as I had wanted to*—and no one in their right minds wanted.

There is not much of the jungle going north. We passed the Hai Van Pass north of DaNang and then followed the coast. Drifting by below me were the rice paddies of so many movies and pictures and the endless Vietnamese burial areas with their perfect round covers, as people were buried, I understand, vertically. These round caps were everywhere.

9-2 / CHECKING INTO THE 131ST

I am dropped off on the flight line ramp under the old French-era control tower that is about mid-field and near the exit ramp area of the 131st. I had a duffle bag of new clothes—*and not a clue what I am getting into.*

I had arrived. Armed Mohawks were sitting there! The 85th Evac Hospital is in the lower right, the 131st to the very far right and on the left side were the helicopter groups.

I was *expected*, but no one came for the new guys. I had to lug my gear down the ramp and find my way to the administrative 131st Orderly Room where I was to report to the First Sergeant. It was interesting. Remember, we went from basic training directly to flight school for nearly a year and then to the Mohawk course at Ft. Rucker and Ft. Huachuca, Arizona and then right to Vietnam. Other than some of the guys that had been previously enlisted, or NCOs and then went to warrant officer flight school—*none of us had ever been in a real military unit of any sort*—just schools.

I was there! I got a hooch assignment, and one of the enlisted guys gave me a rundown on what to expect and what to say or more importantly—*what not to say or do.* The new CO is not there, a replacement for the 131st CO that had just died at Phu Bai in a flight training accident a few weeks before. I would not meet any of the other officers until that evening in our little shack of an officer's club (previously blown up by rockets), called the Spud Club.

I had arrived. The sensation is a bit surreal to be sure, but it was much like Charlie Sheen in *Platoon* when one comes one-by-one, not as part of a unit or group, just one replacement after the other—*alone*. This was itself a troubling situation the Army did start to change until after Vietnam.

9-3 / THE SPUD CLUB

It is the *Officer's Club* for the 131st, and like most Officer Clubs lacked the polish and support that the more member-driven NCO or enlisted clubs had, mostly because there were so few of us to support it. The club is the size of two of the wooden hooches set just slightly down and behind the flight hangars. One end of the small wooden shacks is set at a right angle to the other and is the entrance and bar area. Not so large, maybe thirty feet long by slightly less wide.

A large Hawk emblem is set into the floor tiles. If you were to step on the Hawk, or get thrown onto it, and you had to buy a round of drinks for whoever is at the bar. From time-to-time, depending on the drinking, suddenly someone is jerked off a stool and tossed onto the Hawk. Just the way it was.

Spud Club (Officer's Club) and surely another Frank Lloyd Wright Design

One came into the club off the dirt/mud street, a single vehicle wide slosh of gooey mud that is not much more than a pathway, really, going further down to the 571st Medivac hooches and the dual pads for their Dustoff helicopters. The 571st then shared, inside the unsecured Phu Bai airfield, the 131st' inner compound, the clubs, and the mess hall with our unit.

The relationship with the Dustoff guys was prized for other reasons—starting with we sometimes used the hot Dustoff helicopter to hover-taxi down to the 85th Evac Hospital, pick up some of the nurses, and bring them back to our O-Club. We did this just so we could avoid the hassles the 85th Evac commander had with the nurses leaving the hospital—however, a few Dustoff helicopters on and off the hot pads at night did not draw any attention at all.

This is the new and *improved* Spud Club after a 122 mm rocket tore out the far end

Right outside the bar's front door, and across the road, is the officer's showers, which is just a wooden hooch with open showers and toilet stools. From there, to the right, were about ten of the officer's four-man hooches set up on wooden pegs to keep out of the mud, the rats, and the snakes.

Once inside the O-Club bar to the far end, maybe only twenty feet, and beyond the Hawk in the floor, is a stone bar, built before I got there, with maybe ten bar stools and room for a single bartender, one of the NCOs, working behind it. Drinks were limited to the basics including the old rusty beer cans of those days.

To the right end of the bar is another door that opened only to *Piss Valley*, as it is known. There might have been something else there before, but a recent 122 mm rocket had blown out the end wall and left a large crater hole outside that was never filled in. You could stand there and take a piss, but you did not want to risk falling out *that door*. A brass bell is positioned by the door to Piss Valley and would be rung whenever someone had stepped on, *or tossed on*, the Hawk signaling another round of drinks is being poured.

To the left then, as you came into the bar area, is a room with about ten or so four-person round tables. To the right from there is a small stage area. Behind the stage is a kitchen area where we had Vietnamese women making food from—*well, we were not sure what the food is made of*. But we would have some *mystery meat* sandwiches from time-to-time and even steak, assuming someone had gone to DaNang and stolen some from the Air Force clubs.

Must have left my then good looks in Vietnam

At the end of the table area, the wall area is used for our near nightly running of 8 mm porno flicks made in a dirty hotel room. Such is the case then—how far we have come today!

The club is somewhat protected outside by stacked 55-gallon drums of sand one-on-top of the other. The roof was covered with PSP like is used for runways and was then covered over by more sandbags.

X-Spud Suits

Many aviation units have their own party suits, and we were no different. One did not have to be there but a few days before a new black party suit is ordered from the tailors in Ubon and brought back from a beer run flight—most correctly identified as a *forced* diversion to Ubon—over the flak in Laos, because you could not land at Phu Bai. Something about the airfield being down to zero-zero conditions, or it was to get laid, get some real food, do some shopping and *only then* fly back across Laos? There was a vast and ever growing number of emblems one would have sewn on. Some were standard for our Mohawk unit, like SLAR, or IR or VR emblems.

We were really a class act, to be sure

A Ski Mu Gia Pass (North Vietnam) patch is typical, but only if you had earned the patch by having done that dangerous and deadly event either on a VR or IR flight. So if not an IR or VP pilot, and no wanted to be one and die young, then you did not have one. The general use patches for the 131st were always enough to decorate the best of suits. If we went someplace to show off, let's say the Udorn Air Force O-Club, then showing up in a Spud Party Suit is standard fare.

Tiger Hound represented Steel Tiger North & South (southern Laos)

Notice the wall images

Upholding the warrant officer's good name.

You either sat on your damp bed by the mud or went across the muddy road and into our club and conducted educational discussions—or drank a lot.

Grady Wilson and Mary Ann.

Captain Gray Wilson and Mary Ann at our club. Grady went through flight school with me and to the 131st as our maintenance officer and pilot extraordinary. Years later Grady is on the *60-Minutes* show as a whistleblower on the deadly Bell/Boeing V-22 Osprey program (good for him!). I do not know how he got from being a fixed-wing Mohawk pilot to being the *Chief Test Pilot* for Boeing on the Osprey. He was flying the third V-22 out for testing and that one rolled over and crashed. Later, Grady is flying trail, when during flight-testing, a V-22, with seven Marines on board, while transitioning from airplane mode to vertical mode—came apart and killed everyone in front of him.

Mary Ann was truly one of the most wonderful of the nurses and a great human being that suffered probably more than we all did. As you can see, she had her own Spud Party Suit too.

9-4 / AIRBORNE TV VERSUS OUR PORNO MOVIES

My, how far we have come these days in adult entertainment. Each night we received a couple of hours of military TV news from a circling C-121 Super Constellation aircraft. There was no other programming that I can recall.

Our only other entertainment is the standard fare of 8 mm *made-in-a-motel room*, porno movies running maybe 5-8 minutes—and all obviously with the identical plots. How far we have come! Some guy would come back from an R&R and have four or five of these to pass around the units, and we would try to commandeer one or two of the ever-failing projector bulbs and watch these flicks.

9-5 / RATS - EVERYWHERE IN OUR PHU BAI COMPOUND

Rats were everywhere in our compound—in the hooches, under the hooches, in our clubs, which were just other hooches; the mess hall, walking down the dirt paths, in the showers, and worst of all, in the bunkers and the culverts we had between the hooches and used as quick hiding during rocket and mortar attacks.

Damn . . I really, really hate rats!

We had a rat problem to be addressed from time-to-time. In our Spud Club, the twin hooch setup we loosely referred to as the 131st Officer's Club, we had, even more rats. The rat problem was likely because our club was next to a sewage dump and right across the few feet of dirt from my hooch. And because we did some cooking there, in the back, by a Vietnamese woman making sandwiches and what would pass as *mystery meat* burgers. Because there are no cattle for the markets, what was the *mystery meat burgers* was possibly the closely related kin to the rats we had all over the rest of the club. These were questions you surely did not want to ask, for fear what the answers might be.

We had two interesting rat incidents. The first was *Herbie the Rat*, a furry creature that lived under the stone bar in the front section of the club area. Herbie was sometimes seen to be scrambling from under the bar, where no doubt he is getting the best of both foods and spilled liquor, and going outside through the side door that opened, literally, to *Piss Valley*.

As it was, *Herbie* was a bit of a barroom fixture until—*Herbie*, who was apparently really *Herbette*, had a litter of little *Herbie* and *Herbette's*. Now we had, even more, rats right under the bar. This open house status for rats apparently gone too far and had to end. Perhaps it was a shortage back in the cooking room of *mystery meat*, but whatever the reasons, there was a *first rat shooting* one night at our bar. Not unusual, except it was unannounced, but not entirely unexpected. The NCO that is bartending that night pulled out his US Army issued 1911 .45 caliber pistol and started unloading on *Herbette* and her young kin—to the utter amazement of some the pilots that are sitting right there at the bar, some of whom allegedly fell back off their seats. In a flash, without warning, the pistol is violently and brutally unloaded onto this unsuspecting young rat family. Slaughtered, most of them, though some surely did escape out to *Piss Valley*. That was the end of openly tolerating the rats under the bar.

Our other significant live rat event led to some changes in the handling of personal guns in the club. There was an open wall area between the stone bar, which seated maybe 6-8 guys, and the other room is just another wooden hooch section built at an angle to the bar where we had a TV and a half-dozen round tables and chairs.

It was probably going to happen sooner or later, but after a fatal, or a near fatal (for a local rat) shooting in the club, that we adopted this *no-gun rule* for the club. You always had a pistol belt on, *always*, with either a Browning .45 automatic or, more likely, a Colt .38 Special, your choice, but we decided you had to hang-up your gun belt inside the bar door, just like in some old cowboy movie.

What had prompted such action is that one night one of the guys, who had long passed the point of good reason, is sitting at the end of the bar and watching whatever is the night's 8 mm porn features and a *big* rat—probably having only recently escaped from the back cooking area—is going back and forth along a ledge immediately behind where a movie is being projected onto the wall.

The rat may not have been one of Herby/Harriet's kin, but nonetheless with a dozen guys slouching in chairs and with the tables full of bottles—gunfire erupts from the end of the bar going across the room in pursuit of the rat. We assumed the rat—considering the stage of impaired consciousness of the shooter—was never really in any danger of being hit. Anyway, the shooter ~~from the grassy knoll,~~ err . . . from the end of the bar unloaded his pistol *towards* the rat who did escape—but it left more than a few of the guys down on the floor.

So it started that we would leave our guns at the door on wall hooks. This lasted for only a month or so because no wanted to be without his pistol while anywhere inside of our unsecured compound.

9-6 / Bodies Left Hanging Along Side Our Compound Gate

The bodies of local VC or NVA that were killed at our Phu Bai airfield, usually blowing up in the three layers of minefields or shot trying to come through the multiple layers of wire, were often simply hung onto posts beside the main airfield entrance and left hanging there to rot and decay away.

We need to stop war . . everywhere . . for every reason.

What is so tragic is that these decaying bodies were mostly of the local young men and boys. Like the Vietnamese, who worked inside our compound, the hooch maids and cleaning staff or construction workers, each day as they came through the main entrance had to look up and see the village men and boys hanging there, often decaying for weeks on end.

9-7 / OUR HOOCHES

And this is before FSB Barbara tried to level the officer's hooches

We lived for years in this mud, in the monsoon rains, and these little windowless wooden shacks you would not keep as a tool shed. The officer's latrine is at the end, on the right, and the Spud Club, post 122 mm rocket-damaged, is on the left. The Dustoff helicopters were down at the far end of the mud road.

Who says you cannot get used to living in any condition, ***even for years at a time?***

9/ As it Was – Hue/Phu Bai

The monsoon rains lasted for six months' steady at a time.

My hooch is two off on the left; the officer's latrine is on the right, the Spud Club across the muddy road, and the maintenance hangar and flight line up above and behind. You lived within these very few yards, for a year at a time: Just between the hooches and flying. No going anywhere, no leaving the base at all. This situation is especially challenging for the non-flying guys of all the ranks, as they lived in this mud all the time—though still better than the infantry or the artillery firebases.

At least the flying guys, the pilots, and the TOs got to divert from time-to-time over to Ubon, Thailand, maybe with an overnight maintenance issue, get a dose of the real world and then come back to the mud and the mortars and the rotten food.

We had apparently pissed off some of the enlisted guys because one night a hand grenade is placed on a stick at the door of the latrine, with a string to pull the grenade pin out. It is in the mud, and when one of the officers, in the dark, stepped down onto the string—not swinging his foot over it—the stick holding the other end is only pulled over, and the grenade pin is not pulled out. *Lucky, lucky, lucky.*

We lived in standard windowless wooden hooches that were lifted up on blocks or support posts. This kept us out of the water, mostly, and the snakes and various other creatures that live in a jungle. The roofs were metal PSP, usually, so we had some protection from small 82 mm mortars. Sandbags placed all over and added another limited layer of protection.

Depending on what stuff you could get ahold of, you might have had a row, or two, of sand-filled metal barrels around your hooch just as our Spud Club had.

While I did see some hooches with rooms, for most of the flight officers there were four of us openly in the hooch with each staking out a corner area and a bit of privacy from stacking up more junk or ammo boxes. The NCOs had the same arrangement, but I think the other enlisted guys, in their hooches, had six to a building rather than four. The NCOs always had it better, as they controlled the supply lines, the equipment, the food, the *whatever could be stolen* from the Air Force and thus lived a better life all around.

Someone else put the artwork up on my wall before I got there . . and that is the story I am sticking with.

It was 1970 and not complaining, because before I got there, the guys had lived a couple of years in tents, in the mud! Unlike those aviation units to the south of us, at the 131st, our beds were metal frames (versus just bare Army cots for my predecessors) with a two-inch mattress that offered only the barest of bedding support. Our sister units at least had real beds to sleep on. Sheets and Army blankets made up what you needed. Should not complain considering how the infantry or artillery units lived.

A single wooden footlocker kept your personal stuff. Bearing in mind that you had to be able to leave or relocate with just what you could have in a duffle bag, so not much personal stuff. As it was, from time-to-time, someone might have gotten a tape player from the PX at the 101st Airborne's nearby Camp Eagle. But, how could you move with it? You could not.

There were a few window-type air conditioning units, but those were only in the CO's hooch, operations office, and a few other places. There were no windows in the hooches so holes had to be into the wall and the units stuck in. Otherwise, you had only fans to move the hot, stinking, air, around, and no windows to open when it is hot and not raining.

Right to the side of my bunk I would put my boots and then tuck my pistol down into one of them. I used to keep my gun under my pillow, but more than a few excessively alcohol indulgent nights convinced me that fluffing up my pillow could have a bloody and dangerous outcome.

The officer hooches, maybe a total of 7-8 of them, lined up along this little single vehicle dirt and mostly mud road just across from the back of the maintenance hangers. Between these hooches and the flight line is our little officer's Spud Club.

9-8 / BUNKERS, CULVERTS AND UNDERGROUND HOLES

No matter where you were, an Army base, Air Force base, or wherever, you kept conscious of *where the bunkers are*. Mostly they were concealed in case the bad guys got inside the compound, and you did not want to point them to your protective shelters so they could toss in explosives.

X-Personal Bunkers at Phu Bai:

Our personal bunkers at Phu Bai. Notice the excellent architectural designs.

I lived in these windowless, monsoon rain-soaked, leaking, wooden sheds for nearly two years.

These were the bunkers located right next to your hooches. At Phu Bai, we had metal culverts half buried in the mud between the hooches that you were to crawl into for protection. What!? Sandbags were stacked around and over the upper part of the exposed culverts. Because the culverts were just half-buried, they were then usually half-full of muddy water or, least we checked, with *snakes*. I never, ever, never went into our personal hooch bunkers, the flooded culverts, at Phu Bai. Never. No matter how many rockets or mortars were raining down on us, never, ever, never go into the small water and snake-infested bunkers. Never!

At Marble Mountain, 90-miles to the south—and a world apart from us, most of the personal bunkers were metal Conex containers buried near the hooches and had a hole in the top so you could climb down into them. These larger containers were covered by several layers of PSP, more reinforcing timbers, and sandbags. The comment about water and snakes was even more so at Marble Mountain, so I never once went into my personal hooch bunker there either. A little time on our hooch's floor, smoking and with a beer, offered just as much protection from the 82 mm mortars, which were up to several hundred a night, but nothing would have protected you from the 122 mm rockets—*so why to worry about it.*

X-Operations and Work Area Bunkers:

Everything had barrels and layers of sandbags and PSP coverings

Usually, but not always, these were above ground at Phu Bai and were heavily fortified with PSP, timbers, and sandbags, with several layers of each. These larger, above-ground bunkers, could take an 82 mm mortar hit, but not a 122 mm rocket. These bunkers were large enough for a dozen or more people and included, as needed, tables, bunks, radios, and more stored weapons.

On my first combat tour, when I arrived at Marble Mountain and was waiting to be assigned and transported to the 131st at Phu Bai, I stayed for several days and nights in a large underground operations bunker that was neat, clean, mostly so, and heavily fortified. On my first night at Marble Mountain, we had mortar attacks, which is why it was called *Marble Mountain Rocket & Mortar Proving Grounds*. The living for a few days in a bunker in Vietnam was incredibly exciting – at that time it was. I am in *the war!* In a bunker while enemy rockets and mortars are impacting above ground—just like in a war movie! Mostly, the dozen or so guys that would venture down into the bunker were just smoking, playing cards and drinking until the all-clear was signaled an hour or two later.

X-Mortars and Rocket Hitting Phu Bai

On my first tour at Phu Bai, in 1970, we had occasional 82 mm rocket attacks, but mostly they were limited to maybe 60-80 rounds, at most. If they wanted to fire at the helicopters, which were a better use than shooting at us, then the mortars were hitting on that side of the airfield and other than the sirens we would just ignore the incoming explosions.

If the 122 mm rockets fired at us, then that is something else because they could not be aimed accurately—just pointed and fired like in the first story of this book. As such, they could impact anywhere, including taking out the end of the Spud Club, right across the mere 25-feet from my hooch. And hiding from them is not realistic at all because the bunkers—if anyone is foolish enough actually to get into one of them in the wet season—is not adequate protection from the rockets.

On my second tour, as the 1972 Easter Offensive started and while we are getting ready to flee to Marble Mountain, we sometimes got *several hundred mortar rounds a night*. Hundreds of them are pouring in for hours and hours. Then fire bases to our west that used to be the ones getting hundreds of incoming, sometimes now were getting more than a thousand mortars a night. That did get our attention!

We got mortared *a lot* at Marble Mountain and right onto the Mohawk ramps. My good friend, Gary, and fellow warrant officer, IR pilot, and all-around good guy (and our guitar player for drunken songs in the club) got a well-deserved Purple Heart from mortar shrapnel he got one night while out preflighting his Mohawk.

For the most part, the mortars and rockets, on the initial incoming barrage, before people were in bunkers or on the floors, were equal opportunity killers—and one's rank is no protection.

There were times of pretty regular mortar attacks, and it is then not unusual to be walking around with a protective flak jacket on, even in the mess hall or club.

A bigger issue for the pilots at Phu Bai is that the runway lights would be off if there were any *incoming*. The airfield tower controllers *might* turn them back on during our last half a minute just before touchdown—might, but not always, and if you had fuel issues, which you usually did, then landing at night to a blackened airfield during frequent mortar attacks was the norm.

9-9 / HOOCH MAIDS

The local Vietnamese population is allowed to work on the military bases in a variety of support roles, from cleaning to warehouses, to food services.

As an officer, you contributed to a joint pot of money to be used for nominal payments to men and women to work in the offices and other non-sensitive areas. Then you had your personal hooch maids that did your housekeeping, as little as there is in a wooden hooch up on stakes and for the hand washing laundry.

Laundry was interesting, as they did this along an internal dirty creek, at least in our area it was, and then hung out to dry in the non-monsoon times. Otherwise, it is hung on ropes strung around the inside of the hooches. Review the movie *Bridge on the River Kwai* for a look at how we lived in Phu Bai. They actually had it better.

The hooch maids were middle-aged women, but I suspect they looked much older than they were. Missing teeth were common and most had blackened teeth supposedly from betel nuts or leaves they liked to eat.

The younger women usually worked in the clubs and mess halls or kitchens.

To be sure, some probably were spying on our equipment and things, but little we could do about that. Most likely the men were interested in our weapons and their location. The majority of the VC and NVA attacks are directed towards the helicopter units on the other side of the runway as there was very little intelligence they could get from watching any of us.

Payments to the locals were in MPC, the <u>M</u>ilitary <u>P</u>ayment <u>C</u>ertificates, or as we referred to, the Monopoly Money that is the only official use money. You were not allowed to possess any real America money in Vietnam, for a variety of reasons, but as flightcrew, as we were back and forth to Thailand, the flight crews did usually have *greenbacks*.

We paid the locals in MPCs, and the hooch maids could convert that to the local currency. Several times a year there was the sudden, *unannounced*, currency exchange days, known as *C-Days* and the base would suddenly lock-down, and all the money would change again. These sudden, unannounced events had to do with black market issues. On a never announced *C-Day* the Vietnamese would be standing outside the fences trying to throw over their MPC at half rate to get new money. Pretty ugly.

9-10 / MESS HALL

Towards the center of our unit compound, was a common mess hall. One of the shortcomings of the Army is the lack of accommodating various working hours. An Air Force pilot, or us too if at an Air Force base, could walk in and get crew meals at any time, day or night, or have them boxed to take with us.

At the Army mess halls, it is more or less standard hours. If you worked late at night and missed breakfast, that is your tough luck. You would just have to do without the endless powdered eggs, powdered milk, too often hot dogs, *even for breakfast*, and find something else to eat.

Our problem was that Phu Bai, other than Quang Tri a few miles to the north, is at the far end of the supply line coming up from Saigon: a world away. Everything, everything from food to supplies, equipment, radios, clothes or whatever, was siphoned off before they even got to DaNang, much less up to us in northern I Corps. The cooks did a good job with what little they had to work with that managed to get even to Phu Bai.

So basically, through no fault of the cooks, the food is not very good. We looked forward to the periods when we would get Army bagged C- or K-rations, which were a whole lot better than anything we would otherwise get to eat.

We understood the Air Force mess halls sometimes were *limited to only two or so flavors of ice cream,* and the steaks were limited to just two apiece at any meal. **WHAT!?**

Occasionally, we did get boxes of steaks, or we had someone go to DaNang and steal them from the Air Force, and then we had cookouts at the Spud Club, and ditto for the NCO and enlisted men's clubs also. The NCOs were always better at trading—or stealing—food, liquor, and other supplies, so they usually got better food and steaks too.

Our other food source was that the Vietnamese were allowed to set up little food kiosks inside the compound during daylight hours. They all had to be out of the compound by nightfall. They had food—*of some sort*. A hamburger there was made of—*something*, which was never determined. Not beef probably, but some *mystery meat*. It was always one of those questions you did not want to ask for fear of what the answer would be. Eating dogs was not, and still being not, uncommon.

9-11 / 85TH EVAC HOSPITAL
X-How It Made Phu Bai Tolerable

How could we have gotten by without at least the moral support of the 85th Evacuation Hospital, located at the far end of our side of the airfield at Phu Bai? This field hospital is the farthest north evacuation hospital in the South Vietnam theater. The 85th Evac supported the immediate medical care, emergency and otherwise, for all of northern I Corp.

Because the Phu Bai airfield compound was itself never a secured base, each unit or organization there is in and of themselves little mini-compounds of sometimes mine fields, concertina razor wire, gun emplacements and armed patrolling guard forces. The hospital had the added responsibility to protect the nurses from the US military forces—mostly from the Army pilots as it was. To that end, the hospital commanders had a formidable array of guards, checkpoints, wires and more. The nurses were the only American military females in Vietnam, or at least in any part of Vietnam that I saw. As I understand it, there were no enlisted women in Vietnam, only the officer nurses.

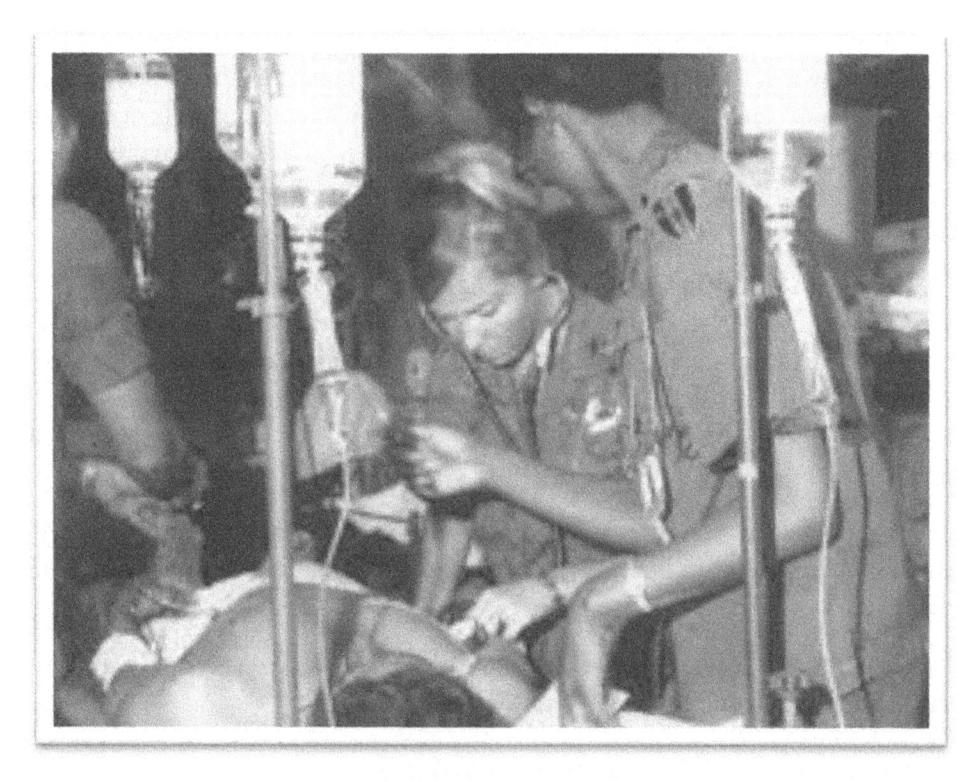

Just getting into the evac hospital compound was a task, and involved an MP security screening at one of the two gates to be sure that one is not *on the list* as it was—wherein my name had shown up a number of times. To be banned from the evac hospital was, at the time, somewhat of a subtle badge of honor amongst all the Phu Bai pilots, be they airplane or helicopter pilots.

Once inside the compound you had access to better bar food, to be sure, a better O-Club, some entertainment, which was not surprising for the number of doctors and nurses there. There was also overall better access to some of the sundry items we could not get over at the PX at nearby Camp Eagle. It is a rare treat just to get into the hospital compound.

For the 131st pilots, it is especially useful, and we were always in some competition for the attention of the nurses with the other *mere helicopter pilots* from the other side of the runway, and more specifically, with the Dustoff pilots who had near constant interaction with the hospital anyway, and with the staff and nurses as they would be flying onto and off the two helipads, often several times a day.

Helping our cause, for the 131st guys, is that we were at the far opposite end of the runway from the 85th Evac and there, for reasons unclear, the Dustoff unit shared our secured (?) mini-compound, our clubs and our mess hall. Most importantly our relationship with the Dustoff guys was that they could crank up a Dustoff helicopter and hover taxi it directly to one of the two hot pads at the hospital; pick up some of the nurses and hover-taxi them down the airplane side of the airfield to be deposited near the Spud Club. From there, we would party into the night, and later the standby Dustoff crew that is on call would crank up the helicopter, put the nurses on board, and they would get back into the hospital compound without logging in or out of the hospital gate. Remembering, that the *hospital* at that point is nothing more than just hooches, a bit nicer than ours, and an assortment of medical rooms, hooches, and these metal curved small buildings used as operating rooms and bed wards.

Near the hospital's hot pads is a morgue where bodies, and at times—*stacks of bodies or body bags*—were kept cold while waiting to be transported south to DaNang. The remains are taken to the DaNang *Graves Registration* facility—one of about thirty such installations in South Vietnam—a vast and sad place, where the bodies, or what pieces there might be, were prepared for movement back to the states.

While our current wars are, as all are, horrible, as it was in Vietnam, especially in northern I Corp, that we had days of over a hundred young men dying, *in a single day!*

I am pretty confident the brave men and women that worked at graves registration have carried an enormous mental scar their whole lives.

X-New Year's Eve and We Were in Trouble

Well, the hospital did have a better club and much better entertainment on the traveling USO shows. Down at our poor guy's end of the runway, in our little partially destroyed officer's club, we had a small stage area that at best we may be, only a couple times, had a no more than C-, or D-grade, USO entertainment, usually just a couple of people. Most of whom we saw, in our little remote club, were Australians. Besides, our club was well infested with rats as you find here in the book and no one wanted to be there, *including us*.

The 85th Evac, likely having dozens of doctors and nurses as the staff, got at least some B+ grade entertainment for their club. So it was that New Year's Eve of 1970. On that night, down at the Spud Club, it is just another bar night, nothing special. But some of us, some that were on *the list*, had other plans for the evening.

That New Year's Eve night several of us, maybe six or so, took a unit jeep and headed to the 85th Evac. We had to bribe our way through the MPs at the entrance gate, but it is New Year's Eve, and that was workable for the good booze we would continually be bringing back from Thailand as the currency of choice to bribe your way in, or out, of some places—or else the folks would be drinking warm beer from rusty steel cans. With a number of flights a week going back and forth to our base at Udorn, or a diversion over to Ubon, and having in our possession US currency that is illegal to have in South Vietnam, we could supply *anything* on short notice and even more with a few days' notice.

So getting through the gate that night was no big deal.

Within an hour or so we had met up with a few of the helicopter pilots that had also made it into the club that night to watch this great Aussie show. We were a little drunk; a given for that evening. Being outsiders, we were forced to stand around at the back of the hospital's officer club, and we felt we were treated, well, *rather shabbily*. The doctors and a variety other higher-ranking officers from Phu Bai had good table areas towards the front of the club while we, against the back walls, could hardly see what is going on with the entertainment. As it was, not being able to see much toward the front we had the chance to look around at the back of the club.

What we found back there were several cases of champagne, in coolers, in the way back of the club waiting, we guessed, for the magic midnight hour to approach.

Being a little drunk already, we decided to liberate two newly, and cold, cases of champagne—as the doctors *obviously* had more than they needed, in our view anyway. We almost got away with the goodies until one of the doctors that were outside taking a pee, at the time recognized what we had. Ouch! The chase was on.

In less than a minute, there were six of us, both helicopter and Mohawk pilots, inside of and sitting on the hood of our one jeep and now driving around their compound. We figured we could get to the exit gate and out before being caught. Even as we approached the hospital's gate, it looked like something is amiss with four of us inside the jeep and two sitting on the back and hood—and the MPs put down the stop bar.

We stopped, and turned around, and heard them yelling for us to stop. Now we had a situation. We drove around for maybe 15-minutes trying to decide what to do next as it is sure that we would not be getting out of the gate that night. Maybe the saving grace was that midnight is approaching, and the ones that saw us, and could identify us, were back inside the club to see what is happening.

We could not get a Dustoff to come for us, but one of the helicopter guys that I did not know until that event, got a radio call over to his unit and fifteen minutes later there was a Huey slick settling onto the hospital hot pad. We were out of there, on the helicopter, hover-taxiing down the Phu Bai flight ramp and dropped us off at the entrance to our aircraft revetments. We were home safe and still with some of the loot.

The night is not over yet.

I lost track of things soon after that. When it was daylight and by then midmorning on January 1st, 1971, that I woke up, in my bunk, partially covered in mud, my flight suit still on, one boot on and one off with a swollen foot. I got up, shuffled out into the monsoon rains, and down the walkway to the officer's showers, still in my muddy clothes. I went in and stood under the cold water until I was cleaned off, still in just one boot, and a soaking flight suit and a big, and hurting head to boot.

I came out of the showers and carefully crossed the now very muddy, single-lane, dirt street to the front of our broken down officer's club and went in and directly to a seat at the stone bar. I needed at least some tomato juice and the club was the only place to get it.

I carefully shuffled to the bar, avoiding our big Hawk in the floor tiles, and took a seat. One of our operations officers is also sitting there and maybe a couple of others. I said nothing. I pulled out a barstool and asked for some juice. I am still dripping wet from the shower, one shoe only, and looking pretty rough. At least I am not still covered in mud. However, I surely liked, and probably still smelled, like I had just climbed out of a horse trough.

As I started to sip my juice, the other officer at the bar asked me how I am feeling? Not so good I admitted.

Then he said that, while he is now on his second tour, and had seen many guys dragged, carried or staggered out of our little club, that just after midnight last night I had pushed the door open and *crawled* into the club, not walked. I was covered in mud from coming up the road and did not have one of my boots on (was still missing somewhere).

Then I had gotten over to the bar, pulled myself up, had a drink, said nothing to anyone, and got back down on the floor and mostly crawled out. He said the guys waited a minute or so and then went outside to be sure I was not passed out in the mud to be driven over by a jeep or truck.

I had to get back to Udorn.

In my defense, if any, I had been in Vietnam only about eight months and two of my best flight school buddies were now dead; Russ Rowe from the FSB Barbara artillery barrage and now, just weeks ago, George Rogalla, my best friend, had disappeared on an IR mission just after we had traded missions.

Within weeks, my last flight school friend, Jack Brunson, and my also roommate at the time, Al Musial, would be shot down in Laos and disappear into the MIA category.

It was shaping up to be a trying year.

I went back to my dirty bunk and slept for a few hours until word came from our commander about the evac hospital champagne raid and that I was fingered (again) as one of the culprits. I am to leave within an hour and go back to Udorn (like that takes much persuasion).

Maybe an hour later I am sitting on a step-up maintenance stand that is up next to the pilot's side of my Mohawk. My helmet is on the ejection seat, and I am using my oxygen mask to suck up what pure, 100% aircraft supplemental oxygen, I could get. I had found my boot, put it on, but I could not get it laced up.

My crew chief came over, *concerned*, very concerned, but less so than the maintenance guy that is riding back to Udorn with me. He is probably scared—and rightfully so; he was about to depart over Laos, in daylight, with what was surely a badly, very badly, hung over 21-year-old pilot.

I would not be back to Phu Bai for several weeks, but nearly two months later the New Year's Eve issue was still a hot topic at the 85th Evac.

X-Surely, Colonel, Sir, I Just Picked Up the Wrong Jacket

After the New Year's Eve adventure and our escape as it was with a helicopter pickup from the hot pad, my name and others were on *the List,* for reasons that were unclear (?); on the hospital commander's list of *undesirables*. I was not so sure if this is an honor—or a matter of some concern? I think the colonel commanding the hospital had in mind something like an Article 32 punishment for what had happened nearly two months before. Or, perhaps they could send us to Vietnam and have us fly nightly combat missions in Laos or helicopter gunship missions in the *A Shau Valley*? Huh?

As it was, two of us, I and one of the captains from my unit, had taken a jeep to the 85th Evac for a bit of a more-or-less private party in the hooch of two of the nurses. Unlike our four-up officer open hooch bedding areas, the doctors and nurses had a hooch with two private bedrooms and an open front room and small kitchen area. *Practically a five-star hotel by our standards,* but still just a wooden hooch up on sticks.

It was nearly midnight, and I had to fly early the next morning, so I – with great reluctance— had to leave. I took the jeep and headed for the exit gate. By fifty yards away I could see not just the MPs at the gate, but the hospital commander, *the Colonel* as it was, himself there checking names and IDs. Did he not have something better to do than gate checking *at that hour of the night*? No wonder we lost the war.

No, the Colonel was there still trying to chase down the New Year's Eve culprits, and it somehow rated very high on his list of priorities. The word might have gotten out that night that two of the pilots from *the List*, were inside his compound— and surely up to no good. *This was partially correct . . .*

Well, no way was I going to get out the gate, and calling for a Dustoff to the hot pad is not going to work either. But what could he do? Any of them do? Send us to Vietnam and put us in combat day and night? In Phu Bai of all hell hole places? Huh?

I drove back to the nurses' hooch and swapped my jacket and hat for that of my captain buddy, who was otherwise occupied in one of the bedrooms—and maybe would be there all night—*if he was that lucky*. This seemed like a good plan, and it worked, to a point. *The Colonel* still at the gate, at nearly midnight, had the MPs check my name on the jacket and the captain bars on the hat. I was waved through and drove back down the road past the control tower to our mini-compound.

The *home-free escape* lasted maybe an hour or two, and it was my commander that was shaking me awake and telling me to get dressed—*I was leaving*. Oh no, not being sent back, *again*, to the Paradise Hotel in Udorn.

My buddy, then with my jacket that had my name badge and warrant officer bars and my hat with warrant officer bars, had been, well, *apprehended* as it were by this colonel. Better him than me. Holding the captain as a hostage, the colonel had called down to my commander—and this is now well past midnight, and he wanted me brought back there, *to be shot*, I suspected. And all this over a few cases of cold champagne we had liberated from the hospital's doctor's officer's club during the New Year's Eve club party. *How petty*.

I quickly dressed in my flight suit as my Mohawk was pulled out onto the blackened Spud ramp. Before my buddy could even get taken back, in this crazy *hostage swap*, this hospital commander was told I had already left on a scheduled mission—and as they were maybe talking about my punishment the cold night swallowed up another Mohawk heading to Udorn and the Paradise Hotel—and that was my punishment.

This whole thing worked out well, and the depth of it likely kept me longer, months longer I suspect, based in Udorn and living the good life at the Paradise Hotel. Tell me there is no justice . . !

Figure 2.—Prompt evacuation increased the wounded soldier's chances of survival.

Terms and Words

AGL

Above Ground Level, versus MSL, Mean Sea Level, or above the ocean waters.

AO / Area of Operations

A term is referencing what the working area is called, such as Steel Tiger, Barrel Roll, the PDJ or wherever.

Bandits

Soviet MiG aircraft of various types.

Barrel Roll

The area in northern Laos—the CIA's Secret War in Northern Laos—that is where the PDJ is. This term used with Alley Cat and Cricket, the Air Force EC-130 C&C crew covering northern Laos.

Bingo Fuel or Bingo Time

Slang used to define when an aircraft had to depart a location to have enough fuel to get back to their base safely.

Call Signs

Spud or *Iron Spud* - the 20th ASTA/131st aircraft

Sandy - the US Air Force A-1 Skyraiders

Nail, Covey, or Raven – US Air Force FACs, O-1 Bird Dog, O-2 Skymaster, or the OV-10 Bronco aircraft

Candlestick – US Air Force C-123 flare aircraft

Spectre – US Air Force AC-130 gunships

Spooky - Laotian AC-47 gunships

Stinger - US Air Force AC-119 Gunships

Dustoff - the Medevac helicopters

Deep Sea – Air Force aircraft in the South China Sea, off the coast of North Vietnam that gave SAM and MiG alerts

Red Crown - Navy controller, as is Deep Sea, off the coast of North Vietnam also for SAM and MiG calls and for coordinating rescues
(There is some question about this and if you know more, let me know)

AIR FORCE EC-130 COMMAND & CONTROL AIRCRAFT
Alley Cat - Night aircraft in the Barrel Roll (PDJ) and Steel Tiger North (Tchepone)
Cricket - Daytime aircraft in the Barrel Roll (PDJ) and Steel Tiger North
Hillsboro - Daytime aircraft in southern Laos, in Steel Tiger South
Moonbeam - Nighttime aircraft in the south of Laos, in Steel Tiger South

COBRA / COBRA GUNSHIPS
The AH-1 gunships with a large, center-mounted, machine gun and pods of rockets hung on each side. Usually flown by two pilots with the front pilot as the gunner with a head-mounted gun targeting system.

A Cobra is often part of a *fire team* of aircraft including, usually, an OH-6 Loach. DMZ

The demilitarized zone separating North and South Vietnam.

DEEP SEA
The call sign of US Air Force airborne aircraft that, along with Red Crown, coordinated the issue of MiGs (Bandits) and SAM missile firing. We had to check in with Deep Sea and Red Crown on all of RP-1 SLAR missions.

See *Red Crown*

DUSTOFF
Medical evacuation helicopters, usually a UH-1 with a red cross painted on it to make it a better target for enemy gunners.

AIR FORCE EC-130 COMMAND & CONTROL AIRCRAFT
Designated as Airborne Command, Control & Communications (ABCCC) missions. In this book, it refers to the USAF EC-130 C&C aircraft that were part of the 7th Airborne Command and Control Squadron. The 7th Airborne Command and Control were based at the Udorn RTAFB.

These were special Air Force EC-130s that had an insertable *control capsule* wherein a dozen or more guys worked communications and mission coordination. There were 24-hour coverage and two sets of control call signs for each.

Over northern Laos in the Barrel Roll (PDJ) and Steel Tiger North, in southern Laos, in the area of Tchepone was Alley Cat at night and Cricket in the daytime.

Over Steel Tiger South, in the south of Laos was Moonbeam at night and Hillsboro during the day.

Also, see call sign *Deep Sea*.

ECM / ELECTRONIC COUNTER MEASURES

The 131st Mohawk had an APR 24/25 passive ECM system with a glare shield mounted scope display and rows of warning lights to identify the types of radar, such as SAM sites, ground radar, air-to-air, and others.

EJECTION SEAT

The Mohawk is equipped with a Martin-Baker J5 ejection seat that had a built-in crewmember parachute. These were dangerous and not always working as was expected, but they did save many lives of crewmembers that had to *punch out* of a crippled aircraft.

FAC - FORWARD AIR CONTROLLER

While the Army used Cessna O-1 Bird Dogs, a single-engine airplane to do recon and to spot for artillery, the Air Force used three different types of aircraft for controlling attack aircraft on strafing and bombing runs.

They used the Cessna O-1 Bird Dog (but a better version than the Army O-1) and the Cessna O-2 Skymaster, a two-engine pusher-puller aircraft and later, the North American OV-10 Bronco, a twin-engine turboprop aircraft.

The OV-1 Mohawk, while technically an observation designation, was seldom used for visual observation, though, of course, we flew armed VR (visual recon) in the 131st. Most of the first Mohawk detachment aircraft units also had the armed Mohawk.

FAST-MOVER

The term usually for an Air Force or Navy jet. ATC might give you a call to point out unidentified *fast-movers* to your side or coming across in front of you.

See *Slow-Movers*

FIRE TEAM

In this book, usually referring to one or two Army AH-1 Cobra gunships and a Loach all working together to find targets (the Loach) and the Cobras to attack. There are sometimes references to a Light Fire Team (one Cobra and a Loach) or a Pink Team or Pink Fire Team.

GCA / GCA APPROACH

<u>G</u>round <u>C</u>ontrolled <u>A</u>pproach. Is radar used on the final approach to a specific runway. Another radar controller, usually GCI, would vector an aircraft onto a long final alignment and then the GCA controller took over with constant nonstop and small corrections to your descent and alignment—right down to touchdown in zero-zero, or near so, weather.

GCI / GCI Control Approach

Ground Control Intercept. The term for the area radar controller usually near an airfield that would bring an aircraft around and hand off to the GCA *final controller* to be talked-down to a landing.

Guard (On Guard)

Refers to the emergency frequencies for both the VHF (121.5Mhz) or UHF (243Mhz) radios. The military radios, besides the set-in or selected in-use frequencies, always have ON Guard receiving with a small switch that takes one immediately to transmitting on the Guard (emergency) frequency. Besides aviation emergencies, calls about SAM missiles and MiGs were transmitted in the blind on the Guard frequencies.

Gunship

Could be any one of a number of aircraft, but in this book, I am usually referring to any one of the Air Force AC-130 *Spectre*, the AC-119 *Stinger* or the Laotian AC-47 *Spooky* gunship, all of which had mini-guns. The USAF ones had advanced cannons and even a 105 mm artillery gun in some of the *Spectre* gunships.

The Gunship term is also about the Army AH-1 *Cobra* and the UH-1C *Hogs*, themselves with miniguns, rockets and more.

Graves Registration

There was a total of some 30 American graves registration facilities in Vietnam where the bodily remains, if any, were taken for embalming and preparation for shipment back to the states.

IFF – Friend or Foe (Transponders)

Is the Mode 4 setting of the military transponders that put out a signal, which while not specifically identifying the aircraft, such as Mode 3 for ATC, nor Mode 2 (mission-specific codes), it does somehow determine the plane to be a *Friend* (our friend to be sure) or a *Foe*.

In The Blind (radio calls)

These are radio calls transmitted to no one in particular, such as calls about SAM missiles or MiGs (Bandits) or other emergencies.

IR / Infrared

The heat sensing system that the OV-1C, Super-C and OV-1D carried. The OV-1D could switch between the IR and SLAR system. The IR system had several hundred feet of IR sensitive film running through the system. The IR had a cockpit display that the TO monitored and adjusted to get the best image and resolution.

Some IR uses were real-time, such as running targets from a SLAR tracking of *Movers* to see if they were tanks or trucks. Other missions were closed, in that we ran the IR mission over predetermined target areas and the Spud Intel guys would later read-out the film looking to discover something, like equipment, vehicles, etc.

LIMA SITE-20A / LONG TIENG

Was the CIA's secret airfield known as LS-20a (Lima Site-20a) at Long Tieng, in northern Laos. At one time, this was the busiest airfield in South Asia, with over 400 flight operations a day, **but it was not on any map**.

As the war was spooling up the village of Long Tieng, north of Vientiane, became the staging city and airfield for Air America, the CIA-funded air operations group. However, Lima Site-20a was never shown on any map and the LS-20a designation, versus just LS-20, was probably meant to get people to think that it was referring to a small sub-site of little consequence somewhere near LS-20.

LOACH

An Army OH-6 Cayuse (Hughes Model 369) light observation helicopter. Usually used with an AH-1 Cobra in a *fire team* group. Some of the aircraft had

MARBLE MOUNTAIN ARMY AIRFIELD / MMAAF

Marble Mountain Army Air Field near DaNang. The 131st moved south to Marble Mountain in the spring of 1972 after the local Mohawk unit flying I Corp missions; the 245th SAC was deactivated. We stayed there until late August 1972, just after I was medevac'd to the USAF hospital in the Philippines.

MIGS (BANDITS)

MiGs were the Soviet fighter jets, mostly the MiG-17 and 19s, but maybe later some newer models.

MIGCAP

These were the overhead, usually round-the-clock, missions of Air Force fighters staying aloft to protect others from the MiGs. Usually, to stay aloft for an extended time, the planes would be sitting with or attached to an Air Force KC-135 aerial refueling tanker.

MOVERS

Our term for little black dots on SLAR screen or the film that showed that something was moving along a road or trail or stream. The Movers then were passed to the gunships or down to the IR aircraft to make a run past them and see what type of target they were.

Also, see Fast-Movers

MSL
Mean Sea Level, or height above the ocean waters.

NKP
Nakhon Phanom (NKP), an Air Force base located in the very northeast border of Thailand and Laos. The AC-119 *Stinger* gunships and the C-123 *Candlestick* flare dropping aircraft operated out of NKP.

PAVN - PEOPLE'S ARMY OF VIETNAM
Usually referred to as the NVA (North Vietnamese Army)

PDJ - PLAIN OF JARS
The area in northern Laos where the CIA's Secret War in Northern Laos was fought mostly by the Hmong tribes people and funded and backed by the CIA. For flight control purposes, this was referred to as the Barrel Roll.

PUNCH OUT
To eject from an aircraft.

RED CROWN
Call sign of the radar-equipped USS Long Beach or the USS Chicago (different times, same mission) stationed in the northern part of the Gulf of Tonkin, that called out Bandits (MiGs) and SAM launches. It was usually Red Crown that we had heard coordinating rescues.

See *Deep Sea*

RP-1 / ROUTE PACK-1
The SLAR track up along the lower coast of North Vietnam to a point south of Vinh, North Vietnam. There were also RP-2 & 3 missions that I think were later flown by Navy P2V aircraft. The SLAR was used to round-the-clock keep track of ground traffic up to 45 miles inside North Vietnam.

RTAFB
Royal Thai Air Force Base, of which many were used by American forces.

RTB
Return-to-Base, going home or wherever they went.

SAM MISSILE
Refers to the Soviet-built SA-2 surface-to-air missile.

SLAR
Side-Looking-Airborne-Radar. What the OV-1B and OV-1D models carried for mapping ground *Movers* up to about 60 miles either side of the aircraft's ground track.

SLOW-MOVERS
Aircraft, other than the *Fast-Movers*.

SPARKLERS
Was the term for small arms gunfire, mostly from AK-47s, shot at overflying aircraft. When flying low and moving fast, is what you saw was sometimes dozens of these **sparklers:** the muzzle flashes from the guns.

SPUD OR IRON SPUD
Call sign of pilots with the 131st. Each pilot had a personal Spud call sign (Spud 22 was mine). The missions were flown with a Spud mission number, mainly to confuse us all.

STEEL TIGER / NORTH & SOUTH
The areas of southern Laos designated as targeting boxes. Each area had its gunships. Usually, an AC-130 *Spectre*, flare aircraft like an Air Force C-123, a 131st SLAR aircraft flying high for finding moving targets and a low 131st IR aircraft to run over the SLAR targets to determine if the gunships should attack.

TCHEPONE
The deadliest and most heavily defended NVA area in Laos, inside of Steel Tiger North, and about 40 miles to the west of the tri-borders of Laos, North and South Vietnam.

TIGER ISLAND
A small North Vietnamese island that was just northeast of the DMZ and was our starting and ending point for RP-1 SLAR missions up and down the coast of North Vietnam.

TO OR TECHNICAL OBSERVER
TO is not an accurate term or was not by the time the Vietnam War came about. The IR and SLAR systems were set up, film loaded and the mission itself run by the right-seater, or TO, who was an enlisted man usually at the grade of E-4, Spec 4, and above. On many of the advanced IR missions, we had the senior TOs, often highly experienced E-6s as the TOs.

The absolute *keep-you-alive* entity on an IR flight was almost entirely the doing of the TOs, keeping you from hitting mountains and dodging the gunfire and flak.

TRAIL, *THE TRAIL*
The Ho Chi Minh Trail was the extensive system of various supply routes, small roads or just jungle bike and walking trails, coming out of North Vietnam and into Laos. As *the Trail* moved down through Laos (Steel Tiger North and South) it branched hundreds of times to other roads and trails that went through the border into South Vietnam.

WILD WEASEL

Refers to the Air Force and Navy aircraft specially equipped to attack SAM sites using a mixture of electronic jamming and missiles that could home in on a SAM site's radar signals.

WOC - WARRANT OFFICER CANDIDATE

The Army primarily used warrant officers, perhaps 80% or so, for the Vietnam pilots. The WOCs, or Warrant Officer Candidates, only had to be 18-years old to start flight school and being dedicated just to aviation. As the years went by the warrant officers were usually the unit Instructor Pilots and Maintenance Officers because the commissioned officers, each assigned to their respective branches (infantry, armor, supply, artillery, etc.), would rotate in and out of aviation assignments while the warrant officers stayed dedicated just to aviation.

Otherwise, a *WOC* was something to throw at a *wabbit* . . .

ABOUT THE AUTHOR

Gerald Naekel

www.GeraldNaekel.com

I had come to Vietnam *the first time* in early 1970 after some 11-months of Army basic training and then a graduate of the Army's fixed-wing flight schools. I am a 20-year old Army warrant officer—a newly minted young WO1, fixed-wing pilot. There were another 5-months of Mohawk flight training at Ft. Rucker, Alabama (the home of Army aviation) and then it was on to Ft. Huachuca, Arizona (learning to fly with the aircraft's sensors, the IR, SLAR and camera systems). I was now a Grumman OV-1 Mohawk command pilot.

It was not like this is my first great adventure; I had learned to fly in high school and in 1968, when I was 18-years old, I am hired by my friends at Emery Aviation in Greeley, Colorado (where I lived and learned to fly) to ferry a slightly used single-engine Cessna 205 from Washington State to Brasilia, the then relatively new wilderness capital of Brazil.

I spent over three weeks *just getting there,* and I had slept some nights, lost, out of fuel, in the Amazon's Great River Basin on an old abandoned airfield at Macapa. It was then, a number or days and nights later, onto the Amazon port city of Belem, and nearly a week later to Carolina and to the interior Brazilian Plateau of Bahia before arriving at Brasilia, *alone*.

As it was then, I had nine countries flying experience, mostly alone, under my belt before I am nineteen years old. There were jungles, swamps, and at times fueling through a chamois from a hand pumped barrel while in remote wilderness areas. Sometimes sleeping in this airplane, a pistol under my belt, and *clueless* of what a dangerous environment I worked in.

When I later flew home to Colorado commercially from Brazil, and as much of an anti-war individual as I later became, I *wanted* to go to Vietnam. I wanted to *be there,* to test my mettle as many young men did. Though many others did not share my enthusiasm for another needless war that took over 58,000 American lives and untold hundreds of thousands of others in the war, I *wanted* to go.

In the fall of 1968, just after turning 19, and at the very height of the war, it took several of us all of just three days to go through the Army flight aptitude tests, get a physical, be sworn in and on our way to Army basic training. Then it was on to the Army's Warrant Officer Candidate (WOC) flight training program. I had even left my car in a recruiting station parking lot in Fargo, North Dakota, for months until I could come back and retrieve it after basic training. That was how fast things moved in the war days.

About the Author

Our 131st Unit Patch

I continued life with flying for a number of CIA-front companies, including Evergreen Helicopters and Evergreen Airlines (the *CIA's Private Airline* as they were known), the FAA, the US State Department in foreign lands, and ultimately working for the CIA in the Middle East on covert activities with IC agents inserted inside my own aviation company as *my employees*.

I hold a US State Department license to export US military equipment, systems, and technology and I have run my own Mohawk programs in Argentina and later asked by the State Department to lead the deployment of Mohawks to South Africa a few years later, though, after months of delays, I did not deploy my team to South Africa.

Ultimately I retired from the US Army as a CW4 with 27-years of service including some years as an Army Special Forces command pilot and instructor pilot in the C-7 Caribou and many years flying Mohawks and later the C-23 Sherpa for the Army National Guard.

I hold Master Aviator Wings and instructor pilot designations in *both* the US Army and the Argentina Army.

THE END

Lightning Source UK Ltd.
Milton Keynes UK
UKHW052252271118
333080UK00010B/322/P